Getting Even

Getting Even

Revenge as a Form of Justice

Charles K.B. Barton

Open Court
Chicago and La Salle, Illinois

To order books from Open Court, call toll-free 1-800-815-2280.

Open Court Publishing Company is a division of Carus Publishing Company.

Printed and bound in the United States of America.

Library of Congress Cataloging-in-Publication Data

Barton, Charles K. B., 1959-
  Getting even : revenge as a form of justice/Charles K.B. Barton.
    p. cm.
  Includes bibliographical references.
  ISBN 0-8126-9401-5 (cloth : alk. paper). — ISBN 0-8126-9402-3 (paperback : alk. paper)
  1. Punishment—Philosophy.   2. Revenge.   3. Lex talionis.
I. Title.
K5103.B37   1999
303.3'6—dc21   99-22765
                                                          CIP

39.95

Mine is a most peaceable disposition. My wishes are: a humble cottage with a thatched roof, but a good bed, good food, the freshest milk and butter, flowers before my window, and a few fine trees before my door; and if God wants to make my happiness complete, he will grant me the joy of seeing some six or seven of my enemies hanging from those trees. Before their death I shall, moved in my heart, forgive them all the wrong they did me in their lifetime. One must, it is true, forgive one's enemies—but not before they have been hanged.[1]

Revenge was a very wild kind of justice, and Hewson was a civilized man. He believed in the Good, in the balance of things, and in an eventual, tremendous pay-day.[2]

"There, Edmond Dantès!" he said, showing the count the bodies of his wife and child. "There! Look! Are you avenged?"

Monte Cristo paled at this terrible spectacle. He realized that he had exceeded the limits of vengeance, he realized that he could no longer say: "God is for me and with me."[3]

Contents

Preface

In writing this book I have relied on many people whose support I would like to acknowledge. Foremost among them are Karen van den Broek, Michael Tooley, John Braithwaite, the late Richard Sylvan, Graham Oddie, and Roy Perrett. I sincerely thank them for their time and generous comments and suggestions. I also wish to thank all the other philosophers who have tested and critiqued my ideas and arguments in the context of conference and seminar presentations in Australia and New Zealand. Finally, I wish to acknowledge the generous support received from three institutions: Massey University, Charles Sturt University, and The Australian National University.

In their own ways, all these excellent people and institutions have contributed to the completion of this project. It is now my pleasure to share with them the credit and the satisfaction.

Introduction

Empowering the Victim

If legal justice perishes, then it is no longer worthwhile for men to remain on this earth.

Immanuel Kant[1]

Justice is vitally important to many people for various reasons: to innocent persons wrongly accused, who want to clear their names; to offenders, who should be protected against excessive or dehumanizing punishment and given the opportunity to make amends for their harmful wrongdoing; and to victims of crime, especially the most serious crime.

What do victims of crime want? Not only restitution, fair compensation, or even the just retributive punishment of their wrongdoers—though all of these may be important to them. Victims of crime also often have a desire to know all the relevant details of, and reasons behind, what happened. They frequently want their side of the story to be heard—by the offender as well as by the general public—and they may find satisfaction in visible signs of remorse elicited by their wrongdoers, especially in heartfelt and sincerely expressed apologies where such are due. Most importantly, however—and quite compatibly with the foregoing—it is important for victims to have the legal right to a substantial say in how their cases are handled and resolved in the legal justice system.

In their purported mission to protect the innocent and punish the guilty, contemporary criminal justice systems marginalize and disempower these three groups of people who, in a sense, are their clients. Most significantly, victims and accused alike are discouraged and are denied real opportunities to take an active role personally in the legal processing and resolution of their cases. In effect, they are reduced to the status of idle bystanders in their own cases, in what, after all, is *their* conflict.

The judicial system has become monopolized by legal professionals, who make a handsome living out of creating drama, and often squabble inordinately among themselves in the process of dealing with other people's conflicts. Especially under the adversarial system, prosecution and defense are often bent on vanquishing each other by fair means or foul. What seems to be of overriding importance to the professionals, unlike the clients of the legal system, is not finding the truth of the matter and applying justice, but which of them can triumph over the other by winning the case. Compounding the problem is the fact that, through all the drama of the courtroom, judges seem content to act as if they were mere referees in a boxing match or a cock fight, and justice, in which victims and accused have such high stakes, can all too often be unnecessarily and recklessly jeopardized.

A consequence of this unsatisfactory situation is that police lose faith in the judicial system, some of them treating it as a joke. As evidenced by the findings of the Wood Royal Commission into the New South Wales (Australia) Police Service, especially in cases where police had no doubts about the guilt of the accused, officers "would perjure themselves or do whatever else was necessary to secure a conviction."[2] Moreover, in the light of the mass violence created by the Rodney King trial in Los Angeles, we cannot altogether dismiss Braithwaite's suggestion that the American criminal justice system, for example, might be

> more a cause of crime than a protection against it . . . It is time to recognize that it, like other Western criminal justice systems, is an abject failure. In fact, the criminal justice system stands out as the greatest failure of any of America's institutions.[3]

Kennedy, who recommends the adoption of the inquiry system[4] of France and other European countries, put the matter in the following way:

> [T]he adversary system of criminal justice which we employ in this country [Britain] and which we have exported to the United States and Commonwealth and is essentially one of conflict, is not only extremely childish, but a most unsatisfactory way of attempting to dispense justice. In a situation where one side is doing its best to vanquish the other, truth is apt to fall by the wayside.[5]

Similarly, in his book *Trial by Voodoo*, Evan Whitton argues that under the adversarial system the law defeats justice and democracy because it does not set out to establish the truth, and punish the guilty.[6] Without discounting arguments to the contrary, the long list of historical examples cited by Whitton and Kennedy—all of them cases where the guilty have gone free while many innocent people have been convicted, due in the main to the adversarial nature of the legal system—strongly suggests that reform of this particular aspect of some judicial systems is overdue.

However, traditional inquiry systems are still not satisfactory in terms of providing for substantial, grass-roots participation by victims and offenders in the legal processing and resolution of their cases. As Braithwaite points out:

> The Western criminal arrest and trial is a sterile production line process dominated by experts (mainly lawyers) who disempower the communities that might be able to plan some solutions to the underlying problems.[7]

This is increasingly recognized all over the world and laws are being modified, even in Europe.[8] This is, perhaps, as it should be. For, given the high stakes held by clients of the legal system, justice is far too important to be left completely in the hands of legal professionals.

But, while justice is very important to clients of the legal justice system, it would be a mistake to think that the quest for justice can, or should, be confined to the domain of centralized legal systems. For one thing, the concept of justice is an essentially moral concept, which is both *older* and *broader* than are our criminal laws. It would not be an exaggeration to say that the quest for justice must be as ancient as mankind, whereas criminal laws are a relatively recent phenomenon. Principles of fair treatment permeate all facets of our private and public lives: in the home, in friendships, in schools, in the workplace, on the streets, and elsewhere, and very few of these are enshrined in criminal law.

At the same time, there is no passion like that for justice and, in spite of apathetic professionalism in our criminal courts, the legal justice system is by no means immune to pressures to reform. Fuelled by a powerful passion for justice, the victim movement especially seems poised to make a major impact on the way criminal justice is done. As evidenced by the increasing legal recognition of victims' rights in criminal laws, as well as by the rapid proliferation of restorative justice programs around the world, a major transformation is taking place at an increasingly rapid rate. Broadly speaking, these changes follow principles of client restoration and empowerment. Victim Impact Statements (VIS) which have been introduced in many states and countries over the past decade represent an unmistakable step in the direction of greater victim empowerment. Similarly, the restorative justice initiatives which have sprung up around the world over the same period, such as the New Zealand Children, Young Persons, and their Families Act 1989, and the New South Wales Young Offenders Act 1997 are not simply about warm and fuzzy healing of the effects of crime. Principally, they are about individual and community empowerment. This trend toward client empowerment in criminal justice systems is not focused exclusively on victims. It is focused equally on offenders, as well as on their respective communities of care, especially involving close family and friends.

While this book concurs with such all-round empowerment of clients in legal justice systems, it has a predominantly victim justice focus in arguing the necessity for substantial victim empowerment. The central claim is that victim justice, to be worthy of that name, requires the substantial empowerment of victims by law, giving them the legal right to become involved in the relevant legal processes, some of which may culminate in impositions of punishment on their wrongdoers. Essentially, victims must be given the legal authority to have a substantial say in how their cases are resolved. As part of such victim recognition and empowerment, legal systems must grant victims the right to fair retributive justice, as well as a corresponding right to show leniency and mercy as *they* see fit in their own cases. Their decisions on such matters should be vetoed only if they display unreasonable leniency or harshness. This is part of what it means to empower victims and treat them with due respect and justice. From a victim justice point of view no criminal justice system can be satisfactory without such substantial legal empowerment.

Perhaps the greatest obstacle in the path of substantial victim empowerment is the fear of revenge, as evidenced by revenge's undeservedly poor image. Especially in contemporary Western societies, revenge is widely thought of as being crazy, nasty, and unworthy of the aspirations of truly civilized people, or of a civilized society. Wanting revenge is frowned upon and is treated with distrust, no matter how badly or unfairly the victim might have been treated and harmed by the wrongdoer. Reinforced by stiff legal sanctions, our present public morality's condemnation of revenge seems so powerful and complete that any admissions to feelings of revengefulness and resentment would be met with distrust and disapproval. Seeking justice is all very well, but it is far from acceptable for anyone to admit that the justice they claim to seek may in fact add up to revenge.

There seems to be a curious ambivalence in attitudes toward revenge in our culture. Notwithstanding the severity with which revenge is condemned, there appears to be no end to people's fascination and preoccupation with revenge in both fiction and reality. The impulse to get even in the face of injustice is one of the most enduring aspects of the human spirit which even the stiffest penalties can only hope to dampen, but never completely eradicate. And, while wanting *justice* is openly acceptable, the false distinction between revenge and justice breaks down even in the courtroom when judges and juries cannot in good conscience deny or disregard the presence of fundamental and legitimate motives for justice behind what are clear acts of revenge. The Owen case in England is a good example: after having admitted to the shooting of his son's reckless and apparently unrepentant and contemptuous killer, Mr Owen was acquitted of all charges by the jury, even of simple ones which the defense did not contest, such as illegal possession and use of a firearm.[9]

Notwithstanding such exceptional cases, the general presumption is against revenge. The mere mention that for the most part of mankind's history revenge has been the only way of securing justice is enough to create unease in people's minds. It would be a standard response to say *Yes, but they weren't civilized, were they?* or *Their revenge practices show a lack of civilization.* Such responses and attitudes imply that we alone, by virtue of openly rejecting revenge, are civilized, and that our rejection of revenge is evidence of our civilization.

Leaving aside the questionable assumption of superiority in such thinking, it represents a costly delusion, the burden of which is borne mostly by victims of crime. The silencing, disempowerment, and severe marginalization of victims in our criminal justice proceedings owe a lot to such views about revenge and to the corresponding official attitudes towards victims who may be all too easily suspected, and accused, of being motivated by revenge. Even historically, the process of victim disempowerment started with a desire by rulers and governments to control feuds and revenge killings and, to be sure, few of us would wish to bring back those practices. However, we have gone too far in our ostracism of revenge when a victim's evidence can be challenged and discredited in our court rooms with such glib phrases as *You only want revenge, don't you?*—as if revenge and justice were incompatible, or had nothing in common, and as if wanting revenge were a most terrible thing, something to be ashamed of.

In response to such techniques designed to silence them, victims usually try to maintain their credibility by denying the accusation, insisting that they only want justice. However, by doing this they have been put on the back foot because *revenge is personal retribution,* and in calling for justice victims typically want the fair but nevertheless retributive punishment of those who unjustly harmed *them.* Thus, both personal and retributive elements being present in a victim's desire for justice, that desire does in fact amount to a desire for revenge. This, I maintain, is a necessary truth, denials of which are likely to be suspect even to the philosophically untrained. Maintaining credibility for victims by way of protestations that they *only want justice, not revenge,* is not really convincing to their audience in court nor even to themselves. The accusation sticks because there is truth in it, and victims suffer more trauma as their motives are questioned.

But victims should never have to justify themselves in this fashion. While retribution may not always be among a victim's reasons for wanting punishment, in those cases where they call for fair punishment on retributive grounds their calls are equally legitimate and justified. There is absolutely nothing wrong with resentment of injustice and there is nothing wrong with victims wanting proportional retribution as a matter of justice for the wrongs they have suffered. One of the aims of this book, therefore, is to expose the sham, and the lack of legitimacy, in such silencing techniques. I show that, far from revenge being an *alternative* to justice, when implemented with appropriate legal and institutional constraints, revenge is a perfectly legitimate and sometimes superior *form* of justice.

The familiar catch-phrase, of course, is that we cannot have anybody, let alone victims, being 'judge, jury, and executioner' in their own cases. But the kernel of wisdom in this phrase is way overrated. While we may agree that victims should not act as *jury* where they themselves are concerned, this is largely beside the point in most instances. The vast majority of cases which are put through the criminal justice system do not require a jury because there is no denial of guilt by the accused. Few victims would wish to be the *executioners* of legally imposed sentences on their wrongdoers, and, since the push for substantial victim empowerment is not along these lines, this element of the catch-phrase is even more beside the point. It is only the first element which is in contention, namely the question whether victims should have a substantial say—in the same way that at the moment only *judges* do—in the way their cases are resolved in terms of the final sentence or resolution to be reached. I argue that victim justice considerations require that they should.

Impartiality is, of course, a very important virtue in the administration of justice. It would be a mistake to deny that. At the same time, the impersonal, alienating processes, and the distant and professional disinterestedness in our courtrooms are the root cause of much dissatisfaction among victims and offenders alike. The question therefore is whether impartiality can be secured without depersonalizing and marginalizing the principal clients of the legal system, and the answer here is affirmative. It is a fallacy to suppose, in the face of evidence to the contrary, that people's capacity to judge fairly and with justice in their own cases is adversely affected. It is simply not true that impartiality and fairness can be secured only through neutrality and disinterestedness. In fact quite the contrary may be the case, as some examples of out-of-touch reasoning by judges may tend to indicate. While that is an arguable point for another occasion, the present claim is that impartiality and fairness of judgment can be secured without the disempowerment and exclusion of victims from criminal justice processes dealing with their cases. While victims are by no means disinterested in the outcome of their own cases, the notion that therefore they cannot maintain impartiality and fairness *vis á vis* their offenders is a myth. Empirical research consistently shows victims not to be more punitive than others, and the generosity of spirit consistently shown by victims toward their offenders in restorative justice programs is further evidence that fears about bloodthirsty and overly punitive victims are fundamentally mistaken.

As to concerns about conflict escalation as a result of greater victim and offender participation, these are best addressed by appropriate institutionalization of the criminal justice process, not by excluding and disempowering the very people who have been most affected by the crime. There is no justification for the state, and the professionals who wish to maintain the status quo, stepping in, taking over, and disempowering virtually everyone who has a stake in the truth of the matter, and the substantive resolution of the case—most notably the victims of crime, but also the accused and their respective communities of care. Instead of helping them, their marginalization and disempowerment in the names of impartiality and fairness become sources of further victimization and collateral damage which only exacerbates the harm from the initial act of crime to both of them, to their respective families and friends, as well as to the wider community.

These problems can be remedied only by reforming the legal justice system. However, if reforms are to make a positive difference, then whenever possible they must empower victims and offenders, as well as their respective communities of care, so that they are allowed and encouraged to deal with the most immediate causes and consequences of the crime. From a victim justice point of view, reforms must provide forums where victims can express their legitimate feelings of resentment and outrage, forums where they can seek satisfaction in terms of adequate material restoration, apology, and even retributive justice, in a controlled and civilized manner for the wrongs committed against them without feeling condemned, or being moralized and patronized, and without feeling that they are thought less of by others for doing so.

A very important dimension of such victim empowerment consists in according victims their rightful status to be the primary bearers of the prerogative and the power to forgive and be merciful. It stands to reason that the forgiveness of wrongs should lie primarily with those against whom those wrongs were perpetrated and their decisions on such matters should be subject to veto only when they show unreasonable leniency or harshness. Victim empowerment in these terms is very important for purposes of victim restoration, and is an integral part of providing due justice to victims.

From an offender justice point of view, such reforms must provide offenders with appropriate opportunities to understand the seriousness of their actions and a chance to put things right with their victims and their community. This is crucial to their own social and moral-psychological restoration, for their being able to reach self-forgiveness, and for repairing the damage they have caused to their own sense of self-worth. It is only fair that offenders be given such chances for restoration. While it would be naive to suppose that all of them will respond constructively, being afforded such opportunities is part of treating them with respect, dignity, and justice.

Outline of This Book's Argument

My argument proceeds as follows. I start by providing a broad framework for understanding revenge and divergent attitudes to revenge in terms of different paradigms of justice (Chapter 1). This is followed (Chapters 2–4) by the critical examination and rejection of various anti-revenge arguments and myths. I then (Chapters 5–7) provide conceptual analyses and philosophical arguments concerning the nature of revenge in relation to other key concepts in the language and philosophy of punishment, such as retribution and justice, arguing that revenge is *personal retribution* and that, just like any other forms of punishment, revenge can be just or unjust, depending upon whether or not principles of justice (such as not punishing the innocent and proportionality) are observed. This is followed (Chapters 8-10) by a philosophical and moral justification of institutionalized forms of revenge from a victim justice perspective, offering two models for sensible victim empowerment within criminal justice systems. One of these models relates to an appropriately modified court system, including cases where, following a plea of not guilty, offenders are found guilty. The other model is an alternative to a court system and covers only cases where responsibility is not disputed by the offender. Issue is taken also with the fashionable but conceptually muddled trend among academics and other reformists of creating a false dichotomy between 'retributive justice' and 'restorative justice' as part of an otherwise worthwhile attempt to spell out the theoretical foundations of restorative practices and of the restorative justice movement. The book concludes (Afterword) with a few pointers for reforming the criminal justice system.

1

Paradigms of Justice

No more tears now; I will think upon revenge.

Mary Stuart, Queen of Scots[1]

Revenge is a kind of wild justice, which the more man's nature runs to, the more ought law to weed it out.

Francis Bacon[2]

The above aphorisms capture well the divergent attitudes that the idea of revenge often evokes. They also represent an interesting polarization of attitudes to revenge, and two very different paradigms of justice: *a pro-revenge paradigm*, and an *anti-revenge paradigm*.

In the pro-revenge paradigm, revenge is held to be the ideal response to injustice. In many cultures, taking revenge is regarded as a genuine and legitimate moral option for victims of injustice. Indeed, there are many situations in which, even if it is not the only option, in the view of the society in question it is the only morally acceptable option. On the basis of his survey of the various revenge practices of pre-industrial societies from around the world, Herbert Spencer points out that "In all these cases we see that either avowedly or tacitly revenge is considered a moral obligation."[3] In his anthropological study of blood revenge in Montenegro, Christopher Boehm observes that:

> After a first killing had occurred, the retaliatory homicide that followed was considered not only to be reasonable and proper but also to be morally necessary by traditional Montenegrin standards.[4]

By contrast, and in spite of the fact that throughout the world the first form of justice has been revenge,[5] an unconditional rejection of revenge is

endemic to modern Western culture where an *anti-revenge paradigm* domi-
nates. In industrialized Western societies, the quest for justice has become
confined almost exclusively to the domain of highly impersonal legal systems to the point where it is a truism that revenge is held in low esteem. If
anything, industrialized Western societies are characterized by norms prohibiting revenge and by corresponding injunctions to forget, forgive, or
turn the other cheek, or simply to let the law take its course. Such strong
anti-revenge attitudes in the Western world have developed under the combined influence of Christianity and policies pursued by powerful, bureau-
cratic States on crucial matters of law and order.[6]

The fact that most contemporary Western philosophers and thinkers
would readily endorse Bacon's exhortation to weed out revenge, and that
they invariably do this by assumption rather than argument, is a good indication of just how pervasive and well-established the anti-revenge paradigm
of justice is. In discussions of retribution, for example, it is not uncommon
to hear the accusation that retribution is revenge in disguise. The implicit
assumption in such claims is that retributivism, the idea that retribution is a
legitimate reason for punishment, is automatically knocked out of contention as soon as it is found to have anything to do with revenge. Observations made by philosophers Nozick and Glover are illustrative:

> The view that people deserve punishment for their wrongful acts . . . indepen-
> dently of the deterrent effect of such punishment, strikes some people as *a prim-*
> *itive view, expressive only of the thirst for revenge*[7] (emphasis mine).

> Among objections urged against retributivism are that 'retribution' is a polite
> name for *revenge, which is more generally recognized to be evil,* . . . *[H]atred and*
> *pleasure . . . combine so unpleasantly in revenge*[8] (emphasis mine).

Philosopher, theologian, and popular writer C.S. Lewis warns that "the
least indulgence of the passion for revenge is very deadly sin."[9] According
to Lewis, revenge is a "vindictive passion . . . [which] is evil and expressly
forbidden to Christians."[10] Nietzsche, though rejecting Christianity and
many Christian values, nevertheless concurs with Lewis and Glover in
rejecting revenge by saying that *"for humankind to be redeemed from*
revenge—that is for me the bridge to the highest hope, and a rainbow after
long storms."[11]

To my mind, both these paradigms of justice are unsatisfactory. The
pro-revenge paradigm is lopsided because its concern for justice is focused
too much on the wronged party's need for retribution, often ignoring the
demands of justice from the point of view of the accused. The anti-revenge
paradigm is similarly lopsided because it ignores the needs of victims for
restoration following an offense and focuses mainly on the accused party's
need for fair treatment and on society's need to deter crime.

However, in rejecting these paradigms, it is possible to preserve what is best from both while seeking to lay the philosophical foundations of a new *empowerment paradigm of justice* which encompasses a reasonable and sensible way of thinking about revenge, a way of thinking which is free from the excesses of the above two extremes. Taking the view that revenge is nothing more than personal retributive punishment, the *empowerment paradigm* respects the moral rights of victims to impose such punishment and to show mercy, and insists only on safeguarding against abuses of such extensive rights by appropriate institutionalization of the relevant processes of justice. The empowerment paradigm also recognizes that such instances of institutionalized revenge are often part of restorative processes aimed at fairness and equity between offender and victim—literally restoring a relationship of fairness and justice between them which, in turn, serve to restore individual and social peace and aid proper healing.

This is an important point which is often lost on advocates of restorative justice who tend to see retribution and revenge as inimical to restoration. But if restorative justice processes are to be culturally appropriate and truly empowering to indigenous people of the colonized world, for example, who tend to have traditional revenge-based systems of justice, then these restorative processes must of necessity make allowances for institutionalized revenge as required, or rendered appropriate, by indigenous customary laws. For the anti-revenge paradigm, which is clearly under threat from indigenous calls for culturally appropriate legal justice systems, there is no way of evading the reality of this problem. With appropriate controls in place, such indigenous legal systems are certain to incorporate culturally accepted acts of revenge by aggrieved parties as part of, and in the interests of, restoration and reconciliation.

Leaving aside the reluctance of letting go of power and control, the idea of legalizing revenge is understandably difficult for the Western mind which has been shaped by an increasingly pervasive anti-revenge paradigm. But no matter how pervasive or influential it may be currently, this paradigm is indefensible where reasoned argument is concerned. Victim empowerment in terms of making lawful allowances at appropriate stages of the criminal justice process for the legitimate needs of victims to express their views and feelings of indignation and anger about the offense, as well as in terms of giving victims *the right* to have a proper say in how their cases are handled and resolved—including *the legal right* to show mercy or seek fair and proportional revenge within limits allowed by law in a civilized manner for the wrongs they suffered as they think fit—leads to superior legal justice systems on account of the enhanced status, social recognition, and the legal empowerment experienced by victims in such contexts. In other words, what I am suggesting is that there is a strong case for abandoning Bacon's advice while maintaining a legal-institutional perspective on justice. Instead of trying to weed out revenge, the law should seek only to weed the wildness out of it.

As to concerns that justice to offenders would be jeopardized by such victim empowerment, there is no rational basis for such fears. Revenge can be measured and proportionate. As Wallace also points out, "there is nothing in the concept of revenge that necessitates injustice to the revengee."[12] Moreover, facing the rightful anger and power of victims in this way has as many benefits for offenders as it has for victims. It affords offenders the opportunity to learn the real consequences of what they have done, to show remorse, offer apologies and make amends and, in return, to receive the potentially healing forgiveness of those they have hurt most.

The healing power of such restorative interactions cannot be overestimated, but its fundamental starting point must be *the victim's prerogative and right to show mercy or take revenge*. Without a healthy and robust sense of empowerment, it would be self-delusion for victims to think that they can exercise mercy. By definition, only one who has the power of punishment can be merciful by forgoing the exercise of that power for the benefit of the receiver of mercy. For victims who are too disempowered to show mercy in the first place, it is very hard emotionally to forgive their wrongdoers and to let go of their anger and the resentment they naturally feel on account of the injustice they have suffered. Indeed, it is an insult to expect them to forgive, when we rob them through marginalization and disempowerment of the chance to be merciful in the first place. And yet there is no healing power greater than those of forgiveness and mercy for enabling victims and wrongdoers to free themselves of the emotionally oppressive and sometimes devastating consequences of what has happened. In Shakespeare's eternal words,

> The quality of mercy is not strained,
> It droppeth as the gentle rain from heaven
> Upon the place beneath. It is twice blest:
> It blesseth him that gives, and him that takes.[13]

Critical observations such as the above are not enough to destabilize a well-entrenched anti-revenge paradigm, and any views recommending a legal right to institutionalized revenge are bound to be controversial. Therefore, besides debunking that paradigm through rigorous questioning, the concept of revenge will also require proper examination. Saying, as Bacon does, that revenge is a kind of wild justice might capture some of its flavor, but can be no substitute for the proper analysis required for an informed evaluation of the concept. By undertaking such an evaluation and defense, I show that, instead of trying to eradicate revenge altogether, in the interests of victim justice the law should only seek to tame revenge, to weed the wildness out of it. In turn, this requires showing that revenge need not be wild and dangerous and that there are perfectly acceptable ways to tame and civilize it through appropriate institutionalization. Of equal importance is to demonstrate the superiority of resultant systems of justice over standard judicial systems, not only in terms of their enhanced ability to ensure justice to victims, but also in their much improved ability to address effectively the causes and consequences of criminal behaviour by assisting, rather than hindering, the rehabilitation, correction, and social reintegration of offenders.

Far from being a threat to fairness, with which offenders must be treated, the new empowerment paradigm of justice provides offenders with opportunities to understand fully the serious consequences their actions have had on others. It also empowers them to take responsibility for their actions by taking constructive steps to repair the damage they have caused to their victims, to their own family and friends, and, derivatively, to repair the damage to their own self-esteem and sense of self-worth. Indeed, withholding from offenders such opportunities to make amends for what they have done is inhumane and is a serious violation of an inalienable human right, a violation of an important principle of justice requiring that they be treated in a humane, respectful, and dignified manner.

Thus, the empowerment paradigm of justice is empowering not only to victims, but also to offenders, and their respective empowerment is best achieved through the empowerment of their respective communities (caring individuals around them, typically their respective families, friends, and colleagues) to deal with the causes and consequences of the wrongful behaviour in question. However, the universal stranglehold of the anti-revenge paradigm of justice in the public, religious, social, professional, and intellectual spheres presents a formidable obstacle to such empowerment. Especially where victim empowerment is concerned, the instinctive rejection of anything that has to do with revenge is bound to stand in the way of accepting the empowerment paradigm in the light of which a new understanding of the nature, rationality and morality of revenge can be developed. But given the increasing influence of the victim movement and the increasingly self-confident calls for autonomy and empowerment by indigenous people in the colonized world—whose cultures often include revenge practices aimed at re-establishing fairness and justice between people following an offense— the days of the anti-revenge paradigm may well be numbered. Civilized and fair institutionalized revenge is already present in many victim-offender encounters and resolutions under restorative justice processes, and it may be only a matter of time before more accepting attitudes to victim empowerment, including the right to revenge and mercy, will be seen to be sensible and desirable.

The relevance of revenge to a new victim justice focus in legal justice settings has been recognized by Robert Solomon.

> To the dangers of vengeance unlimited it must be countered that if punishment no longer satisfies vengeance, if it ignores not only the rights but the emotional

needs of the victims of crime, then punishment no longer serves its primary purpose, even if it were to succeed in rehabilitating the criminal and deterring other crime (which it evidently, in general, does not). The restriction of vengeance by law is entirely understandable, but, again, the wholesale denial of vengeance as a legitimate motive may be a psychological disaster.[14]

Just like Solomon, I am not advocating that victims should take revenge within limits allowed by law no matter what, and I am definitely not advocating that they should act outside the legal justice system by taking the law into their own hands. Rather, I am arguing for the moral *permissibility* of institutionalized revenge and for according victims the legal right to such revenge, and, correlatively, I am arguing for their rightful prerogative to forgive and show mercy to their offenders, if that is the way they are moved. As long as they remain within limits allowed by law, their decisions in these regards should be vetoed or overruled on appeal only if they can be shown to have been unreasonably lenient or harsh, or otherwise inappropriate. Victim justice worthy of that name can consist in nothing less than such victim empowerment, and it is questionable whether victim restoration can ever be complete without according to victims the legal rights in question. Indeed, to be successful, restorative justice requires the empowerment of victims and offenders alike in the respective senses I have indicated for them.

Contemporary criminal justice systems not only ignore but explicitly dismiss such human needs through the marginalization, silencing, and disempowerment of victims and offenders in the course of processing their cases. While such legal systems can re-establish immediate legal order, they have proven unsatisfactory in terms of society's long-term interests in controlling and reducing crime, let alone in terms of being able to bring peace, restoration, and healing to those most affected, the victims, the offenders, and their respective families. In his report to the Queensland (Australia) Corrective Services Commission, Severin stated the problem in the following manner.

> Unfortunately, the criminal justice system does not provide an active role for victims and offenders. In the criminal justice system, victims and offenders are required to enact their roles as witnesses and defendants, but beyond that, they have to remain passive. Once they have stated their immediate cases, the system 'steals' their conflict and takes over. The system is very much concerned with re-establishing legal order, but fails to leave any room for the interpersonal resolution of conflict and the restoration of social peace. [15]

If individual and social peace are to be restored for offenders, victims and their families, and if a feeling of satisfaction is to be engendered in them with regard to the legal processing and final outcome of their conflict—both of which are important for their respective social-psychological restoration and for enabling them to get on with their lives—then they all must be empowered and given constructive opportunities to play an active role in working out a resolution to their conflict which is acceptable to both sides. This empowering restorative justice approach for dealing constructively with criminal offenses is explained by Severin as follows.

> Restorative Justice goes beyond restitution and connotes a dynamic dimension and an interactive process of establishing justice and fairness. With its focus on conflict resolution and the re-establishment of peace (justice and fairness), restorative justice is essentially based on the voluntary and participatory nature of the conflict-resolving procedure. [16]

The early success and popularity of programs based on the concept of restorative justice in countries such as Australia and New Zealand, and more recently in England and the United States, as well as in other European countries, such as Austria and Germany where over the past decade the concept has developed at "breakneck speed,"[17] are signs that the concept of restorative justice is destined to play a very important, if not central, role in the future development of legal justice systems all over the world. But, while I fully support these developments, my call for the empowerment of victims and offenders goes beyond the way in which restorative justice has hitherto been conceived. There are three main differences.

First, with respect to victims, proponents of restorative justice tend to think that restorative justice is opposed to retributive justice.[18] This is mistaken. Far from being inimical to restorative justice, acknowledgment of victims' rights to retributive justice is a fundamental first step to promoting their restoration. Moreover, as indicated earlier, effective restorative justice can include retributively imposed sanctions and penalties on the offender as a proper and sometimes necessary part. There is no reason for excluding considerations of the wrongdoer's moral desert (just deserts), especially if the offender and their supporters[19] accept what is being proposed as fair in the light of the offense. As indicated above, this is no longer uncommon in practice but some advocates of restorative justice tend to shy away from acknowledging that such personal retributive motives and considerations by victims are often part of the restorative justice processes they support.

Second, with regard to offenders, restorative justice models have tended to focus on the importance of socially reintegrating offenders with the aim of reducing the likelihood of re-offending. The empowerment paradigm emphasizes, in addition, the moral and ethical imperative that offenders be given constructive opportunities to apologize to their victims and make amends for their wrongful actions. Providing offenders with such opportunities is a matter of fairness and justice. This is one of their basic human rights and forms part of treating them with humane consideration and dignity. Denying offenders this right is inhumane because it unnecessarily hinders recovery of their damaged sense of self-esteem and social-psychological restoration. Unfortunately, restoratively motivated conferences also fail to respect these rights when, through ignorance or negligence victims are not invited to participate, and where poor facilitation fails to bring the parties to this crucial healing stage where expressions of remorse and apology from the offender, and corresponding expressions of forgiveness from the victim can be exchanged.

Third, advocates of restorative justice mostly have in mind restorative justice in a mediation or a conferencing setting where the victim, the offender, and their respective communities of care come together to discuss and find resolution to an incident away from the courtroom. My call for empowering the key participants under an empowerment paradigm of justice holds equally for our courts, where appropriate empowerment of victims, offenders, and their communities is sorely needed. Moreover, from a restorative justice point of view, victim empowerment in terms of participation and substantial contribution to the resolution of a case is an imperative, even where the offender or the victim do not wish to engage the other in dialogue. This would entail that judges and magistrates share their sentencing powers with the appropriate victims. This no doubt controversial claim will be supported with arguments in later chapters. But first, in the next three chapters, I examine and reject what appear to be the basic building blocks of the anti-revenge paradigm.

2

Pious Myths about Revenge

Vengeance is the emotion of 'getting even', putting the world back in balance.
                                                          Robert Solomon[1]

Revenge has had a bad press in modern times. Especially in the Western world, revenge has been dismissed and condemned as an excessive and perverse reaction which is evil, vindictive, nasty, and contemptible, something to be avoided by self-respecting, civilized persons. Robert Nozick, for example, claims that "revenge involves a particular emotional tone, pleasure in the suffering of another,"[2] and Jonathan Glover makes a similar assertion that "hatred and pleasure . . . combine . . . unpleasantly in revenge."[3] Again, C.S. Lewis warns that "the least indulgence of the passion for revenge is very deadly sin."[4] According to him, revenge is a "vindictive passion . . . [which], of course, is evil and expressly forbidden to Christians."[5] Moreover, according to Lewis, revenge is a "perversion."[6]

I disagree with these charges against revenge. They are myths born of unreflecting thinking, misguided piety, and an irrational fear of strong emotions such as anger and resentment. But, whatever their origins, there is no philosophically defensible foundation to any of them. Three main mistakes or 'myths' are discernible from the above passages, and I consider them in turn.

Myth 1: The desire for revenge is perverse.
Myth 2: Revenge is an evil, vindictive passion.
Myth 3: Revenge has a nasty emotional tone, taking pleasure in suffering.

Myth 1: The Desire for Revenge is Perverse

According to Lewis,

> The good thing of which vindictive passion is the perversion comes out with startling clarity in Hobbes's definition of Revengefulness; "desire by doing hurt to another to make him condemn some fact of his own."[7] Revenge loses sight of the end in the means, but its end is not wholly bad—it wants the evil of the bad man to be to him what it is to everyone else.[8]

Lewis claims that the aim of revenge is *to make the evil of the bad man to be to him what it is to everyone else,* and that while this would be a morally acceptable motive to have, in revenge it is typically lost sight of and perverted. In other words, what Lewis may be claiming is that "vindictive passion," the desire to hurt one's wrongdoer is not good enough by itself as a motive. What may be good enough is when one wants to hurt the wrongdoer with the aim of *making him condemn his own evil*—regret what he did and feel remorse, perhaps.

This is an interesting but nevertheless fallacious position. By calling the desire for revenge a "vindictive passion," Lewis misdescribes the nature of the desire in question. The desire for revenge does not simply consist in wanting to hurt the wrongdoer for the sake of hurting that person. Rather, it is a morally motivated desire for *equity* and *justice* retributively conceived as *reciprocity*—hence the expressions 'paying back' and 'getting even'.

In addition, since revenge is a form of retribution, it does not have, and it does not need, forward-looking, consequentialist motives or rationales such as inducing regret and remorse, or *making the bad man condemn his own evil.* Indeed, Lewis's own defense of retribution does not mention any such forward-looking, consequentialist goals or motives. Quite the opposite. According to him, it is misguided to punish for any other reason than "because we have deserved it, because we *ought to have known better.*[9] In fact, Lewis is vehement in his repudiation of such well-meaning, forward-looking reasons for the so-called good of the offender, considering it a "kindness [which] stings with intolerable insult."[10]

> [W]hat can be more outrageous than to catch me and submit me to a disagreeable process of moral improvement without my consent, unless . . . I *deserve* it?[11]

Getting a wrongdoer to *recognize and condemn his own evil* seems to be the kind of moral improvement Lewis is arguing against where the justification of punishment is concerned and, therefore, it is inconsistent of him to claim that the desire for revenge is a perversion of a desire for unsolicited moral improvement. The contradiction in Lewis's philosophy, I suggest, is due to his failing to realize that revenge and retribution are not opposed to each other, but that revenge is a form of retribution, just as judicial and vigilante retribution are forms of retribution. In his pious eagerness to condemn revenge he unwittingly tries to subject revenge to criteria which he himself repudiates where other forms of retribution and punishment are concerned.

It might be thought, however, that there is a morally significant distinction between retribution and revenge in that while revenge is the getting of one's own back, getting even, or paying back the offender, retribution is the giving to offenders their just deserts. But even if we left aside for the moment that retribution can also be unjust—for, just like any other form of punishment, even judicial retribution can get the wrong person and it can be overdone—there is nothing to warrant drawing such a distinction between retribution and revenge. Take the real life example of a Sydney rape victim who "stabbed his attacker to death seven years later."[12] His simple explanation for the murder was that he had been raped by this person. If we were to elaborate on that further, no explanation could be more natural, credible, or more compelling, than to add that his rapist *deserved what he got and that it would have been unfair, and wrong to let him get away with it.* As Carlyle says, in the desire for revenge we have an "ineradicable tendency to . . . pay them (scoundrels) what they have merited."[13] An explication and defense of such retributive justificatory claims will be provided in Chapter 8. Now it is time to consider the next myth about revenge.

Myth 2: Revenge Is an Evil, Vindictive Passion

Lewis points out that there is a truth behind "the universal human feeling that bad men ought to suffer" and argues that "it is no use turning up our noses at this feeling, as if it were wholly base."[14] For,

> On its mildest level it appeals to everyone's sense of justice. . . . On a sterner level the same idea appears as 'retributive punishment' or 'giving a man what he deserves'. Some enlightened people would like to banish all conceptions of retribution or desert from their theory of punishment and place its value wholly in the deterrence of others or the reform of the criminal himself. They do not see that by so doing they render all punishment unjust. What can be more immoral than to inflict suffering on me for the sake of deterring others if I do not *deserve* it? And if I do deserve it, you are admitting the claims of 'retribution'. And what can be more outrageous than to catch me and submit me to a disagreeable process of moral improvement without my consent, unless (once more) I *deserve* it?[15]

Lewis's defense of a retributive position on punishment is basically correct. I shall argue later for the philosophical defensibility of such a position. However, as indicated above, I disagree with Lewis's attempt to categorize revenge as something distinct from, and opposed to, retributive punishment:

> On yet a third level we get vindictive passion—the thirst for revenge. This, of course, is evil and expressly forbidden to Christians.[16]

For Lewis, revenge is intrinsically evil, something barbaric by nature, something which automatically and necessarily destroys the morality of anything that partakes of it. But there are no defensible reasons for holding such a grim view of revenge, especially if we accept, as Lewis does,[17] a retributivist position on punishment. There is no doubt that the ideas of retribution and revenge are very closely allied especially in this respect: *that some unpleasant treatment is meted out to someone as desert for a wrong they had done,* and regardless of whether or not that treatment will have other desirable consequences, such as reformation of the offender, deterrence, and so forth. As in the case of the previous myth about revenge, Lewis fails to see the point, which will be argued in more detail later, that retribution and revenge are not opposed to each other, since revenge is a form of retribution. More specifically, revenge is personal retribution in virtue of its being imposed personally by the victim, or someone close to the victim, as payback, to get even, and as a matter of desert for the offense in question. In short, retribution and revenge just aren't different enough to justify Lewis's position.

In addition, Lewis also seems to make the mistaken assumption that retribution is definitionally guaranteed to be deserved. This is to honorify, embellish, and ennoble retribution by assuming or suggesting that all instances of it are invariably and unfailingly justified.[18] As I shall argue in more detail in Chapter 6, the mistake here lies in supposing that the crucial moral elements of desert and the principles of justice, such as proportionality and not punishing the innocent, are built into the very idea of retribution. But even if this were correct and there were a difference between retribution and revenge so that these sanitizing elements had to be added onto revenge in order to make it fair, just, and morally acceptable, this would surely warrant only caution in the case of revenge, not the vilifying, grim view Lewis takes of it. In the absence of supporting reasons, Lewis's claims that revenge is a vindictive passion and that it is evil remain unsubstantiated assertions. Against Schopenhauer's similar assertion that revenge is evidence of our own wickedness, Wallace contends that moderate and proportionate revenge need involve no such thing.

> Consider the much put-upon domestic servant. For many years she has been in the service of a domineering and petty employer. On her final working day, she prepares madam's soup, pees in it and serves it for lunch. She feels suitably

triumphant. Does revenge require that her martinet of an employer is harmed by the soup? It is unlikely that she will be. . . . Schopenhauer is obviously assuming that revenge must involve wickedness, but our servant example shows this to be too strong.[19]

A similar and equally unsubstantiated assertion to that made by Lewis, is Glover's claim that "hatred and pleasure . . . combine . . . unpleasantly in revenge."[20] Glover makes no attempt to justify this claim. Instead, he seems to assume that the claim is self-evident and uncontroversial. But such assumptions are unwarranted. I shall argue in more detail in the following chapter that the typical emotion behind revenge is not hatred but the retributive emotions of resentment, indignation, and anger, which are aroused by perceptions of injustice and unfair treatment. Only when a seriously offended person is powerless to remedy the injustice in question are such retributive emotions likely to turn into hatred and bitterness toward those responsible for the unfair treatment.

Even if it were the case that some kind of hatred is typically involved in resentment and revenge, it is questionable whether there is anything wrong with hating an unjust act, or even an unjust person who, on top of the wrongdoing, refuses to make amends and remains defiant and unapologetic. The other element of Glover's implied allegation, that revenge is characterized by some morally objectionable pleasure in the suffering of another, is considered below in conjunction with Nozick's similar claim where I argue that the pleasure in question is most plausibly identified as *satisfaction* in justice being done.[21]

Myth 3: Revenge Has a Nasty Emotional Tone

Similarly to Glover, Nozick claims that "revenge involves a particular emotional tone, pleasure in the suffering of another."[22] Nozick makes this claim only in passing, in the context of a comparison between revenge and retributive justice. He does not say explicitly that taking pleasure in the suffering of another is morally contemptible. However, if his exercise of attributing this feature to revenge and denying it to retribution is to be significant, he must at least think that the feature in question is problematic—especially since he makes the comparison as part of the groundwork for an account, and defense, of retribution.

The notion of taking pleasure in the suffering of another is ambiguous. It can be understood in two ways. It can mean either (a) pleasure in the suffering of another *simpliciter*, or (b) pleasure in the suffering of another who (is believed to have) harmed one. Although, strictly speaking, Nozick and Glover are committed by their claim only to the second reading, it is quite possible that in making their claims they have in mind the first one. However that may be, it will be worthwhile to discuss the status of revenge with respect to both types of pleasure.

Revenge and the Taking of Pleasure in the Suffering of Another Simpliciter

To identify the emotional tone in question simply as pleasure in the suffering of another *simpliciter* would be, intentionally or not, to present revenge in an artificially bad light. To be sure, this sort of pleasure is perverse and morally base. It is the mentality of the sick-minded torturer who derives pleasure from the suffering of his victims. But to suggest, as the claims made by Nozick and Glover may be taken to suggest, that revenge is even typically accompanied by an emotional tone of this repulsive sort is not at all plausible.

If in many, or perhaps in most, cases revenge were accompanied by an emotional tone of this morbid sort, given the fact that quite generally human beings have a strong and natural inclination to be revengeful, their claims would seem to commit them to the view that human nature naturally inclines to take pleasure in the suffering of others. But, besides being uncharitable to ourselves, maintaining this of human nature would be mistaken.[23] Experimental studies on aggression consistently show that, with rare exceptions, not only do people not enjoy hurting others under normal circumstances when they could do so with impunity, they will not enjoy doing so even if they are annoyed, irritated or seriously angered by other people in their environment.

This was clearly demonstrated in Milgram's famous study on obedience to authority.[24] In these experiments the aim was to find out the extent to which ordinary people were willing to do certain things under pressure from authority which they would be otherwise unwilling to do. Subjects were required to punish 'learners' in a 'scientific experiment' by administering increasing levels of electric shocks to them when they made mistakes, the maximum being 450 volts. They were told, falsely, that the experiment was designed to monitor the effects of punishment on learning. The real aim, of course, was to monitor their obedience to the authority of the experimenters, who were presented to them as 'experts' and in full charge of the experiment. The disturbing findings of these studies are well-known: the vast majority of subjects (who were perfectly ordinary people of diverse backgrounds and representative of all sections of society) obeyed authority and went on to administer what they believed to be potentially lethal levels of electric shocks to their 'slow-learning subjects' (who in fact were actors, mimicking the effects of such shocks). Two important things were found. First, despite having the opportunity to inflict pain on others without restraint (and with good justification—in the form of an important scientific cause), the subjects were not in the least inclined to do this beyond a point where their 'subjects' started to find the shocks seriously disagreeable. Second, when the experimenters started to anger, irritate, and frustrate the subjects, in administering the shocks, subjects would at most move up one or two shock levels, say from shock level 4 to level 6.[25] Although this represented a genuine increment in aggression, the increase was minimal and negligible. The level of shocks administered voluntarily under both conditions was low and totally reasonable in the context of these experiments. With rare exceptions, the subjects did not display sadistic tendencies, not even when they were annoyed, irritated, and angered.

In view of the fact that revengefulness is a universal human trait, these findings strongly support the view that describing the emotional tone in revenge as pleasure in the suffering of another *simpliciter* would be to misidentify the nature of the emotional tone involved. People do not, as a general rule, take pleasure in the suffering of others. Milgram is very clear on this point.

> In observing the subjects in the obedience experiment, one could see that, with minor exceptions, these individuals were performing a task that was distasteful and often disagreeable but which they felt obligated to carry out. Many protested shocking the victim even while they were unable to disengage themselves from the experimenter's authority. Now and then a subject did come along who seemed to relish the task of making the victim scream. But he was the rare exception, and clearly appeared as the queer duck among our subjects.[26]

The hypothesis that it was sadistic tendencies, the lust for inflicting pain on others which found the occasion to raise its ugly head in the context of these experiments was disconfirmed in several different settings. In one of these, the subjects were confronted with two incompatible commands issuing from separate but equally powerful authorities. At 150 volts the learner started to complain vehemently about the pain but the two experimenters radically disagreed as to whether higher shock levels should be administered. Thus, they left it up to the subject to decide whether to give more shocks to the learner or not. Virtually without exception, all subjects broke off the experiment at this point.

> Not a single subject 'took advantage' of the instructions to go on; in no instance did individual aggressive motives latch on to the authoritative sanction provided by the malevolent authority. Rather, action was stopped dead in its tracks.[27]

In another setting in which the choice was left completely up to them, the vast majority of subjects delivered the very lowest shocks to the victim.

"By and large, subjects were not inclined to have the victim suffer [despite the fact that] . . . the situation provided a setting in which it was acceptable for the subject to hurt another person."[28] The same conclusion follows from the results where the experimenter wanted to halt the experiments but the victim himself insisted that, although the shocks were painful, he definitely wanted to go on. He argued that a friend of his had recently gone through the whole experiment and "it would be an affront to his manliness" to do anything less than that. It was found, however, that "not a single subject complied with the learner's demand."[29] What is more, the great majority of subjects refused to carry on with the experiments as long as the commands came from non-authority figures.[30] Indeed, a number of them took physical action to protect the victim from such over-zealous non-authority figures.[31] While it is true that this picture changed when subjects were commanded to go on with the experiment by figures of authority, there can be little doubt as to how this change should not be interpreted. As Milgram says,

> Those who argue that aggressive motives or sadistic instincts are unleashed when the command to hurt another person is given must take account of the subjects' adamant refusal to go on in these experiments.[32]

Once again, revengefulness being a virtually universal human trait, these findings can leave no doubt that the emotional tone in revenge cannot be identified with any plausibility as one of taking pleasure in the suffering of another *simpliciter*. I find implausible the suggestion that revenge is even typically accompanied by any sort of pleasure in the suffering of another. The empirical findings above show that even if this were the case, as a matter of fact, the pleasure in question could not be of the repulsive sort I have just discussed. Rather, it would have to be pleasure in the suffering of another *who is believed to have harmed one*. Nozick and Glover are committed at least to this interpretation of their claims and this is what must be considered next.

Revenge and the Taking of Pleasure in the Suffering of One's Aggressor

If we identified the emotional tone in question in this way, the hypothesis in question is not disconfirmed by empirical findings. In fact, psychological research has consistently found that, while pain cues from victims who have not angered the experimental subjects tend to decrease the aggression of these subjects, pain cues from victims who have beforehand aroused the anger of these subjects have a markedly opposite effect.[33]

> In angry aggression, [as opposed to instrumental aggression] some form of attack, insult, or annoyance by another person is the stimulus to act aggressively. This leads to anger that can eventually result in aggressive behavior. In this kind of aggression, the intent is to cause harm to the person who was responsible for angering us, and that person's suffering reinforces our aggression.[34]

But, once again, we must be careful how we interpret these findings. For, although the idea that hurting others in revenge involves pleasure in the suffering of those believed to have harmed one is compatible with these empirical findings, these findings are completely silent over *why* pain cues in people with whom we are angry tend to increase our aggression toward them. We could be jumping the gun if we concluded that it is pleasure in the suffering of these people which leads us to increased aggression. It could be this but equally, if not more plausibly, it could be caused by a whole host of other reasons. I shall cover a number of these shortly but first I want to suggest that the phenomenon of increased aggression at the sight of the suffering of those who angered us can be explained without reference to any other emotions besides our anger, indignation, and resentment towards them for what they have done.

However, even if such explanations were inadequate or wrong, and increased aggression were due to some emotional tone, it would still be doubtful whether this tone could be plausibly identified as one of pleasure, except perhaps in a minority of cases. There are several other ways of accounting for the emotional tone in question which are equally, if not more, plausible. One of these I have already mentioned: satisfaction at a job well done, a duty discharged—even if that duty necessarily involved pain for another. This may be applicable in situations where the norms of one's society prescribe revenge as a duty but also in situations where there is injury to one's dignity and self-respect as a consequence of some wrong or affront. In such situations one may consider it owing to oneself not to allow the culprit to get away with it.

The tone in question may also be identified as a sense of relief. When we are wronged and feel 'hard done by', we may feel hurt, demeaned, humiliated, resentful, and angry about the incident and a feeling of relief may well accompany a successful act of retaliation which puts an end to these intense and taxing emotions. Standing up for ourselves through retaliation also boosts our self-confidence that we are in form, that we are safe, that we can cope even if a similar aggression comes our way in the future. Not being able to retaliate or defend oneself against aggressions is likely to make one feel insecure and anxious regarding the possibility or likelihood of similar future aggressions. In other words, being able to discourage similar aggressions reassures oneself of one's ability for self-defense. But what is significant in all this, for present purposes at least, is that as soon as this is done,

one's oppressive feelings that originated from being wrongfully treated by others are naturally relieved. This relief from oppressive emotions and feelings may well be part of the characteristic experience of satisfaction we are trying to identify and explain.

A different but compatible suggestion is that the emotion in question is better identified as satisfaction at *regaining* one's identity and status as a worthwhile person. This sort of explanation would be especially plausible where part of the motivation for revenge is a wounded sense of honor, self-esteem, or even social and public reputation. And if this satisfaction also has an element of pleasure, it is quite plausible to describe it as a pleasure at having been able to do something about the violation against one's personhood, against one's physical, psychological, and moral integrity as a worthwhile, important individual. There is no doubt that being considered significant, at least to the point of being treated with respect and consideration by our fellow human beings, is an essential part of our psychological well-being in a social setting. It matters to us, for example, whether we are greeted by our friends or colleagues at work with a smile, or with a contemptuous, nasty comment. Contemptuous treatment can hurt, let alone the more serious violations of one's personhood, sense of self-worth and dignity.

Yet another way of accounting for the experience in question is by reference to the fact that retaliation, whether instantaneous or delayed (but especially if it is delayed), is extremely demanding and stressful. When retaliation is completed, this stress is released, which may feel good and pleasurable in the same way as the mere relief from an intense and prolonged physical discomfort or pain is often experienced as a form of pleasure. Moreover, it is not at all clear why, at least in some cases, the emotional tone in question could not be identified in the same way in which Nozick is happy to identify the possible emotions involved in retribution. He claims that in contrast to revenge (which, according to him, involves pleasure in the suffering of another), "retribution either need involve no emotional tone, or involves another one, namely, pleasure at justice being done."[35] For if in the end revenge turns out to be not as different from justice as Nozick and Glover seem to believe, if it turns out to be a perfectly possible way of doing justice, then surely this explanation cannot be dismissed out of hand where the emotional tone of revenge is concerned.

Finally, the notion of satisfaction, as an alternative to pleasure, cannot be over-emphasized in the case of revenge. Even linguistically there is ample warrant for emphasizing the notion of satisfaction (such as satisfaction that justice has been done or that duty has been discharged). When challenging someone to a duel to avenge an affront, one says: 'I demand satisfaction' as one throws down the gauntlet;[36] and again, according to the OED, revenge is an act done to *satisfy* oneself with retaliation for an offense on the offender.

It should be noted that all these alternative explanations for the characteristic feeling of satisfaction in question are quite compatible with one another. My suggestion is that, with possible exceptions, whenever that characteristic emotion is experienced by the avenger, it is one or a combination of these which are at work and not pleasure in the suffering of others in the way claimed by Nozick. But even if this were all wrong and the emotional tone accompanying most cases of revenge was in fact pleasure in the suffering of those who have harmed and wronged one, it is not so obvious that these cases of revenge would be morally reprehensible on that account. It is not at all obvious that, on retributive principles, there is anything wrong with taking pleasure in the deserved suffering of wrongdoers. For if one accepts the view that wrongdoers should or ought to suffer, then it is hard to see why taking pleasure in the suffering of a wrongdoer should be objectionable, since one is only taking pleasure in the fact that someone got what they deserved.

Summary of Refutations of the Three Myths

We have seen that all the major myths of revenge considered in this chapter are without foundation. The myth that the desire for revenge is a perversion of the desire to make the bad man condemn his own evil has been found wanting because, since revenge is retributive in character, it is unnecessary and inappropriate to impute such forward-looking, consequentialist goals to it. The myth that revenge is an evil vindictive passion is untenable because revenge is not sufficiently dissimilar to retributive punishment to merit their differential treatment, and because retribution, including revenge, can be justified. The relevant justifications are provided in later chapters. Further, Glover's unexplained and unsubstantiated assertion that revenge involves an unpleasant mixture of hatred and pleasure is doubtful. Hatred and bitterness are likely to develop only when people find themselves too disempowered to address serious injustices committed against them.

Finally, the myth that revenge is characterized by a morally objectionable feeling of pleasure in the suffering of others is equally unsustainable under both possible interpretations. The first interpretation fails because revenge is highly unlikely to involve morally distasteful pleasure-taking in the suffering of others *simpliciter*. This is supported by experimental research findings on the nature and psychology of human aggression. The second interpretation, that revenge might be characterized by a feeling of pleasure in the suffering of an aggressor, is equally suspect. Revenge is not typically accompanied by such feelings of pleasure, and there are alternative ways in which the emotional tone referred to by Nozick and Glover may be more plausibly identified. There is ample warrant to identify the emotional tone in question especially as *satisfaction*. But even if all the suggested alternative identifications should turn out not to be viable or applicable on retributive principles, there seems to be nothing wrong with taking pleasure in the deserved suffering of wrongdoers. This last suggestion, of course, must ultimately rely on a satisfactory account, and defense, of moral retributivism in a later chapter. In the next chapter I consider attempts to exclude revenge from being a kind of punishment.

3

Punishment and Revenge

The impulse to punish is primarily an impulse to even the score.

Robert Solomon[1]

Feuds are a basic element in the history of punishment.

Graeme Newman[2]

It was suggested in the preceding chapters that revenge is a form of retribution, a personal form of retributive punishment. In this chapter I examine views to the contrary, that revenge is not a form of punishment at all, that it is only a personal expression of feeling, with no distinctly moral content. Forming part of the dominant anti-revenge paradigm in the Western world, such views seem to be motivated by a desire to exclude revenge from the domain of morally acceptable actions. According to these views, while punishment is the justified imposition of penalties on an offender by an appropriate public authority for offenses prohibited by law, revenge is just a private expression of hurt, resentment, and anger towards those who interfered with one's interests. As such, there is no moral content in revenge to qualify it as punishment.

There are, in fact, two arguments here, bundled into one. The first argument is that punishment requires a civil authority which determines, by law, what counts as wrongdoing, what the penalties for the various wrongdoings are going to be and which imposes the appropriate penalties. Since private revenge fails this test, it is not punishment at all, but something quite different. Exponents of this view would include, for instance, Hobbes and Rawls.[3] The second argument is that revenge is just an individual, private expression of emotion which has no morally worthwhile basis. As such, revenge falls outside the sphere of the morally worthwhile to which punishment properly belongs. Once again, the conclusion is that revenge is not punishment. Among the supporters of this view are Mill and Kleinig.[4] I want to show that both views are wrong, starting with a discussion of Hobbes.

According to Hobbes, there are certain laws in civil society which are made by an appropriate public authority prohibiting certain actions, such as stealing and murder. Corresponding to each prohibited action there are appropriate penalties which are incurred for transgressing the aforementioned laws. However, in Hobbes's view, transgression of such a law is not only sufficient for punishment, but also necessary.

> A PUNISHMENT, is an evil inflicted by public authority, on him that hath done, or omitted that which is judged by the same authority to be a transgression of the law; . . . harm inflicted for a fact done before there was a law that forbade it, is not punishment, but an act of hostility: . . . punishment supposeth a fact judged, to have been a transgression of the law . . .[5]

As Hobbes also observes, from his definition of punishment it follows that

> neither private revenges, nor injuries of private men, can properly be styled punishment; because they proceed not from public authority.[6]

Such a legalistic approach to defining punishment is indefensible. Firstly, the crucial presupposition of punishment is *wrongdoing*, and not merely an action prohibited by law. Therefore, the question whether some law has been broken is not the only one that it is relevant to ask. The question of whether a wrong has been committed is equally legitimate and perhaps more important. Given that this is so, then, short of giving up his legalistic definition, Hobbes would have to say that it is public authority's task and prerogative to determine what counts as moral wrongdoing. But this move renders the project vulnerable to the familiar criticism that making the state the sole arbiter of what counts as wrongdoing leaves no basis from which to evaluate laws made by civil authority. The only way to avoid the view that in matters of punishment might is right, therefore, is to acknowledge the existence of pre-legal, moral notions of right and wrong that can serve as a basis for punishment. Indeed, in a well-governed society, such pre-legal moral principles inform and guide the legislators.

Furthermore, apart from the possibility of unjust laws, the civil authority might not have laws determining right and wrong behaviour in every area of human life, such as family and close relationships and associations. Even further, in communities with no civil authority to determine codes of behaviour, there are nonetheless moral precepts and understandings at play, perhaps upheld by custom, history, and tradition, which furnish a basis for punishment. In all three cases—that is, where the law is unjust, in areas where there are no laws, and in communities which do not have modern, state-sanctioned legal codes—on the legal positivistic view, such as that espoused by Hobbes, harmful, injurious, and socially disruptive behaviour would have to go unpunished. This would be an unacceptable situation.

A related point is that, as Kleinig points out in his criticism of Rawls, cases which we ordinarily regard as punishment, such as self-inflicted punishments, divine punishment, punishment of children by those other than their parents or guardians, punishment by private individuals where law and order have broken down, and so forth, cannot be accounted for on the 'public authority' definition of punishment.[7] Such a definition of punishment is inadequate on both practical and theoretical grounds and therefore fails to show that revenge is alien to punishment.[8]

This disagreement with Hobbes can be expressed in another way. Hobbes, along with a number of other philosophers, uses 'punishment' not in the ordinary, neutral sense, but in, what Ingemar Hedenius has aptly termed, the "honorific" sense.

> Used in this honorific sense the word 'punishment' always refers to a certain way of intentionally inflicting pain or something normally regarded as unpleasant. By calling this infliction of pain 'punishment' it is suggested that it is justified. It is embellished, ennobled.[9]

Ultimately, the question whether revenge qualifies as punishment is important only if the word 'punishment' is used in an honorific sense. If it is not assumed, as I argue in this chapter that it should not be, that punishment is somehow more moral and justified, then nothing much would depend on whether revenge is punishment. For, arguably, systems of revenge and judicial punishment are both capable of serving very similar, if not identical, functions. Consequently, if punishment were not honorified by philosophers like Hobbes, they would have to leave it genuinely up for argument as to whether judicial punishment or revenge would be the better response to wrongdoing. Such philosophers would also have to recognize that the answer can go either way, depending on the circumstances and the varying degrees of possible focus which can be adopted towards the interests of the offender, the victim or the general public. This, I suspect, is what they might be trying to avoid, but the result of that avoidance is a conceptual sleight-of-hand whereby revenge is definitionally excluded from being punishment which, in turn, is given an honorific interpretation.[10]

That Hobbes's concept of punishment is honorific, rather than neutral, is also evidenced by the fact that his definition rules out the possibility that an innocent person might be punished, even if by an unfortunate miscarriage of justice. Quinton defends this feature of the honorific concept by claiming that "punishment of the innocent . . . is only logically possible if the word 'punishment' is used in an unnatural way, for example, as meaning any kind of deliberate infliction of suffering."[11]

This is obviously not the case. If I damaged someone's car out of envy and jealousy, or sadistically tortured them, that would certainly qualify as a kind of "deliberate infliction of suffering." Yet, it would be most inappropriate to describe my actions as punishment. Contrast that with someone being tried, found legally 'guilty', and sentenced to life imprisonment in accordance with law for some crime she did not in fact commit. It would not at all be unnatural to say in such a case that the process of justice failed this person and, as a result, the poor woman was punished *in spite of her innocence*. Thinking of it in retributive terms, she could complain without contradiction or oddity that she was forced to pay the (retributive) price for someone else's misdeed, that she was forced to endure the imposition of punishment which was properly deserved by someone else.

It would be pointless, if not insulting, to tell such a person that if she is really innocent, she is misunderstanding her situation because, by definition, no one who is innocent can be punished. This would be to use, in Hart's words, "the definitional stop."[12] The pointlessness of using the definitional stop consists not only in its unhelpfulness in addressing the injustice and the tragedy which befalls the individual concerned, but also in its failure to take the problem off the hands of the system or practice of punishment which has to bear responsibility for imposing penalties on innocent people by mistakenly or wrongfully finding them guilty before the law. Punishment of the innocent, even if unintentional, is a blemish and a problem for any practice or institution of punishment. This is a genuine moral problem and it cannot be defined out of existence by resorting to the definitional stop, or by hiding behind an honorific concept of punishment. As Kleinig points out, "in these cases definitions serve only to shift the problems from one point to another."[13]

It was an illuminating suggestion by Hedenius that honorific concepts of punishment are ideal concepts.[14] They are concepts of what punishment should ideally be. Ideally, punishment should be just, in that it should not be out of proportion, or imposed on someone innocent. It should also be justified, in that there should be good, morally defensible reasons for its imposition. Ideally, however, punishment should also be imposed with due process, by appropriately appointed authorities. For this is the best way to ensure that important principles of justice, such as not punishing the innocent and not overdoing the punishment, are observed, and also that there is a finality built into the process, thus eliminating the danger of conflict escalation. This, I suggest, is the reason why the requirement that punishment be imposed by public authority figures so prominently in honorific definitions of punishment, such as Hobbes's. But, as with the possibility of punishing the innocent, while there are good reasons why punishment is often better placed in the hands of some authority rather than left to private individuals, as Kleinig also points out against Flew, "this is quite different from saying that an imposition *is* punishment *only* if it is imposed by some authority."[15]

I turn now to the second argument for the view that revenge is not in the domain of punishment, the argument that, while punishment necessarily has to do with the realm of the morally good, revenge is merely a personal expression of emotion, devoid of positive moral substance. Mill and Kleinig are representative of this position.

> [T]he natural feeling of retaliation or vengeance, . . . in itself, *has nothing moral in it*[16] (my emphasis).

> The key to revenge lies in the motives of the aggrieved party. For the ground of revenge, and the feature which distinguishes it from punishment, is the fact that someone has *hurt me* or someone close to me. Revenge is the getting of one's own back; *the notion of moral wrong is irrelevant to it* (my emphasis.) . . . It is for this reason that revenge can be taken on a person whose actions are recognized to be morally praiseworthy. If X murders Y and is gaoled for it, I, being a close friend, relative or admirer of X, may without logical oddity be said to seek revenge on the policeman who caught him or the judge who sentenced him.[17]

Kleinig's argument is flawed. For while it is true that revenge is personal in a way that some other forms of punishment may not be, this does not render revenge either morally worthless or objectionable. Moreover, this personal element in revenge allows a more plausible alternative explanation in terms of the subjective/objective distinction of the example suggested by Kleinig. Such an explanation could be that while the punishment imposed on X may have been fair and just from an objective point of view, or from the point of view of the law and the public interest, it can still be judged without logical oddity to have been *unfair from Kleinig's subjective point of view*—a subjective point of view which, typically, in their own cases people tend to regard as objectively right.

The crucial point, however, is that, *essentially, resentment is a moral emotion*. It is conceptually tied to the notion of injustice. For, even if it is possible to feel momentary anger-like, non-moral resentment, the resentment which typically characterizes revenge is not fleeting but is of the enduring sort, and, as Butler points out,

> . . . it is not natural, but moral evil; it is not suffering, but injury, which raises that anger or resentment, which is of any continuance."[18]

Contra Kleinig, moral notions such as *injustice*, and *moral wrong* are central to understanding resentment and revenge, and it would be contradictory for him (or anybody else) to seek revenge on the policeman or the judge while believing at the same time that *the policeman and the judge were right and morally praiseworthy for catching and sentencing X.* Unless an explanation appealing to the notion of injustice or moral wrong (while also allowing different points of view, perhaps) was applicable, the most charitable interpretation of such a person, I suggest, would be to regard them as confused. Such a person would have failed the process of socialization in a serious way: he was not taught, or he somehow failed to learn, the appropriate emotional responses required by moral belief.

The failure in this case is the violation of the logic of resentment. For, unless a person is forced to take revenge under the powerful sway of custom or social norm which makes it mandatory in that situation, it would have to be resentment which fuels his desire for revenge; and resentment proper is impossible in the absence of some perceived unfairness, injustice or otherwise demeaning or wrongful treatment. If we tried to understand a person seeking revenge in a situation such as the above, we would want to find out what feature of *X's* punishment he considered unfair, unjust, or improper. What we may discover is that he found the sentence too harsh or inappropriate for *X's* physical and emotional condition, or he thought that the policeman used humiliating or excessive force when arresting *X,* or that *X* was not given a fair trial, or that in sentencing *X,* the judge was reprehensible for ignoring those who depended on *X.* But if the person in question did not think that there was anything amiss with the arrest and the trial and believed that the police and the judge acted in a praiseworthy manner in all respects, it would be contradictory and abnormal if he still wanted to get back at them.

Similarly, in response to Mill we need to ask *why* the natural feeling of retaliation or vengeance arises in the first place. As before, the answer to this question lies in the emotion or sentiment of resentment which in most cases is what explains the desire for revenge. It is resentment that typically furnishes and fuels the desire for revenge. Were it not for the remarkable human capacity to resent someone or something with intensity over prolonged periods of time, revenge would be unlikely to be still with us today.

Resentment, however, as I already intimated, is a complex emotion. It is different from immediate, spontaneous flashes of anger which may arise in response to almost any kind of hurt. Flashes of anger most often die as quickly as they arise, especially in response to accidental hurt. By contrast, however, resentment is a kind of settled, lasting anger and what settles it in the human heart is perceptions of injustice, unfairness, uncalled-for personal violation, wrongful injury, a feeling of having been demeaned or badly done by. For example, one might become momentarily angry at being accidentally hit by a falling tree branch but that is likely to be the end of the matter. The reason why it would make no sense to resent the tree is because the tree is incapable of performing a moral wrong, and therefore an injustice, to anybody. However, one may well feel resentful towards a neighbor if one perceives that they have deliberately lopped the tree in such a way as to hit one with the falling branch. It is such a perception of an unjustified provocation which gives rise to, and fuels, resentment. As Rashdall argued,

> indignation or resentment at wrong arises naturally and spontaneously in the human mind without any calculation of the personal or social benefits to be derived from gratifying it, . . .[19]

It is worth noting again that there is an important difference between enduring resentment on the one hand and other well-known negative emotions on the other. Anger, hatred, envy and jealousy, for example, can be directed against others without the presence of that component which is so crucial to enduring resentment, which is typically present in revenge: the belief that some kind of unfairness or injustice has befallen one. This kind of resentment can be directed against people only when they are believed to bear some degree of responsibility for unfair, morally wrongful treatment.[20] The idea of resenting someone who at the same time is seen to have done nothing wrong (either directly or by association) makes no sense.[21] Therefore, whenever the desire for revenge is fuelled by resentment, that desire cannot lack moral content.

Of course, in the case of resentment the perceived insult, injustice, or wrongful conduct is perceived to have been directed against *oneself,* not against unrelated others. When improper, wrongful conduct is perceived by us to be directed towards someone with whom we do not have a personal or special tie, our moral response, to the extent that we do have one, is one of indignation.[22] When such conduct is directed towards us in particular, the equivalent and corresponding emotion is one of resentment. This is because resentment is *self-,* rather than *other-,* related. Moreover, this response of resentment to injustice against ourselves and those close to us is entirely appropriate. As Murphy points out,

> If it is proper to feel indignation when I see third parties morally wronged, must it not be equally proper to feel resentment when I experience the moral wrong done to myself?[23]

Similarly, Adam Smith in his *Theory of the Moral Sentiments,* writes that

> The violation of justice is injury . . . it is, therefore, the proper object of resentment, and of punishment, which is the natural consequence of resentment.[24]

Finally, in his sermon *Upon Resentment,* Butler speaks in the following vein:

> And this seems to be the whole of this passion, which is, properly speaking, natural to mankind: namely, a resentment against injury and wickedness in general;

and in a higher degree when towards ourselves, in proportion to the greater regard which men naturally have for themselves, than for others. From hence it appears, that it is not natural, but moral evil; it is not suffering, but injury, which raises that anger or resentment, which is of any continuance.[25]

Although Butler does not insist on a sharp distinction between resentment and indignation, as Murphy does, he nevertheless concurs with the general point that resentment is a response to a perceived moral wrong.

This much should suffice by way of showing that resentment is a cognitively based moral emotion,[26] and therefore that revenge and the desire for revenge are as squarely in the domain of the morally worthwhile and important as any (other) form of punishment can be. But there is, in addition, another way of strengthening this case. Hampton and Murphy each point out that another essential part of resentment, besides the perception of a moral wrong, is self-respect.

> [T]he primary value defended by the passion of resentment is *self-respect*, . . . proper self-respect is essentially tied to the passion of resentment . . .[27]

> the ability to feel resentment following a wrongdoing depends upon one's having enough sense of one's own worth to believe that the treatment is inappropriate and worthy of protest. . . . We will also criticize people for not feeling resentment . . . if we believe this shows they have too low an evaluation of themselves.[28]

I find this a plausible line of argument. If correct, it furnishes another reason for rejecting the claims made by Kleinig and Mill that the natural feeling of retaliation or vengeance has no moral content. This particular argument against their claims goes as follows: Self-respect is an essential part of resentment, and "resentment . . . is a good thing, for it is essentially tied to a non-controversially good thing—self-respect."[29] For example, when we see somebody who does not resent what are obvious insults and put-downs, it is very natural to wonder if they are lacking in self-esteem. It is not that low self-esteem is what always explains lack of resentment, but rather that resentment depends on one's having enough self-esteem to believe that what is resented is unfair to oneself and that it must be resisted for that reason. In short, since self-esteem and self-respect which are uncontroversially important and good are necessarily present in resentment which, in turn, is the typical driving force behind the desire for revenge, it cannot be the case that revenge is bereft of any morally good content, that there is nothing morally worthwhile about it.

While this argument leaves open the question whether any particular instance of revenge is morally justified, it might be objected that only the self-respect of respectable people is good. But even if this were true, it would not affect the argument where it matters most: the moral appropriateness of a victim's feeling indignant and resentful in the face of injustice and unfair treatment. Moreover, it is questionable whether the undermining of an offender's self-esteem and self-respect could be desirable. Low self-esteem is a significant contributing factor to juvenile delinquency, domestic violence, rape, and similar forms of criminal behaviour. Rehabilitation and correction from such anti-social behaviour patterns has little chance of succeeding unless there are ways to improve self-esteem and self-respect in the offenders concerned. Indeed, one of the most useful ways to mark the difference between constructive and destructive shaming of wrongdoers is by reference to whether their self-esteem and self-respect is protected (and possibly boosted), rather than being undermined, in the process.

Returning to the question of relating revenge to the moral domain, many thinkers in the history of philosophy have shown a readiness to acknowledge the moral element in revenge, even if some of them were against revenge as a practice. Carlyle, for instance, exalts revenge with the words:

> Revenge, my friends, revenge and the natural hatred of scoundrels, and the ineradicable tendency to revancher oneself upon them, and pay them what they have merited; this is for evermore intrinsically a correct, and even a divine feeling in the mind of every man.[30]

Another example is Bacon who has provided us, perhaps, with one of the most elegant and insightful descriptions of revenge by calling it "a kind of wild justice."[31] Again, Russell in his *History of Western Philosophy,* points out that "revenge . . . [cannot be] wholly condemned, for it is one of the forces generating punishment, and punishment is sometimes necessary."[32]

More recently, in their book *Vengeance: The Fight Against Injustice,* Marongiu and Newman have argued that

> All acts of vengeance arise from an elementary sense of injustice, a primitive feeling that one has been arbitrarily subjected to a tyrannical power against which one is powerless to act.[33]

Although these authors are by no means favorably disposed towards revenge, they do not hesitate to recognize the fact that the avenger's motivation consists of a desire for equality, justice and reciprocity. There is, however, a distinct group of contemporary philosophers who are willing to throw their full support behind revenge. Robert Solomon is representative of this group:

> [T]o seek vengeance for a grievous wrong, to revenge oneself against evil—that seems to lie at the very foundation of our sense of justice, indeed, of our very sense of ourselves, our dignity and our sense of right and wrong.[34]

Similarly, Susan Jacoby argues that

> The personal and social price we pay for the pretense that revenge and justice
> have nothing to do with each other is as high as the one paid by the Victorians
> for their conviction that lust was totally alien to the marital love sanctioned by
> church and state.[35]

Finally, it is worth mentioning Andrew Oldenquist who argues that

> personal accountability makes no sense unless it means that transgressors deserve
> punishment—that is, they are owed retribution; and there is no doubt that retri-
> bution is revenge, both historically and conceptually.[36]

Given the boldness with which Solomon, Jacoby, and Oldenquist
declare their allegiance to revenge, it hardly comes as a surprise that they are
retributivists who identify retribution, including judicial retribution, with
revenge. I find the *identification* of retribution with revenge problematic
and will take up the issue in Chapter 6. What is important to note here is
that while it is right to claim that revenge is accompanied by powerful sentiments and feelings, the presence of these emotions is quite compatible with
revenge being morally good and worthwhile. Injustice and moral wrong
which give rise to the emotions behind revenge provide as good a moral
basis for revenge as there can be. As Solomon argues the point,

> Sometimes vengeance is wholly called for, even obligatory, and revenge is both
> legitimate and justified. Sometimes it is not, notably when one is mistaken about
> the offender or the offense.[37]

Summary of This Chapter's Conclusions

There is no basis for the view that revenge is not a form of punishment. It is
retributive punishment of a personal nature, and just like any other form of
punishment it can be just or unjust depending on whether it violates any of
the principles of justice, such as proportionality and getting the right person. The fact that unregulated, raw revenge can easily get out of hand, or
that it can get the wrong person do not justify banning revenge altogether,
let alone justifying the view that revenge is not a form of punishment.
Judicial punishment can also get the wrong person from time to time, and
it can be more severe than what is merited. If there are similar or greater
concerns for revenge in these respects, then they only give reasons for
building safeguards around revenge. These points will be taken up in proper
detail in the last two chapters.

I have argued that revenge is properly regarded as a form of punishment. The state is not the sole arbiter of what counts as a punishable moral wrong and revenge is normally taken in response to offensive, unfair, and generally wrongful conduct. Therefore, contrary to the suggestions of Mill and Kleinig, revenge does not fall outside the moral domain where punishment is more readily recognized to belong. The sense of self-worth or self-respect which is present in resentment, and therefore in revenge, provides additional grounds for not excluding revenge from that sphere of human concern and activity which we call the moral. Indeed, there is a strong philosophical tradition which does not attempt to write revenge out of the moral script, although it is often ambivalent, if not critical, of revenge. The philosophers who support revenge most strongly are those retributivists who identify retribution with revenge, and their views will be examined in Chapter 6.

4

Rationality and Revenge

Punishment may or may not teach right and wrong. The important fact is that it supports the morality of social order.

Graeme Newman[1]

An important aspect of the anti-revenge paradigm is the notion that revenge is somehow irrational or self-defeating. In this chapter I show that this view is wrong. I do not wish to claim, of course, that revenge is somehow inherently rational. There would be very few human endeavors, if any, that would have an inherently rational or irrational character in and by themselves, independently of context and circumstance. Therefore, what a defense of the rationality of revenge needs to show is that, as with any other undertaking, revenge can be rational or irrational, depending on the circumstances and, therefore, insofar as rationality is concerned, each act of vengeance must be evaluated on its own merits. This, in a nutshell, is my project in the current chapter, starting with a consideration of the importance of rationality, which is followed by a demonstration of the individual rationality of revenge. I then go on to argue for the collective rationality of revenge as an institutionalized practice in revenge cultures. Lastly, consideration is given to the place of honor in paradigm cases of revenge, such as the blood feud.

Rationality and Its Significance

According to standard definitions (from the OED), a rational person is one endowed with reason, agreeable to reason, sane, intelligent, and judicious. A rational person makes reasoned assessment a basis for action. This sounds plausible and accurate in terms of the ordinary use of the term 'rational.'[2]

The ability to make rational decisions is of obvious instrumental value, particularly when the stakes are high. As a tool it can help us considerably in achieving specific short and long-term goals, but also more generally in our pursuit of the good life and the common good. Those who are rational in their choices and conduct are more likely to be successful both in achieving specific goals and in leading the sort of life they want to live than those who are irrational, inconsistent, and erratic.

Exceptions have to be allowed for, of course, as sometimes it can happen that an irrational choice turns out to be the best one for furthering one's interests. For example, on the balance of probabilities, regularly gambling large sums of money is hardly the rational strategy for the average person in the pursuit of long term financial security. Yet it can happen that through a series of remarkable coincidences one ends up making a fortune. But, far from being the norm, cases like this are the exception. By and large, one's success rate in achieving goals is proportional to the extent that one thinks and acts rationally. This point has been argued in considerably more detail, by Max Black who challenges the views of Geach, Singer, and Ayer according to whom the question *Why should I be rational?* is somehow illegitimate, absurd, or that it can be dismissed because "it questions something which is normally presupposed."[3] In his own answer to the question, Black points out that

> The price of poor reasoning, whether through misperception or erroneous anticipation, can be frustration, hurt or extinction. . . . You should respect 'basic reasons' (be basically rational) because not to do so is to expose yourself to almost certain frustration, pain and death.[4]

The rational pursuit of one's interests, especially self-interest and interests arising out of partisanship, however, can be carried too far and an important function of morality is to curtail rational pursuits of individual interests which would unacceptably infringe on the interests of others. Sen's following little story is an illustration of just how undesirable and nasty uncurtailed, self-seeking rationality would be.

> 'Where is the railway station?' he asks me. 'There,' I say, pointing at the post office, 'and would you please post this letter for me on the way?' 'Yes,' he says, determined to open the envelope and check whether it contains something valuable.[5]

Such a relentlessly calculating attitude towards others is as undesirable as it is unrealistic to suppose it of most people. It would be very hard to relate to someone who constantly calculated the costs and benefits to themselves of doing every small thing, especially at close personal levels, such as in friendships and family relationships. Also, as Johansen points out,

No society would be viable without some norms and rules of conduct. Such norms and rules are necessary for viability exactly in fields where strictly economic incentives are absent and cannot be created.[6]

But, notwithstanding the necessary moral limits, prudential arguments lend a strong normative dimension to rationality—a dimension within which theories of rationality can be used not only to describe, explain and predict, but also to prescribe, evaluate, and criticize individual human behaviour. Moreover, even social and moral norms must be open to broad rational evaluation and criticism from the point of view of the overall interests of the community in question, or from the point of view of other communities which are unduly and detrimentally affected by the first community's practices and norms. Especially in a fast-changing world, norms and customs can become obsolete, inapplicable, cumbersome, or even destructive—and not only to the individual but also to the overall interests of those affected by them. Having outlived their usefulness, when norms become no more than the dead hand of the past clutching and strangling the living present through sheer inertia, a burden and an unnecessary liability for the community and its individual members, they ought to be questioned, undermined and abandoned. As with counterproductive and destructive habits and dispositions, continued adherence to such norms is (collectively) irrational and becomes a legitimate target for rational criticism. However, a word of caution is in order here, for it may still be *individually* rational to adhere to a collectively irrational norm. This may be the case, for example, when social sanctioning of defectors is severe enough. I argue this point in more detail in the latter part of Chapter 7.

From here, for purposes of a satisfactory defense of revenge, the significance of demonstrating the possibility of rational revenge is obvious. For, if arguments were successful in establishing that revenge behaviour is inherently irrational, that it is incompatible with and defies attempts at rational explanations, the case against revenge would be serious. A satisfactory defense of revenge must be able to resist Elster's claim that "the most plausible explanation for revenge behavior lies in psychological propensities that do not appear to serve any individual, social, or genetic purpose."[7]

At the same time, we cannot lose sight of the fact that there is a clear distinction between rationality as an attribute of people on the one hand, and theories of rationality which attempt to explain what rationality is, on the other. It is important to keep these two apart. Thus, a claim such as Elster's, that revenge behaviour cannot be explained by recourse to a particular ends-means maximizing rational choice theory,[8] need not, in itself, amount to a reason or objection against revenge, or even against its rationality, which may be demonstrated and accounted for by recourse to a different theory. This in fact is the case where revenge behavior can be shown to have a principally deontological basis. The immediate motivation behind norm-guided revenge behavior, for instance, is mostly deontological: *If a man rapes your mother, wife, or daughter, you must kill him.* Such deontological rules may not by any means be above criticism. But criticizing someone who acted on such a deontological maxim by simply claiming that the person looked to a rule or social norm, instead of his or her future interests to consider the costs and benefits of killing the rapist, would be misplaced.

This does not mean, of course, that consequences are not important. What it does mean is that direct consideration of consequences in every single instance is not the best way to make one's decisions. As Hare argued the point in relation to moral thinking and action,[9] it is often more appropriate and better to act on the basis of established rules and norms, rather than direct cost-benefit analyses in every situation. Such norm-guided behaviour is not different from meritorious promise keeping. If I keep my promises only if and when it suits me in strictly forward-looking terms, I have a questionable claim to merit. If, on the other hand, I keep my promises as a matter of principle, because I accept the fairness and rightness of the moral injunction *Whoever makes a promise, must keep it,* I am living up to a moral ideal. Any criticism that in keeping my promises I am looking backwards, rather than conducting a quick cost-benefit analysis for my future interests, would be repugnant.

Immediate Costs and Benefits in Revenge

According to Elster, by definition, revenge "only involves costs and risks, no benefits,"[10] and

> the most plausible explanation for revenge behavior lies in psychological propensities that do not appear to serve any individual, social, or genetic purpose.[11]

These views are wrong.[12] Rationality in revenge can be demonstrated both from the point of view of an individual and from the point of view of communities whose justice systems are based on revenge as an institutionalized practice. There are circumstances, for example, in which revengefulness is accompanied by substantial material rewards, even though the aim of revenge is not these rewards, but just retribution conceived as reciprocity and deserved payback with the aim of getting even. To this end, consider the following example.

Transylvanian Life: Suppose that Jakob and Julia live as good neighbors in a Transylvanian township, at some time during the *Ceausescu* era. Just like most other people around them, they work hard and are paid little. And, just like most other people around them, they both engage in various unlawful activities in order to make a hard life a little more comfortable. Jakob, for example, regularly steals agricultural goods, such as corn, wheat and potatoes, from the co-operative where he works and whatever he does not use he sells on the black market. Julia is similarly involved in improving her life by illegally importing and selling Western luxury items such as jeans, color television sets, and push-button phones. A third neighbor is involved in diverting building materials from state construction sites to trusted customers of his own, and so on. They all know of each other's activities and also that there is a substantial reward for reporting on other people's illegal activities, say $5,000. Despite the incentives to do each other in, they all keep silent. After all, they are all in the same boat, so to speak.

Now suppose that one day the *Securitate* (Ceausescu's secret police) raids Julia's house, seizes her luxury items and she ends up in a forced labour camp. She is also questioned regarding other illegal activities that she might know of and, as an inducement she is promised not only the usual reward for reporting on illegal activities but also a substantial reduction in her sentence. Obviously, in the circumstances it would be perfectly rational for her to report any of her neighbors. However, having a sense of solidarity, she does not report any of the others despite the fact that in the circumstances it would pay her to do so even more than it would have before she was caught.

Let us put aside for a moment whether her silence over her neighbors' illegal activities is rational or not, and consider only whether it would be irrational of her to take revenge on any one of her neighbors if she found out that a particular one of them was the informer. Suppose, for example, that after a period of bitterness and hard labour in a detention camp she finds out that it was Jakob who reported her. She is outraged by the betrayal and sets about to get even with Jakob, to pay him back for everything she has endured. But will it be rational of her to seek retribution and avenge Jakob's treachery by, say, similarly reporting on his illegal business? Of course it will be. She will be rewarded for her reporting with $5,000. More importantly, her sentence will be reduced.

This example shows clearly, I believe, that the material costs and benefits of revenge are circumstantial. It is a mistake to suppose that on account of its retributive character, revenge can involve only costs and no benefits. A residual worry that some people might express at this point is whether Julia's reporting on Jakob is appropriately described as revenge. Is it not otiose, an objection might go, to call it revenge when it would have been rational of her to report on Jakob even if she were totally ignorant of his treachery? The answer is straightforward enough: Julia's primary motive was fair retribution; she wanted to get even with Jakob, she wanted to pay him back for what he did to her. Her getting back at him is both retributive and personal in the most appropriate senses to qualify her action as a genuine, unambiguous case of revenge.

A further feature of this case is the fact that she did not consider the rationality of reporting on someone whom she believed was innocent (of harming her) as a sufficient reason for getting others into trouble. Her discovery of Jakob's treachery and her desire to hit back was what made the relevant difference. It was her desire to hit back for the treachery which made her reporting a genuine case of revenge, and the fact that her action was also going to benefit her considerably in the particular situation was what made it clearly rational. This is a clear, unambiguous example of rational revenge where one is rational to engage in revengeful behaviour even in a single, isolated case.[13]

This example does not show, of course, that revenge can be rational on account of its own nature. It was never intended to show that, and no one needs to show that. To reiterate, my claim is not that revenge is *intrinsically* rational, that it can be rational independently of any further considerations besides retribution, regardless of circumstances. As already pointed out, there are few, if any, human actions which could meet such stringent criteria of rationality. Rather, I am arguing that in certain circumstances revenge can be an individually rational option to take. There are circumstances in which, far from being counterproductive, detrimental, or self-defeating, revengefulness can be quite compatible with important material interests. Especially where a long-term perspective is adopted, absorbing short-term losses in the interests of greater returns in the future is eminently rational.

The Collective Rationality of Revenge as an Institutionalized Practice

It is widely recognized that revenge practices in pre-industrial societies which have no centralized law enforcement agencies, serve important functions equivalent to functions served by contemporary Western justice systems. To quote Herbert Spencer,

> [T]he practice, alike of immediate revenge and of postponed revenge, establishes itself as in some measure a check upon aggression; since the motive to aggress is checked by the consciousness that a counter-aggression will come: if not at once then after a time. Among human beings in early stages, there hence arises not only the practice of revenge but a belief that revenge is imperative—that revenge is a duty.[14]

Similarly, speaking of the indignation and resentment at wrong which "arises naturally and spontaneously in the human mind," Rashdall speaks of the

> profound ethical conviction that for societies—though not always for individuals—it is morally good and healthy that this indignation should be encouraged and expressed.[15]

Again, Boehm makes the following observations about the (informal) institution of the feud among the Montenegrins:

> In many respects the morality of several thousand people who are living in a per-
> manently settled tribal territory is unlike our own morality. There is less concern
> for legalistic maneuvering, and more for personal and clan reputation. There are
> no specialized police officers or judges, nor are there any prisons. But there are
> very powerful sanctions that shape behavior, and these operate both directly and
> indirectly, intentionally and automatically. Feuding was essentially a positively
> valued institution insofar as the moral system was concerned, in that it involved
> the upholding of honor. In addition, . . . feuding served as a kind of sanction,
> because it suppressed certain immoral behaviors that people knew were likely to
> start feuds. They also knew that feuds were dangerous, stressful, economically
> costly, and generally inconvenient from a practical standpoint. . . . [T]he effects
> of feuding as a social sanction were highly significant for this very aggressive
> people, who deliberately chose to live their lives with the near absence of any
> coercive authority in human form. . . . [F]euding served as a substitute for such
> authority, in that the probability of lethal retaliation and then a costly feud
> sharply curtailed certain socially disruptive behaviors.[16]

As evidenced by these passages, considerations of the collective rationality of revenge as a socially enforced institution or practice tend to be min-
gled with considerations of its morality. The difficulties of keeping the two
spheres apart are due to the fact that the rationality of revenge as a practice
is evaluated by reference to the common good which, recognizably, is a
moral concept. Moreover, in the case of revenge as an institutionalized
practice, the notion of the common good includes not only such considerations as public safety and security (to be promoted by means of deterrence),
but also considerations of such highly esteemed, non-instrumental moral
values as retributive justice and honor which are universally shared among
members of the societies in question.[17]

While the collective rationality and morality of particular revenge practices such as the Montenegrin blood feud may be controversial, it is not at
all clear that, in principle, such informal social institutions are inferior to,
say, contemporary systems of criminal justice. Supposing that a community
of freedom-loving individuals needs to find some kind of (formal or informal) mechanism for achieving the above-mentioned array of values and
goals, and given that they prefer to do this cost-effectively and without the
creation of a centralized state or authority, it is hard to see what better
options there could be than victim-focused, private systems of law enforcement for which we have creditable historical precedents.[18]

As against the idea that legal justice systems such as those currently
operating in contemporary Western societies are rationally preferable to victim-focused traditional systems which incorporate regulated revenge practices, we need to keep in mind that the former are not only enormously

expensive but also questionable in terms of efficiency and integrity, as pointed out in our Introduction. Corruption and abuse of power in public offices, for example, are ever-present concerns, and it is hardly an exaggeration to say that the ongoing tolerance many contemporary legal systems show towards lawyers' excessive preoccupation with winning court cases, rather than finding out the truth of the matter, is a mockery of justice.[19]

It might be retorted, however, that in revenge cultures there is typically an excessive preoccupation with honor and that this is rationally indefensible. This perception is indeed very strong in contemporary Western societies, and it forms part of the *anti-revenge paradigm*. This is the view that needs to be considered next.

The Place of Honor in Traditional Revenge Cultures

Elster's low esteem of honor provides a useful starting point.

> Asserting one's honor, like enjoying other people's envy of one's assets, is an aspect of a deep-rooted urge to be superior to other people. . . . Its aim is sheer self-assertion and self-esteem. . . . I believe the urge for honor, like the enjoyment of other people's envy, are universal phenomena. They can be controlled but not fully suppressed. They arise in the mind spontaneously but need not have any further effect if we can recognize them and avoid acting on them.[20]

Such evaluations of revenge are untenable. They display a serious lack of understanding of the nature and vital significance of honor for the individual in the relevant cultures. In cultures with an honor-based system of morality, honor is constitutive of a person's very identity in the epistemic sense (but not necessarily in the metaphysical sense, of course) in the same way that dignity is constitutive of our identity in contemporary Western societies. Identity in the epistemic sense is a narrative, a story one constructs and tells about oneself regarding who and what sort of person one is. In a culture of honor individuals define themselves in terms of their position, their status, and the roles they have in their community. Failing to fulfill one's roles means losing one's honor and together with that one is losing one's self-respect, and one's identity as a worthy individual. It will be worth quoting Peter Berger in this regard:

> Dignity, as against honor, always relates to the intrinsic humanity divested of all socially imposed roles or norms. It pertains to the self as such, to the individual regardless of his position in society. . . . [By contrast,] in a world of honor, the individual discovers his true identity in his roles, and to turn away from the roles is to turn away from himself. . . . Both honor and dignity are concepts that bridge self and society. While either pertains to the individual in a very intimate way, it is in relations with others that both honor and dignity are attained,

exchanged, preserved or threatened. Both require a deliberate effort of the will for their maintenance—one must strive for them, often against the malevolent opposition of others—thus honor and dignity become goals of moral enterprise. Their loss, always a possibility, has far-reaching consequences for the self.[21]

Since in honor-based cultures honor is an essential ingredient of an individual's identity, self-worth, and self-respect, it is something that in valuing oneself the individual necessarily nurtures and, if need be, fiercely protects. But, a culture of honor is also likely to make different demands on the individual from a culture of dignity.

> In a culture of dignity, people were expected to remain deaf to the same insults that Southern men were expected to resent. "Call a man a liar in Mississippi," an old saying went, "and he will knock you down; in Kentucky, he will shoot you; in Indiana, he will say 'You are another.'" Dignity might be likened to an internal skeleton, to a hard structure at the center of the self; honor, on the other hand, resembles a cumbersome and vulnerable suit of armor that, once pierced, leaves the self no protection and no alternative except to strike back in desperation.[22]

It is clear from this passage that in a culture of honor an injury to one's honor can be as damaging to the individual as injuries to our dignity today would be and, probably, much worse on account of the intense social disapproval which accompanies one's loss of honor. Such threats to one's self-respect and identity as a valuable, worthy individual cannot be ignored. Something must be done about them. In the relevant cultures in particular—where in many cases there is no efficient external authority to take possession of the conflict—it often happens that the best, even if not the only, available defense against such threats is revenge. In such cases taking revenge is perfectly rational in a proper and defensible normative sense. By taking revenge one employs the best available means to save one's honor which is an essential and integral part of one's identity as a worthy individual.

If all this is correct, honor cannot be excluded from being a proper aim of revenge and, therefore, it cannot be excluded from being a goal capable of providing a basis for substantive, rational choice explanations of honor-based revenge. I consider in more detail the rationality of honor-based revenge behaviour in the latter part of Chapter 7. A more detailed case for the rationality of allowing certain formally institutionalized practices of revenge will be provided in Chapters 8–10, where I defend the morality of victim-oriented, institutionalized systems of justice. For now, the above defense of the rationality of revenge completes the case against the anti-revenge paradigm.

Summary of the Argument So Far

Before we move on, in Chapters 5–7, to discuss the nature of revenge, let us briefly review the ground we have covered. The overall context for the book was set in the Introduction and was further crystallized in Chapter 1 with a discussion of competing paradigms of justice. In the pro-revenge paradigm, revenge is held to be the ideal response to injustice, while in the anti-revenge paradigm there is an outright rejection of anything that is even remotely associated with revenge. Both these paradigms are lopsided, but an empowerment paradigm of justice would avoid their excesses, while preserving what is best from both. In such a paradigm of justice, victims and offenders are appropriately empowered by law so that they can become active participants in the criminal justice processes, supported by appropriate legal rights to have a substantial say in how their own cases are resolved. In Chapter 2 the main beliefs and rationales supporting the anti-revenge paradigm were subjected to critical examination and were found lacking in philosophically defensible foundations. They were found to be little more than dogmas and myths, most likely born of poor thinking, misguided piety, or perhaps fear of strong emotions such as anger and resentment. In Chapter 3 attention was directed to the question whether revenge can be properly regarded as a form of punishment. The answer to this question is affirmative. Revenge has all the morally relevant features to qualify as punishment, since it is a punitive response towards the wrongdoer by the wronged person, or by someone close to the wronged person, for the injustices and wrongs committed against them.

In Chapter 4 the claim that revenge is not rational was taken up, and the possibility of rational revenge was defended on both individual and collective levels. Victim-focused approaches in pre-colonial indigenous societies with their reliance on revenge served the same functions as criminal justice systems of the Western world are meant to serve today. (The sensible and rational nature of traditional approaches, including their tolerance of, and reliance on, fair retribution and revenge, is further demonstrated by the fact that these victim-focused approaches are now being re-introduced in the Western world in the form of *alternative dispute resolution processes* to address the failures of the status quo. This radical return to the old approach will be discussed in detail in Chapters 9 and 10.)

5

Retribution and Justice

There has never been a time in history when wrongful acts were rewarded. In fact, such a possibility is plainly ridiculous.

Graeme Newman[1]

I have shown that there is no justification for the Western world's grim view of revenge, and that revenge is a form of punishment which need not be crazy or nasty. In the next three chapters I will argue that revenge is retributive punishment of a personal kind and that, just like any other kind of punishment, retribution, including personal retribution, which is revenge, can be just or unjust depending on whether the principles of justice, such as proportionality and not punishing the innocent, are observed or violated. All this necessitates a thorough examination of the natures of retribution, justice, and revenge, and of the way these key concepts are related to one another.

While it is clear that retribution and revenge are closely related, there is no consensus on what retributivism as a seriously proposed philosophical thesis is. There is a multitude of proposed definitions, rationales, and justifications on offer. John Cottingham, for example, identified no less than nine senses in which the words 'retribution' and 'retributive', are being used. The remarkable diversity of these senses is testimony to Cottingham's claim that "the term 'retributive' as used in philosophy has become so imprecise and multi-vocal that it is doubtful whether it any longer serves a useful purpose."[2]

The main reason for this unsatisfactory state of affairs is that the philosophical literature on retribution contains at least three different clusters of ideas which are often indiscriminately jumbled together. The ideas concerned are as follows: First, the definition of retributive punishment, commonly referred to simply as 'retribution.' Second, the principles of justice appropriate to punishment contexts, such as proportionality and not punishing the innocent. Third, moral retributivism, which is a distinctive philosophical position on the question of what it is that justifies punishment.

Moral retributivism and its justification are going to be covered later. In this chapter I will clarify the notion of retribution and the principles of justice, and in the following chapter I will challenge previous attempts to identify and explain the relationship between retribution and revenge. In the light of these clarifications I will propose, in Chapter 7, a new way of understanding the nature of revenge, arguing that revenge is a species of retribution, that it is retributive punishment of a personal kind.

The Definition of Retribution

While *retribution* may not be an entirely clear notion, there are two familiar ways to make sense of it: *repayment* and *desert*. It is unproblematic to agree with Cottingham that the most basic sense of 'retribution' is the *repayment* sense. This is the primary meaning that most dictionaries give of the term and, apart from its etymology which is the Latin *retribuo = I pay back*, there is an ordinary way of talking about punishment that fits this sense, which is also acknowledged in the literature.[3] In this sense, retributive punishment is some kind of negative repayment, a kind of tit for tat. It is the repayment of some wrong or offense with the imposition of some kind of penalty.[4] However, I also agree with Cottingham that

> our basic (repayment) sense of 'retribution' . . . is not so much a theory as a *metaphor*, a metaphor which . . . is central to the basic signification of 'retribution', but which . . . cuts remarkably little ice as a justificatory device.[5]

A different but popular way of construing retribution is via the idea of *desert*. According to this formulation, retributive punishment is imposed as a matter of negative moral desert for wrongdoing. However, there are difficulties with using the notion of negative desert to *define* retribution. It is not entirely clear, for example, why the desert concept of punishment should be labeled 'retributive.' The idea of imposing punishment on someone because they deserve it does not seem to entail that they are being paid back for what they did. Even if we adopted the view that desert is a function of the free actions of persons, the entailment from negative desert to repayment is still not straightforward, and requires further explanation and argumentation.

It is not rare to find whole discussions of retribution exclusively in terms of desert as if that was the only correct way to define and understand it.[6] This cannot be right, however. The notion of desert is too restrictive to allow the definition to range over cases of retribution where certain principles of justice are violated. For, just like any other kind of punishment, retribution can also get the wrong person, it can be inflicted for offenses which are not moral wrongs, and it can certainly be overdone. The natural thing to say in such cases is that the retribution is unfair, unjust. But in order to allow for this possibility the definition of 'retribution' must be left unbounded by the principles of justice. This is where, unlike the notion of negative repayment, the notion of negative desert cannot deliver. For example, if a massive penalty is returned for a minor wrong, we have draconian, disproportionate retribution in the repayment sense. It becomes rather problematic, however, to express the same judgment under a desert conception of retribution because a minor offense is hardly deserving of a massive penalty, a good example being the cutting off of someone's hand for stealing.[7]

Put in a different way, a desert-based definition of 'retribution' leaves what we would normally call unfair, unjust cases of retribution without a proper name or a natural category of their own. Many construals of retributive punishment, such as the ones put forward by Nozick and Ten, suffer from this kind of malady.[8] The awkwardness can also be seen in Braithwaite's and Pettit's use of the expression 'just deserts' to denote retribution.[9] But if 'retribution' is understood in terms of 'just deserts,' are we to understand 'unjust retribution' in terms of 'unjust deserts'? At best, that would be awkward and the best way to avoid such awkwardness is to think of retribution in terms of (negative) repayment.

Still, the notion of negative desert plays a very important role in discussions of retribution and is not without its proper domain. Its role, however, is not a definitional one, but a justificatory device for what is properly termed as 'just retribution', retribution within the limits set by various principles of justice. In other words, while *repayment* indicates the nature of the activity we call 'retribution', *desert* indicates the nature of the justification for that activity. Thus, in just and fair retribution people are paid back for what they deserve and they are given that repayment (whether they welcome it or not) *because* they deserve it. However, such desert claims are only *shorthand* justifications of retribution and need fuller, more satisfying explanations. I shall give an analysis of such justificatory negative desert claims in Chapter 8. The next task here is to examine the principles of justice with which retribution is often confused.

The Principles of Offender Justice

There are at least two senses in which punishment can be claimed to be just or unjust. In one sense, the claim is a retributive justification for the imposition of the punishment and manifests in such phrases as 'the punishment served the offender right', 'it is only just, fair, or right, that offenders get the punishment they deserve', and that 'punishment serves, or is imposed in the interests of justice'. These are shorthand retributive justifications for punishment and I shall give a fuller account of them later.

In this section I consider a different sense in which punishment can be just or unjust, the sense which depends on whether certain principles of justice are honored or violated. In this sense, the justice or injustice of punishment imposed on a wrongdoer consists essentially in the observance or non-violation of certain basic principles, such as not punishing the innocent and not overdoing the punishment—by keeping it in proportion to the moral and legal gravity of the offense. These principles can conveniently be called 'principles of justice'. Unlike in the former sense, where punishment is said to be just in virtue of such principles, it remains a further question as to whether the punishment (which is imposed on the right person, is not out of proportion, and so forth) is morally justified. Punishment, being generally painful or unwelcome to the person receiving it, has to have good reasons justifying its imposition, and such principles of justice provide none. Their role or function is to set limits to punishment, not to furnish reasons for its imposition. The burden of justification for imposing punishment falls on theories of punishment justification, such as rehabilitationism, preventionism, and retributivism. The principles of justice are not in the business of punishment justification where retributivism properly belongs and, therefore, it is mistaken to regard these principles as retributive in nature. They belong to a category of their own and nothing but confusion is served by placing them in the 'retributive' category.

One principle of justice which has often been labeled 'retributive' forbids punishing the innocent. J.L. Mackie calls this "negative retributivism,"[10] while H.L.A. Hart calls it "Retribution in the Distribution of punishment."[11] But, as the following quotations illustrate, Mackie and Hart are not alone in regarding this principle as retributive.

> [An] important version of the retributive point of view can be called 'distributive'. It insists merely that a penalty should not be inflicted on a person who has not culpably broken a rule.[12]

> Most contemporary retributivists . . . maintain a *minimalist* position. This holds only that no one should be punished *unless* he is guilty of a crime and culpable.[13]

> Essentially, then, retributivism is the view that only the guilty are to be punished.[14]

Another principle of justice which has similarly elicited the 'retributive' label forbids overdoing the punishment. This is the principle of proportionality which sets an upper limit, beyond which punishment is too harsh, in that it is disproportionate to the seriousness of the offense committed.

Thus, according to Braithwaite and Pettit, "the negative retributivist is concerned that punishment should not be imposed on the wrong people or be imposed too harshly."[15] Similarly, Mackie regards the latter principle to be one of the "quantitative variants" of retributivism,[16] while Walker calls it "limiting retributivism":

> Most penal codes are also constructed on lines consistent with limiting retributivism, providing *maximum* sentences which set the upper limit to severity without obliging the court to impose the maximum.[17]

The expression 'distributive retribution' is odd, especially in that it stands for the simple idea that innocent people should not be punished. More to the point, there is no good reason for using the 'retributive' label for basic principles of justice, such as not punishing the innocent and not overdoing the punishment. There is nothing retributive about limiting punishment in these ways. As definitions, they represent "an incredible evacuation of the basic principles of retribution."[18] Retribution and moral retributivism are about the reasons one gives *for* imposing punishment—be those reasons explanatory, such as repayment, or justificatory, such as negative moral desert. By contrast, principles of justice merely place constraints on punishment, and even Walker recognizes this concerning so-called 'limiting' and 'distributive' retributivists by saying that

> all they offer is principles for restricting punishment, not reasons for imposing it. Only the pure retributivist, who argues that penalties should be imposed because they are deserved, is offering a justification of them.[19]

It is true, of course, that moral retributivism looks to the principles of justice to demarcate the boundaries of its claims, for it does not want to justify punishment beyond those limits. But this provides grounds neither for calling these principles retributive, nor for retributivists claiming monopoly over them. Observance of these or similar constraining principles is not unique to retributivism. They are a must in any theory or system of punishment, if it is to be immune to the charge that it perpetuates unfairness and injustice. Braithwaite and Pettit, for example, are quite aware of this point.

> It is clearly vital for a consequentialist theory to be able to give constraints . . . [a]derived status, for no one can be attracted by the prospect of a system in which agents are unconstrained.[20]

However, repeating an argument by C.S. Lewis,[21] K.G. Armstrong does not think that such a non-retributivist project is feasible. He claims that retributivism is an inescapable part of a just system of punishment.

> In the area of the moral justification of the practice [of punishment] a retribu-
> tive theory is essential, because it is the only theory which connects punishment
> with desert, and so with justice, for only as a punishment is deserved or unde-
> served can it be just or unjust. What would a just *deterrent* be? The only sense
> we could give to it would be a punishment which was just from a retributive
> point of view and which also, as a matter of fact, deterred other people. 'But' it
> may be objected, 'you are only talking about *retributive* justice.' To this I can
> only reply: What other sort of justice is there?[22]

There are two ways of interpreting the above argument. As I have
already pointed out, there are two senses in which punishment can be said
to be just or unjust. Accordingly, one interpretation of the claim that the
justice of punishment consists in the person's desert is that a person's desert
is what justifies his punishment. Under this interpretation, the claim is that
only the (negative) desert of retribution justifies the imposition of punishment. The other interpretation of the argument that the justice of punishment consists in the person's desert is that a person's desert is what sets the
proper limits of his punishment. Under this interpretation, the claim is that
only the (negative) desert of retribution can furnish grounds for principles
of justice by reference to which punishment may be termed just or unjust.

Although it is not clear which of these interpretations Lewis and
Armstrong had in mind, in all likelihood they would endorse both.
However that may be, their argument is indefensible under both interpretations. The first interpretation suffers because there are good consequentialist reasons for imposing punishment. To take a familiar example, if other
measures fail to serve the important goal of crime control, deterrence is a
weighty reason for imposing punishment. Protection of the community
from crime is essential and it cannot be dismissed as not being a legitimate
reason for imposing punishment within generally accepted limits. The argument is similarly untenable under the second interpretation because a retributive theory of punishment is not the only theory which can limit punishment in line with the principles of justice. There are at least three different non-retributive ways of approaching these principles, each of which
constitutes a counterexample.[23] The first counterexample is provided by the
fact that it is quite plausible to regard these principles as having an immediate, underived moral authority, independently of any notions of repayment,
desert or, for that matter, utility. This has been recognized by Mackie.

> This is undoubtedly true of negative retributivism, including its quantitative
> variant . . . [that it has] an immediate appeal and underived authority.[24]

The second counterexample is provided by the fact that it is also possible to adopt these principles as utilitarian secondary rules.[25] Braithwaite and
Pettit, for example, derive these principles in their republican theory of

criminal justice from the consequentialist goal of promoting dominion (republican freedom).

> The right of the innocent not to be punished, and the upper limit we put on the punishment of the guilty, are both derived within our theory as measures required for the promotion of dominion. . . . unless such measures are firmly in place the dominion of people in the society at large will be seriously compromised. Although consequentialist in structure, our theory . . . is rights- and limits-respecting.[26]

A third counterexample can be provided by grounding these principles in a Rawlsian concept of 'fairness' along lines suggested by Walker.[27] Suppose that the choice is to be made from a position of ignorance where one has to choose between two kinds of societies while not knowing what one's position in those societies is going to be. In societies of type *A*, the principles of justice, such as not punishing the innocent and not overpunishing the guilty, are honored as inviolable limiting principles of punishment. By contrast, in societies of type *B*, there is no provision for an upper limit on punishment and innocent people may be framed and punished in cases where the police find it either impossible, or too costly, to find and punish the real offenders. This might be done (covertly, of course), in the interests of deterrence and political image management.

Having no way of knowing whether one would in fact be an offender and whether one would in fact fall victim to the above mentioned type of political expediency, which kind of society would a rational person choose to live in? The choice seems fairly clear. A rational, self-interested chooser would opt to live in a society of type *A*. There would be nothing to be gained by choosing otherwise. Since there is no guarantee that a *B*-type society would have a lower crime rate than an *A*-type society, one would only expose oneself to heightened risks of unwanted and undeserved punishments for no discernible gain.[28] Once again, this account is non-retributive and it makes no appeal to any notions of desert. Furthermore, unlike the account by Braithwaite and Pettit, it is not instrumental either. In relation to his Rawlsian account of the principle that the innocent should not be punished, Walker rightly argues that

> Rawls's non-altruistic man is not a utilitarian. The society which he would choose for its fairness is not necessarily the one which would have the lower crime-rate. Nor does Rawls's kind of 'fairness' involve the notion of desert: simply rational choice of a self-interested sort.[29]

None of these three approaches—where the principles of justice are regarded as morally basic, self-evident and autonomous; where they are derived as secondary rules to promote some value in a consequentialist framework; and where they are grounded in a Rawlsian conception of fairness—concedes one iota to ideas of retributivism, the idea that punishment is due as repayment or desert for an offense or wrong. Moreover, none of them appeals to any ideas of desert either. The Lewis-Armstrong argument, therefore, is mistaken under the second interpretation as well. Neither a retributive theory, nor a desert theory is essential in a moral justification of the practice of punishment. The principles of justice which set the limits of fair punishment certainly need not be based on any notion of desert, let alone a retributive one.

If this is right, then it is clear that we have an alternative answer to Armstrong's question "What would a just deterrent be?": Just deterrent punishment is punishment imposed on someone for purposes of deterrence while fully observing the principles of justice which, as I have argued, can be non-retributively grounded. As to Armstrong's rhetorical remark "What other sort of justice is there (besides *retributive* justice)?," the answer is similar: There is *criminal justice* consisting of punishment imposed for non-retributive reasons, such as deterrence and the promotion of dominion, punishment which, at the same time, fully honors non-retributively grounded principles of justice, such as not punishing too harshly and not punishing the innocent.

The above arguments are sufficient to establish that principles which prohibit punishment of the innocent and the overpunishment of the guilty are independent of any notion of retribution. Along with other principles of justice, such as the ones listed below, they have an immediate, underived, but nevertheless powerful moral authority all on their own. Their violations automatically constitute serious moral wrongs which cannot be easily justified. The appropriateness of these principles is virtually unquestionable. Far from belonging to the retributive category, these principles properly belong to, and are a natural part of, a set of principles to which some (if not all) of the following principles also belong.

1. Punishment must be for a moral wrong, or the transgression of some defensible rule, standard, or law.
2. Punishment must not be imposed on the wrong person, an innocent person who is not appropriately responsible for the offense in question.
3. Punishment must not be overdone; it should not be harsher than the gravity of the offense warrants. Punishment is unjust to the extent that it is out of proportion.
4. Punishment must be equitable and comparable to other punishments for similar offenses (at least within the same community). It would be unjust if a person were to be sentenced to ten years in jail for an offense for which other offenders receive only minor fines.[30]
5. Punishment should not be imposed without due process, without giving the accused a fair chance to argue and defend their case.

6. Where the accused admits liability and accepts responsibility, they must be given constructive opportunities to understand the consequences of their actions on others, express remorse, offer their apologies, and take whatever steps they can to make amends and repair the damage they have caused. Withholding such opportunities from offenders is wrong because it violates moral principles of fair and humane treatment, which is the inalienable right of every person.

While this list may not be complete, it is important to reiterate here the earlier point that retributivists can also violate the principles of justice—even willingly, though not with a retributive justification, or without being reprehensible for such violations—without ceasing to be retributivists on that account. Resorting to somewhat provocative examples, with respect to the principle of proportionality, we only need remind ourselves of Biblical and Islamic notions that Divine Retribution for a short, unrepentant sinful life is Eternal Hell.[31] With respect to the principle of not punishing the innocent, we may remind ourselves of the scapegoat of the Old Testament, and of Christ's innocent (even if voluntary) suffering on the cross paying the (retributive) price for our sins in accordance with the demands of God's Divine Law of Retribution, as it is often interpreted in Christian theology.[32]

Turning to more mundane examples, Susan Jacoby made an astute remark about the independence of the core ideas of retribution and the principles of justice when she pointed out that "Retribution *per se* is an integral component of just as well as unjust legal systems."[33] Furthermore, as I already indicated, non-retributivist moral theories of punishment can also adopt these principles either as utilitarian secondary rules, because their adoption maximizes overall utility,[34] or as limiting principles, recognizing their independent moral authority as principles of natural justice which should not be violated.[35] This last possibility also disposes of another misconception about non-retributive moral theories of punishment, that they sanction injustice, such as overpunishing the guilty and the punishment of the innocent. While non-retributivism has the potential to sanction violations of the principles of justice, it does not have to—just as retributivism's inability to justify violations of those principles does not amount to an ability to prohibit their violation, let alone rendering retributive practices immune to such violations.

This Chapter's Main Conclusions

Principles of justice are independent of retribution. Retribution is not in and of itself just or unjust; whether retribution is just depends on whether it conforms to the principles of justice, which have independent moral authority of their own. Their authority is not called into question by instrumental reasons for punishment, and much confusion is created by placing them in the "retributive" category. Retribution *per se* is most plausibly defined with reference to punishment justification. Retribution is owed to wrongdoers as a matter of negative repayment. It is the direct, moral, and logical consequence of their wrongdoing, something that they morally deserve in proportion to the moral gravity of their actions. We need to be careful, however, to distinguish between the concepts of negative repayment and negative moral desert. While the notion of negative desert plays a very important role in *justifying* just retribution (retribution within limits set by various principles of justice), using desert to *define* the concept of retribution leads to conceptual difficulties whereby instances of retributive punishment that violate the principles of justice are left without a natural category of their own. Such difficulties can be avoided if retribution is defined, instead, by reference to the concept of repayment—a solution that fits well with the etymology of the word 'retribution.' Thus, in just and fair retribution people are paid back for what they deserve and they are given that repayment (whether they welcome it or not) *because* they deserve it. Such desert claims, however, are only *shorthand* justifications: they stand in need of fuller, more satisfying explanations—a task to be taken up in Chapter 8.

6

Retribution and Revenge

There is little grace in punishment. Only justice.

Graeme Newman[1]

Having shown that retribution is not, in and of itself, just or unjust—that depending on whether it conforms to the principles of justice—I still have to show that revenge is a form of retribution.

The contemporary literature in the philosophy of punishment is polarized as to how we should understand the relationship between retribution and revenge. According to one view, retribution and revenge are one and the same thing. According to the other view, retribution and revenge hardly have anything in common. I shall argue in this chapter that both these views are untenable, and in the following chapter that revenge is best understood as a species of retribution.

Revenge and Retribution as Identical

The identification of retribution with revenge is particularly implausible in cases where the agent of punishment bears no special tie to the victim of the crime. Nozick also supports this view:

> Revenge is personal: "this is because of what you did to my ———" (self, father group, and so on). Whereas the agent of retribution need have no special or personal tie to the victim of the wrong for which he exacts retribution.[2]

This point, simple as it may be, is a critical one. Yet it seems to be lost on advocates of the thesis of the identity of retribution and revenge. One such advocate is Jacoby:

The very word 'revenge' has pejorative connotations. Advocates of draconian punishment for crime invariably prefer 'retribution'—a word that affords the comfort of euphemism although it is virtually synonymous with 'revenge'. . . . The death penalty is certainly a form of legalized vengeance—revenge writ large—but so is any lesser punishment if a crime is unlikely to be repeated.[3]

While I would agree with Jacoby that the social ostracism of revenge has reached a degree where "the very word 'revenge' has pejorative connotations," she is mistaken in claiming that 'retribution' is no more than a euphemism for 'revenge.' Retributive punishment through a judicial system, no matter how harsh, does not qualify as revenge. On account of its retributive character, such punishment still qualifies as retribution—institutionalized, judicial retribution—but not as revenge, because the requisite personal elements have been eliminated from it.

Robert Solomon seems to be aware of the personal nature of revenge. He correctly points out, for example, that "vengeance retains the virtue of being personal."[4] Yet he also claims that "retribution and revenge are one and the same"[5]; and again that "vengeance and retributive justice are in the end identical"[6]—apparently failing to realize that the personal involvement in question is not always present in retributive punishment, as evidenced by sentences imposed through the court system. To the degree that Solomon is willing to admit that a personal involvement may not be present in retributive punishment, his position in identifying retribution with revenge becomes inconsistent. This comes out clearly when he attempts to reconcile the identity thesis with the highly compelling distinction between the two pointed out by Nozick:

One might, adopting a distinction from Robert Nozick, say that retribution is justified revenge, where revenge is strictly personal but retribution is not.[7]

But how could retribution be identified with revenge, even if the latter is justified? For even if an act of revenge is justified, it still remains personal in a way that an act of retribution might not be. Therefore, the conclusion must remain that the revenge-retribution identity thesis is indefensible. While acts of revenge are necessarily personal, acts of retribution need not be. Cases in point are when criminals are retributively punished through a court system specifically set up for the purpose. As Pincoffs has pointed out, "defenders of the institution of punishment may be defending it precisely on the ground that it rules out vengeance-taking as a practice."[8]

A more interesting version of the identity claim has been put forward by Oldenquist who, in addition to the conceptual identification, makes a historical claim about identifying retribution with revenge.

Can decent people accept the idea that retributive justice is revenge? . . . there is no doubt that retribution is revenge, both historically and conceptually.[9]

While it is true that historically revenge has been the most prevalent form of retribution, it has not been the only one. Retributive punishment has, from time to time, been executed on wrongdoers by vigilantes who did not have the requisite personal relationship to the victims.[10] Furthermore, judicial retribution, where the victim and those close to the victim are deliberately prevented from taking part in the process of punishment, has been part of our history for a long time now. In cases like these, where the personal element is absent, it is inappropriate and misleading to identify retribution with revenge. Contra Oldenquist, there is a clear difference both historically and conceptually between purely institutionalized retribution and vigilante retribution on the one hand, and personal retribution on the other. This difference is marked by the presence or absence of a personal or special tie between the victim of the injustice or offense and the agent of retribution. This view, I believe, is essentially right, and is not undermined by the subtleties in Oldenquist's position:

> [J]udicial retribution is not mere revenge but 'sanitized' revenge, revenge over which a moral community assumes stewardship . . . [and which is] administered predictably, impartially, publicly, and relatively effectively by police and judges who are not the criminal's victims or relatives.[11]

I agree that there is a sanitizing process involved in moving from simple revenge (which is set and carried out by the victims or their relatives) to judicial retribution. But this move, or evolution, is not from one form of revenge to another. It is, rather, a move from one form of retribution to another. What is common in both forms of punishment is not revenge, but retribution pure and simple, regardless of whether retribution is construed as, for example, repayment, desert, or fair play.[12] For, to repeat an earlier point, once there is no personal involvement left in the process of punishment, it is no longer appropriate to talk about revenge. If the personal element were retained through this process of institutionalization, if the victims and their relatives retained their involvement, if they had a say or a hand in the punishment of their wrongdoers, the imposed punishment would quite appropriately be called institutionalized or sanitized revenge. But where all personal involvement of this nature is excluded and the institution takes the retribution completely out of the hands of the victims concerned, it is most inappropriate to regard such punishment as still revenge.

A slightly different way of understanding Oldenquist's claim, one which is in fact present in his own work but is run together with the above ideas, is to think of institutionalized retribution in our institutions where no personal motives are involved as being "society's revenge on its own members who harm and betray it."[13] But this is to overextend the meaning of the word 'revenge'. For there is no personal involvement here in the relevant sense of the word that would make it appropriate for purely institutionalized punishment to count as revenge. There are two reasons for this. The first is that society, and those involved in enforcing the law and administering punishment, are equally closely related, or not related at all, to the victim or the offender, so the tie in question is the same to both. The second reason has to do with the motivation of those who determine and mete out the punishment in the institutionalized legal system. They are not motivated by a personal tie to the victims, whom they customarily would not know or identify with. They are public servants, appointed to serve the common interest which they must place above their own.

Both these points contrast with the case of revenge. First, as a general rule, the avenger has a closer tie to the victim than they have to the offender.[14] Second, the avenger becomes involved in the punishment of the wrongdoer at least in part because of this personal tie they have to the victim. These are compelling reasons for the view that judicial retribution visited on the offender does not qualify as revenge in any serious sense of that term. It is rather institutionalized retribution which is distinct and clearly distinguishable from both vigilantism and revenge. The claim that institutionalized retribution in our institutions is society's revenge on its own members, therefore, can hardly be more than a metaphor. Taking it as literal truth would require an unacceptable dilution, if not trivialization, of our notion of a personal or special tie, which is such a distinctive feature of revenge.

Apart from ignoring the fact that the requisite personal involvement is not always present in retributive punishment, a conceptual identification of retribution with revenge not only disregards, but also allows no satisfactory account for, the differences between the various forms of retribution which are clearly there at the pre-theoretical level. A situation where we have both the words 'retribution' and 'revenge' standing for one and the same thing, with the added result that certain compelling pre-theoretical differences are rendered hard to account for, is far from satisfactory. Taking seriously the presence or absence of a personal involvement as described above provides an immediate and straightforward solution to these theoretical difficulties. The presence or absence of a personal or special tie seems to provide the best basis all around for a satisfactory explanation of the highly compelling distinction between revenge and other forms of retribution.[15]

Finally, perhaps the most subtle version of the identity thesis has been expressed by John Stuart Mill. The crucial claim that Mill makes is that people's desire to punish for the sake of retributive justice is but a desire for revenge.

> The sentiment of justice, in that one of its elements which consists of the desire to punish, is thus, I conceive, the natural feeling of retaliation or vengeance, rendered by intellect and sympathy applicable to those injuries, that is, to those hurts, which wound us through, or in common with, society at large.[16]

However, in addition to the problems already raised for such views, and which must be faced by any version of the retribution-revenge identity thesis, there is one more objection to which Mill's claim is vulnerable. In claiming that people's desire to punish for the sake of justice is but a desire for revenge, Mill seems to have put the cart before the horse. As I have already indicated, some notion of fairness or justice is necessary for explaining resentment and resentment in turn is necessary for explaining the desire for revenge. Therefore, it is circuitous and mistaken to appeal to the desire for revenge to explain the desire to punish for the sake of justice. Resentment is a feeling that is aroused and maintained by perceptions of injustice and unfair treatment. But such perceptions *presuppose* some kind of sense or idea of what is fair and unfair, just and unjust. Hence, the sentiment of justice can hardly have as its basis the natural feeling of vengeance. If anything, it must be the other way around. If this is right, Mill's attempt to identify the desire for retributive justice with a desire for revenge is untenable. Hence, this particular version of the identity thesis fails as well.

Having shown that an identification of retribution and revenge is untenable, the question remains: how exactly are the two related? In the following section I consider the suggestion that retribution and revenge are different species of a common genus at best, and that they are therefore in different moral categories.

Revenge and Retribution as Different Species

Being a defender of retribution, Robert Nozick seems to be troubled by the fact that retributivism—which he defines as *the view that people deserve punishment for their wrongful acts even if such punishment fails to act as a deterrent*—"strikes some people as a primitive view, expressive only of the thirst for revenge."[17] In response, unlike Solomon or Oldenquist, Nozick attempts to distance retribution from revenge as much as possible by arguing that there are several key differences between the two. These, according to Nozick, are that:

1. Retribution is done for a wrong, while revenge may be done for an injury or harm or slight and need not be for a wrong.
2. Retribution sets an internal limit to the amount of the punishment, according to the seriousness of the wrong, whereas revenge internally need set no limit to what is inflicted. Revenge by its nature need set no limits, although the revenger may limit what he inflicts for external reasons.
3. Revenge is personal: "this is because of what you did to my ———" (self, father group, and so on). Whereas the agent of retribution need have no special or personal tie to the victim of the wrong for which he exacts retribution.

4. Revenge involves a particular emotional tone, pleasure in the suffering of another, while retribution either need involve no emotional tone, or involves another one, namely, pleasure at justice being done.

5. There need be no generality in revenge. Not only is the revenger not committed to revenging any similar act done to anyone; he is not committed to avenging all done to himself. Whether he seeks vengeance, or thinks it appropriate to do so, will depend upon how he feels at the time about the act of injury. Whereas the imposer of retribution, inflicting deserved punishment for a wrong, is committed to (the existence of some) general principles *(prima facie)* mandating punishment in other similar circumstances.[18]

Commenting on Nozick's account of retributivism, C.L. Ten is of the opinion that "Nozick usefully distinguishes between retributive punishment and revenge with which it is sometimes confused" and claims that there is in addition "one other important difference between revenge and retribution, which could be added to Nozick's account."[19] This is the following:

6. Retributive punishment is only inflicted [knowingly] on the wrongdoer, whereas revenge is sometimes inflicted [knowingly] on an innocent person close to the revengee, either because this is an easier target, or because it is thought that this would hurt the revengee more.[20]

With the exception of the third one, with which I agree, all of these claims are flawed. Though neither author spells this out, judging from the context, and adopting a familiar classificatory terminology from biology, their view is that revenge and retribution are, at the very best, different species of some common genus. With the exception of the third point, these comparisons are incompatible with the view that retribution and revenge might be more closely related. For want of a better name, I shall refer to the position held by Nozick and Ten as the (no closer than) *species-species categorization* of retribution and revenge, and I shall contrast this later with the genus-species categorization, which, as I shall argue, is more plausible.

The first reason for distrusting the species-species categorization arises from the fact that under such a schema miscarried acts of retribution under, say, an entirely institutionalized system of punishment, have no natural category of their own. Suppose, for example, that punishment is imposed on someone for retributivist reasons through an institutionalized system, for something that is not a wrong or for something of which the person is not guilty, or that the punishment is out of proportion to what is morally justified in the circumstances. Such punishment is clearly unjust. Normally, if it were imposed for retributivist reasons, we would call such punishment misplaced retribution or unjust retributive punishment.

Yet the species-species categorization does not allow us to do this, at least not in the way constructed by Nozick and Ten. In their sense, punishment of this kind cannot be either retribution or revenge. It is not retribution because it is incompatible with what they claim about retribution as part of their attempt to ground the species-species categorization, namely, that retribution is always in accordance with the principles of justice. It cannot be revenge either, since such punishment is not personal in the requisite sense of the word. But, if such a case of unjust punishment is neither retribution nor revenge, there seems to be no straightforward answer to the question as to what it is.

Difficulties of this kind are only the tip of the iceberg for the above comparisons by Nozick and Ten. Before dealing with them individually, I start with a general criticism that has to be leveled against comparisons 1, 2, 5, and 6. In these Nozick and Ten compare revenge pure and simple not with retribution pure and simple but with *just* retribution, that is, retributive punishment which is in accordance with principles of justice, such as that punishment must always be for a wrong, that it must get the right person, that it must be proportional to the seriousness of the wrong, and so forth. But, as I have already argued above, these principles are quite independent of the notion of retribution as such, regardless of whether retribution is construed as repayment, desert, or whatever. Wittingly or not, Nozick and Ten choose to build into their notion of retribution these principles of justice and it is in virtue of this that for them retribution is necessarily for a wrong, that it is necessarily proportional, that it necessarily gets the right person, and so on. Since they do not build the same principles into their notion of revenge, it is hardly surprising that for them these are not defining features of revenge. But, in order to get a proper, and fair, contrast between retribution and revenge in these respects, the principles of justice will have to be built either into both of them, or into neither of them.

I move on now to consider each comparison individually:

1. Retribution is done for a wrong, while revenge may be done for an injury or harm or slight and need not be for a wrong.[21]

Nozick is mistaken in claiming that retribution must always be for a moral wrong and he is mistaken in thinking that retribution differs from revenge in this regard. Retribution *per se* is a perfectly possible response to morally good actions. A good example is provided by the Stewart Inquiry into the administration of Australian soccer. Soccer personalities were reluctant to testify about corruption in the administration of the game for "fear of retribution in terms of promotion within the sport" and "fear of actual physical violence." In Justice Stewart's words,

There were grave misgivings, many of which were justified, that if material of this nature were to find its way into the hands of vengeful people . . . retribution would follow.[22]

Justice Stewart and Nozick can't both be right about the proper use of the term 'retribution'. My claim that the mistake lies with Nozick is further confirmed in the case of the NSW Police Royal Commission conducted by Justice Wood. According to reports, police officers (whistle-blowers) who report police misconduct fear and face "retribution" in the form of "a series of old or trivial complaints against them" and "disciplinary matters."[23]

Moreover, just like revenge, even retribution which is institutionalized through the legal system need not be for a moral wrong. As pointed out earlier, it is possible that the legislators create morally unjust laws through bad advice, poor judgment, error, corruption, or undue pressure from small but powerful interest groups. The laws being unjust in the first place, transgressing them may well not count as a moral wrong. Nevertheless, such a transgression still amounts to an offense and may be retributively punished through the standard channels. The retributive character of such punishment is not changed by the injustice of the laws concerned. In such cases we would say that the punishment was unjust because the person being punished did no moral wrong.

Consider the following example: The ruler decrees for self-serving reasons that all boys under two are to be slaughtered, and that anybody who hinders this order be put to death as retribution for their defiance. The parents who hide their son when approached by the authorities are later discovered and are put to death. Even though these parents committed no moral wrong, indeed they acted in a morally praiseworthy way, the retributive nature of their punishment remains. We may quite coherently suppose here that their punishment was not instrumental with a view to deter, but genuinely retributive, as desert or repayment for daring to disobey the ruler's decree. Such instances of punishment, retributive or otherwise, where there were no moral wrongs committed, are unjust. For punishment to be just, it must not violate certain basic principles of justice, and one such principle is that punishment may not be imposed unless a moral wrong has been committed.

In claiming that "retribution is done for a wrong," Nozick is assuming that retribution has built into it this principle of justice. That is, he assumes that retribution is always just retribution. In fact, as we have seen, retribution may be just or unjust depending on whether the principles of justice are observed. A similar situation applies in the case of revenge, indeed for all forms of punishment. Nozick is correct when he says that "revenge may be done for an injury or harm or slight and need not be for a wrong." Revenge can be just or unjust, depending, again, on whether the principles of justice are observed, in this case whether the offense for which the revenge is taken is a moral wrong or not. This brings us back to the earlier point that Nozick's contrast between retribution and revenge is only apparent, obtained by (wrongly) building the principles of justice into his notion of retribution while (rightly) leaving the same principles out of the notion of revenge. In conclusion, this first comparison made by Nozick between retribution and revenge is indefensible.

But even if this contrast were defensible, nothing significant would follow from it regarding the moral status or justifiability of revenge. It certainly does not follow from it that there is something intrinsically wrong with revenge. The mere fact that it is possible to exact revenge for slights, harms, and injuries which are not moral wrongs need not prejudice in any way the possibility of morally acceptable and just forms of revenge. Moral condemnations of revenge for injuries and harms which are not wrongs, because they were unintentional, perhaps, are quite compatible with revenge having moral approval in cases where it is a response to unambiguous and unjustifiable wrongs.

2. Retribution sets an internal limit to the amount of the punishment, according to the seriousness of the wrong, whereas revenge internally need set no limit to what is inflicted. Revenge by its nature need set no limits, although the revenger may limit what he inflicts for external reasons.[24]

Inflicting a penalty which is disproportionate and in excess of what is fair and appropriate is to commit an injustice. The notion of proportionality— the idea that the severity of the punishment should not exceed the seriousness of the offense—as I have already observed, is a principle of justice. While this notion is necessarily built into the very concept of just retribution, it is not, I should think, built into the concept of retribution as such. As with revenge, these limits are external to the notion of retribution. They are added onto it, rather than built into it, and it is here that Nozick goes wrong by departing from ordinary usage. For, to be sure, it is possible to overdo the punishment, not only through revenge, but also through vigilantism and even through institutionalized systems of punishment. More punishment can be inflicted than what, in all fairness, would be just in the circumstances. For example, many people would find unacceptable the stoning of women for adultery and the severing of hands for stealing, as has been the practice in some Islamic societies. Other, potentially more controversial, examples demonstrating the point are the criminalization of alcóhol during the prohibition years in the United States and the criminalization of soft drugs, such as marijuana which, on the balance of evidence, do not seem to be more harmful than tobacco and alcohol.

These considerations show that the concept of retribution is a wider one than Nozick and Ten are willing to allow, for both the concepts of just retribution and unjust retribution fall under it. My analysis which allows for both unjust and just retribution still to be regarded as retribution concurs more closely with the ordinary understanding of the term than does the explication put forward by Nozick and Ten. We may still regard, for example, the state's infliction of the death penalty upon a criminal as excessive punishment even if it were imposed for purely retributive reasons, such as repayment or desert for what the criminal has done. We would simply say that it was excessive and, therefore, to that degree unjust, retribution. Its retributive nature is by no means nullified by its excess. The explication put forward by Nozick and Ten is not only unable to account for the possibility that an excessive amount of punishment may be inflicted out of retribution, but leaves no room for discussion or dispute about the amount of punishment which morally can be exacted in the name of retribution. Their definition simply legislates that retribution is by nature fair and that it cannot be overdone, even by mistake. This is clearly not the case.

While on the topic of proportionality in punishment, it is worth mentioning that quite generally, in societies with revenge-based systems of punishment, there are clearly defined limits as to what is appropriate to inflict as punishment in retaliation for injuries and wrongs. This limit may vary from society to society, just as there is variation between the limits set by the institutionalized systems of various states and countries. Some of them sanction the death penalty for murder, for instance, while others do not. But what is significant here is that, in cultures which legitimate and institutionalize revenge as an accepted practice, excessive acts of vengeance or acts which are considered unusually cruel or dehumanizing are not acceptable. Avengers can meet with stiff moral and social disapproval from their communities and "social life could become painfully uncomfortable" if they inflict too much in retaliation, as judged by established community standards.[25]

These considerations, it seems to me, point in a definite direction, that revenge can also be just and that *just revenge* is a form of just retribution, a form of retributive justice. More specifically, it is a form of retributive justice in which the executor of the punishment is someone with a special tie to the victim of the original offense and who becomes involved because of personal retributive reasons but who, notwithstanding, does observe all the principles of justice in punishing and getting even with the offender.

3. Revenge is personal: "this is because of what you did to my ———" (self, father group, and so on). Whereas the agent of retribution need have no special or personal tie to the victim of the wrong for which he exacts retribution.[26]

This comparison captures much of the essence of the difference between revenge proper and its genus, retribution. But, although I have already expressed agreement with this comparison, it will be useful at this point to consider in more detail the question of what constitutes a personal or special tie. Two observations need to be made. First, this tie is relative in nature, in that, for some reason, such as familial, friendship or group membership ties, the avenger identifies more closely with the victim than the offender. For example, on one level of identification I can take revenge on someone, say P, for what P has done to me or my family, while it is also a possibility on another level of identification that I take revenge on someone else, say Q, for what Q has done to P, where I identify more closely with P than Q in virtue of the fact that P is a compatriot of mine, while Q is not.

The second observation is that this closer identification with the victim forms part of the reason for the avenger becoming involved in the punishment. This identification is part of what provides the necessary reason for the avenger making it his or her business to become involved in the imposition of the retribution in question.

4. Revenge involves a particular emotional tone, pleasure in the suffering of another, while retribution either need involve no emotional tone, or involves another one, namely, pleasure at justice being done.[27]

I have already debunked this particular revenge-demonizing myth in Chapter 2, arguing that the pleasure in question is most plausibly identified as a victim taking (self-related) satisfaction in having done justice in their own case. While this kind of satisfaction may be present in revenge, it is not relevantly different from, say, the (non-self-related) satisfaction a judge, or a bystander might derive from the deserved retributive punishment of a wrongdoer in a court setting. Trusting that this point is compelling enough, I simply move on to consider the next comparison. To elaborate on this point, a useful distinction can be made between two types of satisfactions that may be present when punishment is meted out. One is the sense of satisfaction which is felt by victims and those close to them when due punishment is imposed on their wrongdoers. This feeling of relief and satisfaction is not tied to any particular form of punishment. It can be experienced by victims regardless of whether due punishment is imposed on their wrongdoers by themselves personally, or by someone close to them (revenge), or by independent, non-legal third parties (vigilantism), or by legally and institutionally appointed persons for the purpose (judicial punishment). The other type of satisfaction that may be present when punishment is meted out is a more impersonal, abstract satisfaction at justice having been done which may be felt by anyone who cares about retributive justice, whether they be the victim, the executor of the punishment, or any member of the community.

The feeling described by Nozick in the case of revenge as a "particular emotional tone, pleasure in the suffering of another" can be explained by reference to the fact that the victim of the crime is also the person (or someone close to the person) who is imposing the punishment. If my earlier arguments are right, that the feeling in question is largely the satisfaction victims take in justice, then Nozick's comparison becomes vulnerable to the following two criticisms: the first is that he wrongly attributes to the avenger, as the *executor* of the punishment, a satisfaction the avenger feels as the *victim* of the wrong in question. The second criticism is that to the degree that the emotional tone he is referring to is indeed victim satisfaction, he is mistaken in his claim that the emotion in question cannot be felt in retribution. Victim satisfaction can be as much present in judicial retribution as it can be in revenge. This is why it is so important for victims of serious crime that their wrongdoers are convicted and duly sentenced in court.

The avenger may, of course, also feel some closely related satisfaction as the executor of the punishment on account of having been *personally* able to impose punishment for the wrongs done to him. But, once again, this satisfaction is felt by him because he is the *victim* (or someone close to the victim) of the offense or wrong in question. What is important to note here is that neither this particular feeling of satisfaction, nor the previously mentioned victim satisfaction, is perverse sadism to which revenge gives vent—a major point on which Nozick's simplistic and misleading description of these satisfactions as "pleasure in the suffering of another" goes awry.

All the same, Nozick is right in observing that administrators of, say, judicial retribution are not going to experience exactly the same feelings and satisfactions as avengers might do. The reason for this lies in the fact that revenge is highly personal in the way already explained, whereas judicial retribution is not. Since imposers of judicial retribution bear no personal or special tie to the victim, theirs can only be the abstract satisfaction of knowing that they have successfully imposed due retribution on *a* wrongdoer. They can also feel an even more abstract and impersonal form of this satisfaction, that of knowing that retributive justice was successfully imposed on a wrongdoer. But, as I already mentioned, this satisfaction can be experienced by anybody who values retributive justice in general.

5. There need be no generality in revenge. Not only is the revenger not committed to revenging any similar act done to anyone; he is not committed to avenging all done to himself. Whether he seeks vengeance, or thinks it appropriate to do so, will depend upon how he feels at the time about the act of injury. Whereas the imposer of retribution, inflicting deserved punishment for a wrong, is committed to (the existence of some) general principles *(prima facie)* mandating punishment in other similar circumstances.[28]

This comparison is both ambiguous and problematic. One reason for the ambiguity is that, strictly speaking, it does not live up to the requirements of a proper contrast. A basic requirement for contrasting two things is that they be compared in the same respect. If we want to contrast, say, apples and oranges, then it is inappropriate to say that they are different because apples are red but oranges are soft. To make a proper contrast between the two we would need to compare them either with respect to their texture or to their color. In the above comparison Nozick seems to ignore this basic rule. Revenge is claimed to lack generality because the revenger is not committed to *avenge* similar acts done to himself or to others while retribution is claimed to have generality because the executor of retribution is committed to the *existence of principles* which only give a *prima facie* mandate to punish similar acts. To get a proper contrast, the two must be compared either with respect to their commitment to *actions* of the appropriate sorts or with respect to their commitment to the *existence of principles* of the relevant sort, but not in the way done by Nozick.

The ambiguity is made worse, no doubt, by Nozick's wording. In particular, the claim that the imposer of retribution is committed to the existence of certain principles makes no proper sense. If we are to talk sensibly about principles (or, for that matter, about anything in particular), then we either have to talk about their existence (and, by extension, about our belief or non-belief in their defensibility, validity, existence, and so forth), or about our commitment to (live by) them, but not about our commitment to their existence. What exactly am I committed to if I am committed to, say, the existence of the principle of truth telling? Am I committed to live by that principle and tell the truth in all things, or am I merely acknowledging that there is such a principle—a principle to which I do not give significance in my life if it doesn't suit me, a principle to which I am not committed? As with Nozick's claim, it is not clear. Nozick's claims, therefore, need interpreting. The most generous and plausible interpretation seems to be the following:

The difference between retribution and revenge with respect to generality consists in the grounds on which their respective executors act. The avenger acts merely on inconstant, variable, and unprincipled feelings about the act of injury at the time, whereas the executor of retribution acts on general principles which render permissible, or else obligatory, the imposition of retribution, not only in this instance, but also in all other relevantly similar circumstances.

But even if it is something like this that Nozick had in mind, the comparison remains problematic. For, although Nozick is right in pointing out that generally revenge has strong emotions or feelings associated with it, he is mistaken both in suggesting that these emotions are whimsical and in claiming that these emotions are the basis on which the avenger's actions must rest. I argued earlier in Chapter 3 that the predominant emotion associated with revenge is the cognitively-based feeling of resentment. As such, resentment does not simply rise and die in an unstructured, whimsical fashion. It arises in response to injustices and wrongs against ourselves or those to whom we feel close. But, if the feeling of resentment is anchored in the ideas of injustice and moral wrong, if it arises in response to injustices and wrongs, then it is at least arguable that, therefore, (the existence or presence of) resentment can provide a general, consistent and legitimate moral ground for punishment in the form of revenge, (*prima facie*) mandating revenge in other similar circumstances.

But, while this is arguable, we can, and perhaps must, do better. For, while a strong feeling of resentment might be associated with revenge, this feeling is no more of a justification for taking revenge than is the feeling of indignation experienced by imposers of judicial retribution in the case of judicial punishment. The crucial principle which mandates punishment in relevantly similar circumstances is the same for both revenge and judicial retribution. This is the general principle which renders permissible, or mandates, the retributive punishment of unjust and wrongful conduct in a way which does not violate the principles of justice. What justifies retributive punishment is the fact that the person has committed a punishable moral wrong, a moral wrong for which she is responsible.[29] Retributive punishment is rendered permissible by this fact alone and not at all by the presence of retributive emotions, such as resentment, indignation, and anger, which typically arise in response to wrongdoing—although it is plausible to suppose that the function of these moral emotions is to reinforce the need for an appropriate response. But, even though the principle which permits the imposition of punishment is the same in both judicial retribution and revenge, its range of application is different in the two cases. In the case of judicial retribution the principle ranges over all members of the community. Revenge being personal in nature, the principle has a more limited scope, being restricted to offenses against oneself and those closely connected. But that is quite different from the claim that there is no general principle that mandates revenge in other, relevantly similar circumstances.

What could be more plausibly argued, perhaps, is that the imposer of, say, judicial retribution is morally *obliged*, as opposed to merely *permitted*, to abide by the principle of equality in justice, the principle that *like cases must be treated alike* and, therefore, that unlike the avenger, he is morally obliged always to give due weight to general principles which, *prima facie* mandate retribution in all relevantly similar circumstances. But this formulation is equally unsuccessful. For one thing, retributive punishment can be imposed not only through the judicial system but also through vigilantism. Similar to lone avengers, vigilante imposers of retribution are not required or obligated to impose fair retribution for all relevantly similar wrongdoing. Not being part of an institution of punishment, their decision to punish wrongdoing in particular cases is voluntary, beyond the call of duty. Unlike imposers of judicial retribution, they are under no obligation to do so. If Batman or Superman bring a couple of criminals to justice today, their action is supererogatory and is a bonus for the community. But tomorrow, they can hang up their costumes and go fishing without being answerable to anyone for not doing the same as today.[30]

Furthermore, with institutionalized forms of revenge, such as when social norms tightly regulate all aspects of revenge behaviour, revenge can be as mandatory in all relevantly similar circumstances as can be the imposition of retribution in the case of an institutionalized, judicial system. This point is well illustrated in the following passage.

> A man slow to kill his enemy was thought 'disgraced' and was described as 'low-class' and 'bad'. Among the Highlanders he risked finding that other men had contemptuously come to sleep with his wife, his daughter could not marry into a 'good' family and his son must marry a 'bad' girl. . . . He paid visits at his peril; his coffee cup was only half-filled, and before being handed to him it was passed under the host's left arm, or even under his left leg, to remind him of his disgrace. He was often mocked openly.[31]

Clearly, in communities with a revenge-based system of punishment, the social ostracism which can await those who fail to carry out their duty of revenge can be crippling. The pressure is enough to pull into line even the most reluctant and it can be justified by reference to these communities' reliance on everybody carrying their own share of the burden of punishment for purposes of retributive justice and deterrence. In the light of these observations and discussions, it becomes evident that the contrast furnished here by the principle of like treatment of like cases is not between revenge and retribution as such, but between institutionalized and non-institutionalized forms of retribution.[32]

> 6. Retributive punishment is only inflicted [knowingly] on the wrongdoer, whereas revenge is sometimes inflicted [knowingly] on an innocent person close to the revengee, either because this is an easier target, or because it is thought that this would hurt the revengee more.[33]

Revenge can be, and sometimes is, exacted by inflicting suffering on those close to the wrongdoer, although this is not a defining feature of it. The avenger may choose to inflict suffering on someone close to the offender, say, a relative, for two possible reasons. In the first instance, the avenger makes the offender suffer by making the relative suffer. It is interesting to note that in these cases the relative may not be *punished,* as such; their suffering is merely used as a *means* to an end, namely, the end of punishing the offender by hurting them in an indirect way. Nonetheless, inflicting suffering on an innocent person in this way can be objected to both because it treats that person merely as a means to an end and because it is morally wrong to make an innocent person suffer as a means of punishing the guilty.

The other reason why the avenger may choose to inflict suffering on someone close to the offender, say, a relative, is not simply because, as Ten suggests, they are easier targets. Rather, it is because, given the prevailing norms regulating revenge, in many societies the avenger may not be required to distinguish sharply between the offender and their family or group. Hurting any member of the offender's group may be considered to be either as good as hurting the actual offender, or at least good enough. Consequently, the target of the punishment in these cases may not be just the individual who committed the offense, but the whole group (usually the family) with which the offender is identified. In many cultures all members of the group are held responsible for an offense committed by a member of that group because, as with most things, when it comes to punishment, people are identified with their larger groups. Their identities (in the epistemic, rather than the metaphysical sense) are very closely tied up with, and are largely derived from, those close to them—usually their families, friends, clan or tribe.[34] Their moral responsibilities, that is, their liabilities for praise and blame, reward and punishment are inextricably tied to this extended sense of identity. This basically means that it is quite legitimate and proper for any member of the wronged family to direct the retaliation towards any member of the wrongdoer's family, since wrongs and their punishment are matters to be settled between families and clans, not merely between individuals. Feuds, many of which are completely bloodless, are good examples where cycles of revenge and counter-revenge take place between families, not individual people. A feud is made possible primarily in contexts of shared identity and responsibility between family members.

Insofar as it is this kind of context that lends initial plausibility to Ten's observation about revenge, it should be easy to see that Ten's comparison depends on an individualistic paradigm of responsibility which cannot explain, let alone do justice to, the phenomenon under consideration. So-called revenge on the innocent is not explained by a lack of concern for ethical principle, but by a wider notion of responsibility according to which any member of the offending group constitutes a legitimate target for revenge because they are all guilty on account of their shared group identity. Patterson explains this beautifully in connection with the revenge practices of the Maori of New Zealand.

> Whereas Pakeha [Europeans] tend to concentrate upon an individual actor, Maori tend to see the actor as a family or other tribal group. In Pakeha terms, I insult you and so your uncle obtains utu [repayment] by insulting my elder brother. In Maori terms, my family insults yours and so your family obtains utu

by insulting my family. So, seeing the situation in Maori terms, it turns out that it is an ethical requirement in the case of utu, just as it is in the case of punishment, that the recipient be the offender. It would definitely be a mistake, according to Maori values, to inflict utu upon the wrong tribal grouping, just as it is a mistake, according to Pakeha values, to punish scapegoats.[35]

Ten's corresponding claim about retributive punishment, that it is knowingly inflicted only on the wrongdoer, may be true of some judicial systems, but this is not a necessary feature of retributive punishment itself. Judicial retributive punishment can be as unjust in this respect as revenge can be. Unknowing company directors or shareholders, for example, can be punished for the wrongdoings of employees.[36] We can also imagine situations where the legislators determine that, once a person is found guilty of an offense, the punishment which is imposed for retributive reasons must be shared among immediate family members. As a matter of fact, something like this was the practice when it came to punishing disgraced samurai in medieval Japan,[37] and also among the Maori of New Zealand in the form of *muru* (plunder) and *utu* (repayment).

> A standard method of resolving a dispute in traditional Maori law is the practice of muru. In this practice, an aggrieved family may directly confront the group that has caused their trouble, and confiscate goods in payment for the injury.[38]

> If, for example, I insult you, that calls for utu. . . . The responsibility for taking utu falls not on the individual but on the whole family. Likewise, the responsibility for the insulting behaviour is borne not only by the individual who delivers the insult but by a whole family group. A suitable retaliatory insult could be directed against any or all members of the family of the offender.[39]

Again, from an individualistic mode of thinking it might be tempting to say that such punishment is unjust, since one person cannot be held responsible for the actions of another, no matter how closely they might be related. But, apart from being questionable,[40] an attack along these lines would be beside the point in the current context. For even if it were unjust, that would not change the retributive character of the punishment itself, which consists in *the reasons proffered for its imposition, that it is imposed because it is deserved as repayment.* Ten commits the same mistake as Nozick in his comparison of retribution and revenge. He builds the principles of justice into the concept of retribution but not into the concept of revenge. Evidently, this is not the way to obtain a real contrast between the two.

Response and Summary

It has been suggested to me[41] that the disagreement I have with Nozick and Ten is mostly verbal, rather than substantial. Responding to this suggestion will serve the purpose of summarizing the essence of the arguments advanced in this chapter. I disagree with Nozick and Ten on just about every important point that concerns retribution and revenge. First, I disagree with them over what the correct analysis of revenge is, as well as over the question of how revenge is related to retribution. Through their comparisons, they exclude the possibility that revenge might be a kind of retribution. They also exclude the possibility that retribution and revenge might be more closely related than are two species of a genus. In my view they are mistaken on both points. Revenge is essentially retributive in character. The core reasons behind revenge are the essentially retributive notions of payback, getting even, and ill-desert. But since, in addition, revenge is personal in a way that other forms of retribution need not be, the correct way to analyze the relation of the two is in the form of a genus-species categorization. The final analysis and justification of these points are contained in the next chapter.

Furthermore, Nozick and Ten give a distorted analysis of retribution by failing to distinguish it from what are properly regarded to be principles of justice. Nozick and Ten unacceptably restrict the scope of the term 'retribution' by conceptually tying it to principles of justice. The result is an implausible account according to which retribution is necessarily for a wrong, it is necessarily proportional, it necessarily gets the right person, and so on. This is mistaken because it is possible to impose unjust retribution. Retribution can be overdone, it can get the wrong person and, as the example of reprisals against whistle-blowers illustrates, it can be imposed for offenses which are not moral wrongs. The correct analysis of retribution, therefore, must be one in which retribution is independent of the principles of justice. I offer such an analysis in the next chapter.

7

Revenge: Its Nature and Definition

'A wrongful act must be punished' is not only a statement of fact, but verges on being a social law, which is the norm of reciprocity.

Graeme Newman[1]

In this chapter I consider the logical space of punishment with a view to defining revenge and to giving a visual representation of its relation to other key punishment concepts. I define revenge as personal retribution which is typically accompanied by feelings of indignation, anger and resentment for wrongs suffered in one's personal domain of concern. The map I intend to give consists of two parts: (a) a *typology* of the various reasons for punishment; (b) a categorization of the various *forms* of punishment on the basis of two criteria. But it is important that neither of these criteria be confused with what I call, respectively, the *modalities* and the *process* of punishment. Therefore, I start with a brief discussion of these, before proceeding to draw a map of the logical space of punishment with a view to locating revenge on it.

The Modalities of Punishment

There are as many modalities of punishment as there are ways of imposing penalties and deprivations on someone. Imprisonment, fines, shame, embarrassment, deprivations of freedom, actions such as a negative vote in the board room, or arriving late for dinner, all can be ways of punishing someone. They can be conveniently labeled as the 'modalities' or the 'manner' of punishment, as they are modes and manners in which punishments occur.

There are two points worth mentioning about the modalities of punishment. First, there is room for constructing a rich typology of the possible modalities. For example, some broad categories are suggested by the fact that punishment can be physical, freedom-depriving, economical, psychological, sexual, and so on. Possible categories under, say, punishment by deprivation of freedom might be concentration camps, labour camps, standard imprisonment, solitary confinement, house arrest, exile, and so forth. Lists of the categories and sub-categories could go on almost indefinitely, since there are as many ways of imposing punishment on someone as there are ways of penalizing them.

The second point is that the modality of punishment is a legitimate moral concern. There are two dimensions to this, one of which relates to the offender, the other to the victim. With regard to the victim, there is a good moral case for choosing the manner of the punishment in such a way that it not only compensates the victims for their loss but also maximizes their restoration from the trauma of having been victimized. This might mean that, whenever possible, the offender ought to be given a chance to express regret and sincere apology directly to the victim for their behaviour and pay the victim compensation as a constructive way to make amends. In turn, this requires that those punished should be kept economically productive whenever possible. Part of their earnings might also be used to cover the costs associated with the handling of their case.

With regard to the dimension relating to the offender, there is a principle of justice the violation of which seems automatically to constitute a serious moral wrong. This principle is that, regardless of the offense, punishment should not be imposed in grotesque, dehumanizing modes. For example, physical and psychological torture, mutilation and disfigurement are dehumanizing to those punished and are, on that account alone, serious moral wrongs. Not being punished in dehumanizing ways is, perhaps, an inalienable human right. A difficulty here might lie in the fact that there can be radical disagreement about what kinds of punishment would count as dehumanizing. Indigenous people such as Aboriginal Australians and the Maori of New Zealand, for example, consider imprisonment to be dehumanizing and cruel, whereas Europeans perceive the spearing of the offender's thigh, for instance, to be cruel and barbaric. Western culture also condemns the cutting off of people's hands for stealing, to use another example, as evidenced by strong reactions in the West to reports that the practice has been revived in at least one Islamic country.[2] Such culture-specific differences may be irreconcilable because they are often a reflection of the prevailing values and the different ways of life adopted by different people. Interfering with these, in turn, creates moral problems of its own because it raises questions about political autonomy and about rights to national and cultural self-determination. However, discussion of such difficult, but nevertheless important, problems falls beyond the scope of this book.

The Process of Punishment

A somewhat different dimension of punishment from its modality is the process punishment follows. Invariably, punishment in any of its modes is preceded by certain deliberative processes. These can be very short and simple, or long and involved. Using the judicial model as a benchmark, four distinctive stages of the process of punishment seem to be the following: the *gathering of evidence;* leading to the *plea* and/or verdict, which is the determination of whether the accused is guilty or not of the alleged offense; the *sentencing,* which is the determination of both the appropriate mode and the amount of punishment, if the accused is found guilty; and, finally, the *execution of the sentence,* which is the punishment itself.

The process of punishment is also a moral concern, again, for both the criminal and the victim. It would be wrong to accuse and punish someone even if they happened to be guilty without giving them a fair hearing, without giving them a decent opportunity to explain and defend themselves. Insisting on extremely elaborate processes regardless of the circumstances may well be unnecessary, if not undesirable. But the absolute minimum must be that, as far as possible, the process safeguards against abuses and violations of what may be regarded as basic human rights, and that it operates according to the principles of justice outlined in Chapter 5. As with dehumanizing modes of punishment, there seems to be a good case here for not being punished without due process.

The process of punishment can be a moral concern for victims as well. Their recovery could often be greatly helped if they were given their rightful place, and a substantial say, in the process of punishment, as this would empower them in a very tangible way to feel again in control of their disrupted lives. I return to this point again in Chapter 9 where I discuss victim empowerment and greater victim participation from a victim justice perspective.

Concepts of Punishment: A Motive-based Typology

The following typology relies on motive-based reasons and justifications for punishment. A fine and a prison sentence are just that, a fine and a prison sentence, and whether they constitute retribution, or deterrence, or simply the community's way of denouncing the wrong and expressing its disapproval for it, depends on motive-related reasons, justifications and rationales for their imposition. Whether some particular punishment falls into one or the other of the above categories does not depend on external considerations such as the time, place or circumstance of the offense, or some other feature of the punishment itself. Thus, when punishment is imposed in order to reform, or to deter future would-be offenders, the punishment is clearly instrumental because it is used simply as a means to an end, namely to prevent and reduce crime. It is an interesting feature of this kind of justification for punishment that if crime could be prevented and reduced equally well or better by some other approach, such as a generous reward system for good behavior, for example, then impositions of punishment would no longer be justified.

By contrast, when the same punishment is imposed as repayment (payback, getting even) or as a kind of negative desert for some wrong or offense, the punishment in question is recognizably retributive in nature, and this kind of reason for punishment would not disappear even if a reward system would achieve a lower crime rate. Retributive punishment is justified by reference to ill-desert in the wrongdoer and is based on the responsibility they bear for their actions. It cannot be justified by reference to other good consequences their punishment might have, such as a reduced crime rate. Again, when the same punishment is imposed as an expression of disapproval, or as a symbolic affirmation of society's fundamental values, it seems to have a strongly functionalist character. The most familiar reasons for punishment can be listed and broadly categorized as indicated below.

Concepts and Types of Punishment

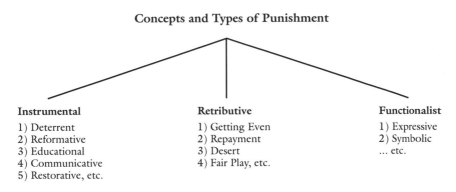

Instrumental	Retributive	Functionalist
1) Deterrent	1) Getting Even	1) Expressive
2) Reformative	2) Repayment	2) Symbolic
3) Educational	3) Desert	... etc.
4) Communicative	4) Fair Play, etc.	
5) Restorative, etc.		

Figure 1

A number of observations are called for at this point. One is that the various reasons for punishment, the natures of which underlie this typology, are not incompatible with one another and several of them can be appealed to in explanations and justifications of punishment. Thus, there is no difficulty in imposing punishment for the combined reasons that it is due as repayment or desert, that it deters future would-be offenders, and that it also expresses disapproval of the offending conduct. Also, not all of the reasons for punishment invoked by this list have to function as justifying reasons. For example, to say that some punishment was imposed as payback for a prior offense can easily be a mere indication or explanation of the motive, rather than being an exhaustive exercise in justification. A full justification of punishment as negative repayment certainly requires a more detailed account of *why* this kind of repayment is morally acceptable. Indeed, we must reserve the right to examine and criticize any, or all of the reasons claiming to justify punishment. No reason is, and none should be, beyond questioning as to whether it really is a good reason for imposing what are potentially unwelcome measures and impositions on people.

Returning to the earlier point on typology construction, there are two reasons why typologies of punishment such as the above should include explanatory motives, both of which have to do with retribution. One reason is that a person imposing punishment, say, as repayment prescribed by law, social norms, and customs, might not be able to formulate the proper justifying reasons for the imposition of punishment. However, that should not present an obstacle to identifying the punishment in question for what it recognizably is: law-, or norm-driven retribution. The other reason why such a typology is preferable has to do with a particular philosophical position about the possibility of justifying retribution. According to J.L. Mackie, for example, it is misguided to look for a justification of retribution. In Mackie's view, there is no such justification to be found, but only a sociobiological explanation.[3] While I reject this view in Chapter 8, Mackie's position on retribution is coherent; making sense of and categorizing such a position would be difficult by reference to justificatory reasons alone because a position like Mackie's disputes the very existence of such justifying reasons. Mackie, however, is mistaken, and a justification for the right of victims to personal retributive punishment within the criminal justice system (institutionalized revenge) will be provided in Chapters 9 and 10 of this book.

Finally, I must re-state the essential difference between *instrumental* and *retributive* reasons for punishment. Instrumental aims, such as deterrence, rehabilitation, and correction, are linked to punishment only contingently and circumstantially. It is possible, if not probable, that deterrence and correction could be better achieved quite often through other means than punishing. Deterrence, for example, might be better achieved through a reward system for good behaviour, while correction and rehabilitation could often be better served by therapy and friendly education. This does not hold true, however, for retributive reasons, where there is a necessary link between the retributive aim of the punishment and the punishment itself. Any response to criminal activity would necessarily fail to achieve or actualize such retributive aims as giving the offenders their (negative) just deserts and repaying them in kind for the wrong they had done, if the response in question were not punishment of some sort. Retribution is impossible without the imposition of punishment in the form of some penalty for the wrong or offense in question. But while retributive punishment is necessarily punitive, it would be a mistake to think that only retributive rationales lead to punitive practices. Severe penalties are often imposed in the courts with instrumental rationales in the name of deterrence and the community's need to feel safe and be protected from crime, and more controversially, in the name of rehabilitation. This last one, incidentally, is an idea repudiated by C.S. Lewis, who argues against forcing onto wrongdoers "supposed kindnesses which they in fact had a right to refuse, and finally kindnesses which no one but you will recognize as kindnesses and which the recipient will feel as abominable cruelties."[4]

Basic Forms of Punishment: A Typology

Once it is established that there are good reasons for punishing someone, it becomes important to decide two further questions. First, who has the right and, possibly, the duty to be involved in the various major stages of the process of punishment? Second, what form should such involvement take? To answer these questions, we need a conceptual framework with clear categories that enable us to distinguish between importantly different forms of punishment. I will now provide such a framework, although an in-depth consideration of the above two questions will have to wait until the last two chapters. A more immediate role of the framework will be to aid us in locating revenge in the logical space of punishment. My proposed framework is based on two criteria. The first criterion is whether or not the process of punishment is institutionalized. Punishment is institutionalized if it is regulated by, and is carried out in accordance with, some established law, custom, or practice. An obvious example of institutionalized punishment is our current judicial system where the process is undertaken by neutral third parties in accordance with relevant legislation. Thus, to the extent that an institution punishes people retributively (for, it does not have to) to that degree the punishment exacted by the institution in question is *institutionalized retributive* punishment. To the degree that the institution punishes people instrumentally, the punishment is *institutionalized instrumental* punishment. An example of non-institutionalized punishment could be where a wife divorces her husband upon discovering his infidelities.

The second important criterion on which my proposed typology is based is whether punishment is imposed for a personal reason or not. A necessary, though not a sufficient, condition for this is the existence of a personal tie between the victim of the offense for which punishment is being imposed and the person who is involved in the process of punishment. A personal tie is conceptually presupposed by the notion of a personal reason and, therefore, the former is necessary for the latter. Very briefly, someone has a personal reason for getting involved in the process of punishment if that person gets involved *because* of the personal tie he or she has with the victim. Typically, the involvement of such a person is going to be accompanied by a feeling of resentment on account of their personal and emotional tie to the wronged person.[5] These two criteria, that is, the institutionalization of the process of punishment and the existence of a personal reason for one's involvement in that process, provide the basis for four basic forms of punishment. The way in which they are individuated can be easily seen in the following Figure (where 'I' stands for 'Institutionalized', 'P' for 'Personal' and '~' for 'Not'):

	Institutionalized	Non-Institutionalized
Personal	I & P	~I & P
Non-Personal	I & ~P	~I & ~P

Figure 2

I shall run through these in order of familiarity. *Institutionalized non-personal punishment* is punishment imposed by a person, or persons, who are specifically entrusted (with or without pay) with the task of ensuring fair, equitable, and systematic ways of punishing people for their wrongdoings. In this form of punishment the punishment is completely taken out of the hands of the wronged party. The victim has no decision-making power in any of the major stages of the process of punishment. Clearly, it is this form of punishment that is exemplified in our courts within the framework of Western judicial systems. By contrast, *non-institutionalized personal punishment* is punishment imposed by a person (or a group) who has a personal reason for being involved in the process of punishment. This personal reason is that they are either the primary victim, or that they have a personal or special tie to the primary victim of the offense or wrong. In this form of punishment the punishment is completely in the hands of the wronged person(s), rather than in the hands of an impersonal institution set up for the purpose. The offended side decides over guilt and degree of responsibility, the amount and type of punishment, as well as the execution of the punishment.

Non-institutionalized non-personal punishment stands in contradistinction to both institutionalized and personal punishment, as well as to their combination. It is both useful and correct to refer to this form of punishment as *vigilantism*. Vigilante punishment is imposed by a person or a body of persons who are neither specifically appointed by law to punish some wrongdoing nor do they have the above mentioned personal reason for taking on the task themselves. Typically, vigilante punishment is carried out by persons who are personally unrelated to either the victim, or the offender. Vigilantes, in a sense, are self-appointed agents who take up the task of punishing criminals in the name of fairness, justice, and the protection of the community through deterrence. Most often these agents take it on themselves in times of great need to see to it that wrongdoing is appropriately punished and that life and property are protected against criminal activity. They take on the responsibility of supplying the deterrence and the retribution if in the circumstances these cannot be ensured either privately by the wronged parties, or institutionally because of the inefficiency, or the total absence, of such a system. Sometimes, however, vigilante involvement may only be partial. Fictitious vigilante figures like Batman and Superman are well known. Real-life examples are the Vigilantes of Montana[6] and the Guardian Angels of the New York City subways.[7]

Finally, *institutionalized personal punishment* is a cross between the first two basic forms. In this form of punishment the victims of the alleged wrongs and offenses become involved in the process of punishment within an institutionalized framework. Viking law, revenge practices of Medieval Japan, and the earlier mentioned Maori practices of *muru* (plunder) and *utu* (repayment) are good historical examples.[8] Notwithstanding the abundance of historical precedents, until very recently, substantial victim involvement has been virtually unknown in contemporary Western systems of institutionalized criminal justice. However, there are good reasons for giving it serious consideration and I shall return to consider personal forms of punishment in the last two chapters where I argue the merits of institutionalized revenge. I move on now to represent the above-mentioned basic forms of punishment in logical space. One way of doing this is as follows:

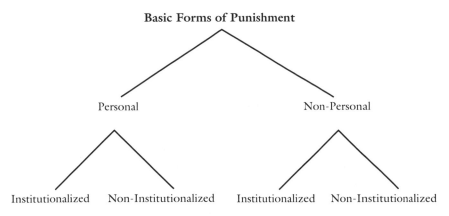

Figure 3

These four basic forms of punishment are pure forms and there is scope for mixed cases. There certainly is scope for degrees of institutionalization with respect to the process of punishment. There may also be scope, perhaps, for ambiguity in certain cases as to the presence of a personal reason for becoming involved in the process of punishment. As I have suggested in the Introduction, it is supposedly for guarding against this reason being present in judicial proceedings that current institutionalized systems exclude the victims and those close to them from having any substantial role in the process of punishment. This much said, the stage is ready to identify revenge on a combined map of the logical space of punishment.

Revenge: Its Definition and Domain in Logical Space

The taxonomy of punishment I presented in the previous section is conceptually and terminologically independent of any ideas of revenge. In this section I provide reasons for identifying certain kinds of punishment as revenge. The strategy here, of course, will have to consist in pointing out the conditions which seem to be individually necessary and jointly sufficient for revenge. If revenge is to be found within the framework set up so far, these conditions and features should already figure on the relevant maps of the logical space of punishment. Indeed, these features must be there, if previous arguments, that revenge is a form of punishment, are correct.[9]

In order to locate revenge on that map, however, we need to take into consideration both the typology of the various specific concepts of punishment and the typology of the forms of punishment. Starting with the typology of the concepts, the most obvious clue is the fact that revenge is essentially retributive in character. Revenge is motivated by the desire to pay back the other, to even the scores, to impose on the other what they deserve in the retributive sense described in Chapter 5. If an act of punishing someone is not done at least in part out of such retributive reasons, be that by reference to repayment, desert, or whatever, then it cannot be a case of revenge. We cannot properly talk of revenge in cases where the punishment is purely instrumental. Take the example of the parent who punishes the child purely to discourage the child from playing a dangerous game, even if that game has already hurt the parent. That sort of punishment cannot by any stretch of the imagination be taken to be a case of revenge. This is because the punishment is purely instrumental and not at all retributive in character.

But, as I have already argued against Solomon and Oldenquist, not all cases of retribution are cases of revenge and, therefore, we need to look further. More specifically, what needs to be done here is to capture or accommodate the personal nature of revenge in the sense already explained. This feature figures prominently in the typology of the basic forms of punishment, and locating revenge on it is straightforward. Combining the two typologies, the domain of revenge can be located in the logical space of punishment in the following way:

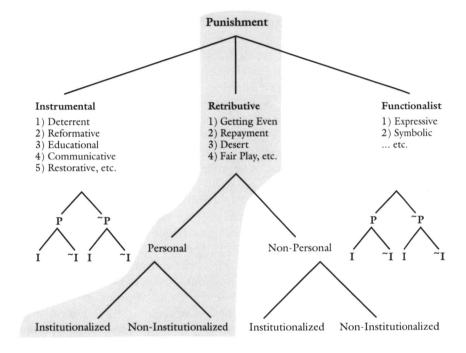

Figure 4

The necessity for a personal reason for revenge selects two and excludes the other two of the four basic forms of retributive punishment as being possible forms of revenge—save by way of being instruments for someone's revenge. *Non-Institutionalized Personal Retributive Punishment* is what we commonly refer to by the word 'revenge.' But, clearly, this is not the only form of retribution to which the term 'revenge' properly applies. For, although the phenomenon had been until recent years virtually absent in industrialized Western cultures, *Institutionalized Personal Retributive Punishment* has not been unknown as a practice and this is also a form of revenge. In medieval Iceland and Japan, for example, individual intentions to take revenge often had to be first registered with, and normally approved by, higher authorities. State sanctions applied for failing to do so.[10] This is what might be called *Institutionalized Revenge.* The remaining two categories, of course, are the familiar *judicial retribution* and *vigilantism.*

To summarize, the place occupied by revenge in the logical space of punishment corresponds to the following definition of revenge: *Revenge is personal retributive punishment,* typically accompanied and fueled by feelings of indignation, anger, and resentment for wrongs suffered. That is, revenge is a form of punishment which is imposed for retributive personal reasons to satisfy the requirements of, and a corresponding personal need for, retributive justice for wrongs suffered in one's personal sphere of care and concern. If this is right, then the earlier arguments about retribution and the principles of justice are as applicable to revenge as they are to judicial retribution. Like judicial retribution, or indeed vigilante retribution, revenge can be just or unjust, depending on whether the relevant principles of justice for offenders are respected.

While the above definition captures well the nature of revenge, the retributive element in revenge remains compatible with instrumental considerations of one's interests. For example, someone could adopt a policy of personally paying back for offenses only when the costs of doing so are not too high. But, what is most important to note here is that the compatibility between retributive and instrumental considerations goes so far that there are many cases of revenge which seem to be largely instrumental, their retributive element fading considerably in the immediate, direct reasoning behind the decision to take revenge. Many pre-industrial societies have, or had, an honor-based system of morality and norms of revenge frequently occupy an important place in their respective codes of propriety and honor. For an individual living in such an honor-centered culture, honor, good reputation, and a good name were precious, if not vital. Importantly, honor and good name were in jeopardy if one failed to live up to society's norms and customs—the relevant ones here being those which regulated the appropriate occasions for, and other aspects of, revenge. Although the codes of honor and the norms of revenge would generally allow a limited number of alternatives, such as accepting an apology or a negotiated settlement, in special circumstances they could conspire to leave the individual with no viable alternative to revenge, but only the loss of face, disgrace, ridicule, becoming the object of gossip and, in extreme cases, of social ostracism. Especially in such cases, but also more generally where honor and social standing were on the line, there was a considerable shift in focus and emphasis away from the importance of retribution pure and simple towards the importance of maintaining the honor and good reputation of the individual and of the whole family. It is not difficult to see how in certain circumstances this shift in focus could be so marked that the individual seeking revenge hardly considered the underlying point and rationale for revenge (which is retribution) and made his decision by reference to the relevant retributive norms and codes alone.

The blood feud is a good example of revenge where individuals and families are primarily moved by concerns to maintain honor, and avoid the disapproval of the community, which, as we have seen earlier, can be crippling. The blood feud being one of the severest forms of revenge, it might be wondered whether retribution really does form part of the concept of revenge. The answer to this question is affirmative. The fundamental rationale of revenge is retribution even in cases where instrumental considerations of honor and social standing figure as prominently in the avenger's reasoning as they do in the feud. The retributive idea of negative reciprocity, or repayment (payback, getting even) is an essential element in any satisfactory analysis of the feud, and so is the idea that retaliation is due, and is justified, on the basis of the responsibility the targeted person bears for the offense avenged. In other words, what ultimately justifies any particular case of revenge in the course of a feud is not merely the preservation of honor and social standing, but the retributive liability of the targeted person (or family) for some prior offense. This liability is based on their moral responsibility for the wrong in question.

Though the concept of honor is essential to understanding the feud, the desire to preserve honor and social standing is part of a powerful mechanism of social control which reinforces the value and the importance of retribution in moral communities where, often by choice, there is no centralized system of punishment. These communities evolved alternative, largely revenge-based, systems of punishment by requiring that everybody pull their own weight within their own spheres of concern and responsibility. Thus, in communities with no centralized system of punishment, but which, nevertheless, want to hold their own members responsible for improper, wrongful conduct, the two critical elements of revenge are explained in the following way: The fact that they are moral communities explains their insistence that offenders be retributively punished for their wrongful behaviour, while the absence of a centralized system of punishment explains their insistence that this be done personally by the offended parties concerned. Those who fail to carry out their moral duties in these matters are punished by the community as a whole through gossip, open ridicule, and other sanctions.

The earlier quote from Hasluck leaves no doubt that social sanctions can be severe enough to make it individually rational even for the faint-hearted to carry out the duty of revenge. Nevertheless, ultimately it is retribution, based on moral responsibility, which provides the justification or the rationale, not only for revenge, but also for the reinforcing social mechanisms encompassing the relevant codes of honor, norms of revenge, the gossip, and the social sanctioning of those reluctant to discharge their duties. These mechanisms of social control have evolved in cultural contexts so that it becomes individually rational for everybody to live by the law of retribution, even if, and when, their other interests and fears would tempt them to do otherwise.

Such mechanisms of social control are not unique to the area of punishment. Analogous ones which control other aspects of people's behaviour often operate in traditional, conservative societies. For example, in traditional Montenegro "in choices such as hospitality versus stinginess, honesty versus overuse of deceit in casual transactions between people, or sexual transgressions versus sexual propriety, gossip was the primary sanctioning mechanism."[11] Similarly, "in the segmentary society of the Bedouins of the Western Desert, which have only recently been submitted to a strong governmental authority, honor has played, and still plays, a most vital role in the field of social control, besides providing an effective code of morality."[12]

The existence of such mechanisms of social control also explains how overdetermination of certain behaviour can take place. To the marital difficulties which would be brought about by extramarital affairs, for example, people are given additional powerful reasons to resist temptation by the gossip and the scorn with which society would regard them. Similarly with revenge where internal feelings of resentment and the moral need for retribution often suffice, immense social pressures of the kinds described earlier can give additional, and sometimes weightier, reason to carry out one's duty of revenge. That said, it is once again time to pull together the many threads of the ideas covered so far.

The Argument So Far

Following the debunking, in Chapters 2–4, of the anti-revenge paradigm, Chapters 5–7 have sought to disentangle from one another the various key concepts in the philosophy of punishment. Essentially, this involved an examination of the natures of retribution, justice, and revenge, and of the way these key concepts are related to one another. In Chapter 5 it was shown that retribution is not in and of itself just or unjust, but that this depends on whether it conforms to the principles of justice which, in turn, have independent moral authority of their own. This is evidenced by the fact that their authority is not in the least diminished in the presence of instrumental reasons for the imposition of punishment. Principles that prohibit the punishment of the innocent and the overpunishment of the guilty are in a separate category of their own and nothing but confusion is served by placing them in the 'retributive' category. Retribution, essentially, has to do with punishment justification. It is identified by a particular kind of reason for the moral permissibility of imposing punishment on wrongdoers, namely that punishment is due to wrongdoers as a matter of negative repayment. They deserve it in proportion to the moral seriousness of their wrongdoing—a view for which justification will be provided in Chapter 8.

Chapter 6 examined the relationship between retribution and revenge, especially focusing on the polarization of views evident in the contemporary literature. Both views, that retribution and revenge are one and the same thing, and that retribution and revenge are in different moral categories, are untenable. The first view is wrong because revenge is personal in a way that other forms of retribution, such as judicial retribution, might not be. The second view is flawed because revenge is essentially retributive in character; it is a form of retribution. These critiques were followed up in Chapter 7 with a positive categorization of the relationship between retribution and revenge, namely the proposition that revenge is best understood as a species of retribution.

Apart from a brief consideration of the moral issues involved in the modalities and process of punishment, Chapter 7 focused on providing a defensible definition of revenge in terms of necessary and sufficient conditions. There are two important typologies of punishment that are particularly relevant for the purpose, namely a categorization of the various concepts of punishment, and a categorization of the various forms punishment can take. In the first typology, the various reasons for punishment fall into instrumental, retributive, and functionalist categories. The second typology highlights and relies on the fact that, whatever the reasons for punishment, the process of punishment can occur in institutionalized as well as non-institutionalized settings and that it can be done with personal or non-personal involvement of the wronged persons in question. These two criteria serve to identify four basic forms of punishment. With the help of the above two typologies revenge can be usefully identified on a visual representation of the logical space of punishment. In relation to the reasons for punishment revenge is retributive, whereas with regard to the forms of punishment revenge is personal, and there is scope for it to take institutionalized, as well as non-institutionalized forms. Essentially, revenge is best defined as personal retributive punishment, a definition that accords well with popular understanding and usage of the term.

The retributive element in revenge remains compatible with consequentialist considerations of one's interests. Indeed, in certain cases, such as the feud, instrumental considerations of honor and social standing can become the primary considerations in the direct reasoning leading to a decision to take revenge. However, this phenomenon of strong instrumental focus does not disconfirm an analysis of revenge in terms of retribution because the fundamental or ultimate rationale of revenge is still retribution. The retributive idea of negative reciprocity, or repayment (getting even, payback) is an essential element in any satisfactory analysis of the feud because the most basic point of justification for retaliation is not the need to maintain honor and social standing but the retrospective responsibility the targeted person bears for the offense in question and, correlatively, a deontologically based moral duty of the offended party to activate such retrospective responsibility through appropriate retaliation. Honor merely acts as an additional stake and serves to reinforce the importance of such retrospective responsibilities and duties.

Having shown that revenge is properly understood as personal retribu-tive punishment and that, therefore, like any other form of punishment, it can be just or unjust depending on whether it violates the principles of jus-tice, I now move on to consider its moral grounding and practical relevance to contemporary institutions of justice.

8

A Defense of Moral Retributivism

In cases which outrage the moral feelings of the community to a great degree, the feeling of indignation and desire for revenge which is excited in the minds of decent people is, I think, deserving of legitimate satisfaction.

J.F. Stephen[1]

Personal accountability makes no sense unless it means that transgressors deserve punishment—that is, they are owed retribution.

Andrew Oldenquist[2]

I showed in Chapters 5–7 that the principles of justice are independent of retribution and that, in virtue of being a form of retributive punishment, revenge can be just or unjust and that it can take institutionalized as well as non-institutionalized forms. In the remaining chapters I defend the moral justifiability of institutionalized revenge, by which I mean personal retribution within frameworks provided for by a legal justice system rather than informally institutionalized practices in revenge cultures.

I am not advocating the unconditional, inherent moral desirability of actually taking revenge in legal institutionalized contexts. Rather, I am arguing for the moral *permissibility* of institutionalized revenge and for the importance of extending such legal rights to victims by legal systems making revenge permissible, not obligatory. Taking victim rights and victim justice seriously requires, among other things, the validation of the legitimacy of victim resentment and anger. It also requires acknowledgment of the moral legitimacy of victims' need for retributive justice, when such a need is present. An equally important part of victim justice is victim empowerment which, in turn, requires legal institutionalized forums where victims can express their legitimate feelings of resentment and anger, forums where they can demand satisfaction in terms of adequate restoration, apologies, or retributive justice in a controlled and civilized manner for the wrongs committed against them, without their being trivialized, moralized, or patronized on account of such needs and feelings, or on account of actions taken on the basis of such needs and feelings. Subject to possible vetoes on grounds of unreasonable leniency or harshness, such forums must also invest victims with the prerogative and the power to forgive and show mercy to their offenders. Without according such substantial rights and powers to victims, notions of victim justice and victim empowerment ring hollow. Such victim rights and powers are also important for purposes of victim restoration in social-psychological terms and are an integral part of providing justice to them.

To be satisfactory, however, a defense of institutionalized revenge must show three important things. First, revenge being retributive in character, the defense must show that retribution is a legitimate and morally acceptable reason for punishment. This is the task of the current chapter. Second, revenge being personal in nature, good reasons must be provided for bringing the personal element back into the justice system in the form of greater victim participation and empowerment. Third, concerns must be addressed over possible violations of the principles of justice with respect to offenders, as well as other fears and reservations about revenge, the danger of escalation being a good example. I argue in these regards that, under appropriate institutionalized conditions, the personal and retributive components in revenge neither endanger justice to offenders, nor do they lead to morally repugnant, or otherwise unwanted, results. The last two of these three main points are addressed in the two remaining chapters.

The Thesis of Moral Retributivism

A satisfactory defense of institutionalized revenge must show that retribution is a legitimate and morally acceptable reason for punishment. This, in turn, requires clarification of the key notion of moral retributivism. Moral retributivism, sometimes referred to simply as retributivism, is a philosophical position which answers the question: What justifies punishment? Consequentialist and other ways of connecting wrongdoing and punishment make the moral status (value or disvalue) of punishment completely dependent on its (good or bad) consequences[3] or functions.[4] By contrast, while being compatible with other connections such as the above, retributivism makes a positive, approving moral connection between wrongdoing and punishment independently of the consequences or functions punishment might have.

Punishment of wrongdoing, according to this view, is good in itself. In other words, retributivism is characterized by the thesis that there is a positive moral connection between wrongdoing and punishment, which is not derived but *intrinsic,* as it is not dependent on extrinsic, derived benefits punishment might (and might not) have in terms of its consequences and functions.

We need to be more precise, however, because moral retributivism does not concern itself with the whole domain of retributive punishment. Its claim is not that all retributive punishment has positive moral value, or is good in itself, but only that retributive punishment within the limits set by the principles of justice, such as proportionality and not punishing the innocent, has positive moral value simply in virtue of being punishment of wrongdoing. This core retributivist thesis provides the basis for two familiar versions of moral retributivism which in the literature are variously referred to as 'pure', 'hard', and 'positive' retributivism, and 'soft' and 'permissive' retributivism, respectively. Pure, hard, or positive retributivism is the view that those found guilty of wrongdoing *should,* or *must,* be punished in proportion to the seriousness of their offense. Soft or permissive retributivism is the view that while those found guilty of wrongdoing *may* be punished in proportion to their crime, they do not have to be so punished.

There is, however, another kind of retributivism which could be added to these two. According to this view, although the retributive just punishment of wrongdoing is right and good in itself, mortals and their institutions possess no moral warrant to impose it on the wrongdoer.

> It is only just and right, Bradley and Kant would argue, that the guilty should suffer. Yes, I agree; their punishment is morally right and just. But that proposition doesn't imply whether *we* ought to punish them or how. . . . What is just when the Fates or the natural world brings it about is unwarranted—morally unwarranted—for human agents. No one and no institution is morally justified in doing such things.[5]

This is a somewhat curious retributivist position. The primary purpose or function of moral judgments, presumably, is to guide action, especially *human* action. Indeed, moral judgments are supposed to have prescriptive force which requires agents to act in specific ways: what is judged to be good or right, morally speaking, ought to be pursued and whatever is judged to be bad or wrong should be avoided. But this version of retributivism turns these fundamentals on their head. It morally forbids us doing what it judges to be morally right and good, namely the imposition of due punishment on wrongdoers. But since this form of retributivism allows the *gods* and the forces of nature to pursue or bring about what in this instance is judged to be good and right, it raises an important issue with regard to punishment. This is the question of who has the right to be involved in impositions of punishment.[6] I discuss this issue in the next chapter with respect to the rights of victims to be substantially involved and have their say in the legal resolution of their cases.

For now, what is important to note about moral retributivism is that, although it is concerned with *just retribution*, it does not beg the question as to the need for an independent explanation or rationale for the moral defensibility of just retributive punishment. For the justness in this context consists solely in the non-violation of certain basic principles of justice, such as those prohibiting the overpunishment of offenders and the punishment of the innocent. As argued earlier, such principles do not provide reasons for imposing punishment, they have only limiting roles. They demarcate the moral limits of punishment by an appeal to independent standards of fairness and justice, standards which are, or can be, autonomous and independent of the reasons for which punishment is imposed. This notion of just punishment is different from the notion that retributive punishment is imposed as a matter of justice, that justice demands the punishment of wrongdoing. Whatever else might be meant by such claims, it is clear that they appeal to the notion of justice more as a justificatory device for imposing punishment, rather than as a device aimed at placing limits on it. I shall discuss in more detail the notion of justice as a justificatory device below.

Another crucial point to keep in mind in any discussion of retributive justifications is that no moral view or theory should be labeled 'retributive' unless it subscribes to, or implies, the thesis that punishment of wrongdoing within the limits set by the principles of justice is intrinsically good, that it has positive moral value, that it is right and good simply in virtue of being punishment of wrongdoing. As Cottingham points out, some construals and justifications of 'retribution' are blatantly consequentialist. An example is the claim that retribution is justified by the fact that punishment of wrongdoing brings satisfaction to the aggrieved, which in turn helps to prevent vendettas in the interests of social stability.[7] There is nothing retributive about such explanations or justifications. Braithwaite and Pettit have raised similar complaints and point out that, in spite of retributivists generally being critical of consequentialism, "sometimes they themselves move into a consequentialist mode of thinking" and that, even if the phrases used in framing retributivist rationales bear the mark of retributivist concerns, "what we are being offered may still be a consequentialist theory."[8] Honderich's account of retribution is a good example of this. The critical feature of Honderich's account is the claim that

> the penalty will give satisfactions equivalent to the grievance caused by his (the offender's) action.[9] The truth of the retributivist tradition, more precisely, is that it seeks to justify punishment partly or wholly by the clear reason that it satisfies the grievances created by offenses, through causing distress to offenders.[10]

But, as Atkinson points out, even "garden variety" retributivists would disown this characterization of retribution.

> Although Honderich contrives to take the sting out of the retributivist position, he does so by a fundamental misrepresentation. He in fact seems to have followed just those "Serpentine wanderings of the Happiness theory" that Kant so emphatically warned us against.[11]

It would be difficult not to agree with Atkinson that through those "serpentine wanderings" Honderich lost retributivism from his account. His justification is recognizably consequentialist in nature. That his account is not retributivist is also shown by the fact that if grievance satisfaction could be maximized through some less painful method, then punishment would no longer be justified by it. For example, a system of rewards, combined with counseling and hypnotherapy for those aggrieved, could be an alternative to punishment as far as grievance satisfaction is concerned. Moreover, there may be cases where the aggrieved party has been murdered and there is no one around who cares about him to derive the satisfactions necessary for justifying punishment along lines suggested by Honderich's account. It is a necessary feature of a retributivist account or justification of punishment that it is able to render an offender liable to moral censure, blame and punishment simply by reference to the moral wrong committed. The challenge facing moral retributivists, therefore, is nothing less than giving a coherent and plausible explanation of the intrinsic moral connection which it claims to exist between wrongdoing and punishment.

This criterion has proved notoriously difficult to meet, and remains unsatisfied even by so-called 'communicative' theories of retribution, such as Hampton's. Apart from being functionalist in nature, Hampton's account rests on the dubious premise that punishment is the best way to communicate to the offender and to others an important moral truth about the relative worth of the offender and the victim. This moral truth, or the message which is claimed by Hampton to be best communicated through punishment, is that, contrary to the assertion implicit in the wrongful act, the victim is not less valuable than the offender, and therefore that "better treatment of the victim is required."[12] To be sure, there is no reason to suppose that such a message is not implicit in punishment. What is implausible is the suggestion that a functionalist explanation of this kind should count as a theory of retribution, let alone an adequate one.

Retributivists need not deny, of course, that good consequences, such as deterrence or grievance satisfaction, and desirable functions, such as communicating moral truths, expressing disapproval, or emphatically denouncing the crime, are highly relevant to justifying punishment in instrumental and functional ways. But such instrumental and functionalist justifications and explanations are of no help where a justification of retributive punishment is called for. The core retributivist idea that there is an intrinsic moral connection between wrongdoing and liability for punishment is not supported by justifications which make only a consequentialist or functionalist link between the two. It is fundamentally mistaken to think that retribution may be given some consequentialist justification, such as when it serves the purposes of grievance satisfaction, individual and social restoration, and deterrence. Such justifications are vulnerable to the obvious objection that those desirable ends should not be pursued through morally distasteful means, such as retribution and revenge, if these are morally indefensible in their own right. Therefore, no credible justification of retributive punishment can fall short of justifying moral retributivism as I have defined it. What must be shown, in other words, is that the moral responsibility borne by people for their wrongful actions is itself a *prima facie* good reason for justly punishing them, where the qualification "justly" merely indicates the need for constraints on punishment, such as proportionality and not punishing the innocent. This is the task of the next section.

A Moral Retributivist Justification of Punishment

According to Hume, and as argued more recently by Morris, imposing punishment on offenders is justified because criminal acts alter the moral status of wrongdoers in that such acts affect their moral rights that stand in the way of their being punished and lead to their forfeiture.[13] Even if this line of argument is correct on a more general level, the task of giving a satisfactory justification of *retributive* punishment in particular requires further argumentation. This can be an intricate, if not daunting, task. In spite of there being a plethora of justifications and rationales, retributivism seems to remain a largely unpopular and unconvincing theoretical position. Yet, it is likely to remain an issue on both practical and theoretical levels. For, as J.L. Mackie points out, while many people are inclined to say that

> only some possible future benefit, such as deterrence or reformation, can justify punishment, . . . when we consider actual or possible cases of crimes or wrongdoing of kinds that we really regard as unmitigated and inexcusable, then we do after all tend to see them as in themselves calling for the infliction of some adequate penalty.[14]

Mackie goes further than this, however, and claims that what we have on our hands is nothing short of a paradox, the paradox of retribution.

> The paradox is that, on the one hand, a retributive principle of punishment cannot be explained or developed within a reasonable system of moral thought,

while, on the other hand, such a principle cannot be eliminated from our moral thinking.[15]

Mackie identifies the crucial, problematic retributive principle as the view that *one who is guilty ought to be punished,* but it is clear from the context that he would regard as equally problematic the permissive variant that *one who is guilty may be punished independently of the good consequences such punishment may effect.* Mackie then mentions the major attempts to make sense of that principle as a principle with immediate, underived moral authority. Some of these he dismisses because of their respective shortcomings, while others he simply dismisses out of hand. He unjustifiably dismisses, for example, the possibility that the principle in question may be justified with reference to the idea of negative desert,[16] concluding that the principle in question cannot be explained or developed within a reasonable system of moral thought.

Having deemed moral justification of retribution an impossibility, Mackie proceeds to give a sociobiological explanation of it in a broad, emotivist framework of the nature of morality and moral judgments. According to this, ultimately, our moral thinking itself has both its origins and its substance in our retributive (both kindly and hostile) emotions. The explanation is in two broad stages. First, he gives a purely biological explanation for the tendency to feel non-moral resentment of injuries and gratitude for benefits. Second, he gives a sociological explanation for the development of moral resentment from its non-moral counterpart.[17] Mackie's claim is that unless we accept an emotivist framework in which the retributive *emotions* form the basis of our moral beliefs and reasoning, we cannot solve or explain the paradox of retribution.

However, such a scientifically minded, sociobiological explanation of retribution leaves retribution in almost as much need of moral justification as before. As Mill points out, "that a feeling is bestowed on us by nature, does not necessarily legitimate all its promptings."[18] Moreover, even if there is merit in such an emotivist sociobiological explanation, Mackie has failed to show that the retributive principle can only be explained, but not properly justified.[19] Apart from the fact that the list of possible justifications covered by Mackie is far from being exhaustive, many of the attempts covered by him are given very short shrift, while others simply aren't taken seriously. Given this state of affairs, he is not entitled to conclude that the principle in question cannot be explained or developed within a reasonable system of moral thought. Not having established this crucial thesis also raises the question as to whether there really is a paradox of retribution in the sense suggested by him. Finally, even though Mackie is right in saying that a retributive principle of punishment is ineliminable from our moral thinking, absence of a paradox would render his emotivist, socio-biological explanation redundant.

I, for one, do not think that there is a problem here, let alone a paradox. Contra Mackie, a retributive principle of punishment can be explained and developed within a reasonable system of moral thought. I suggested in Chapter 5 that while the notion of negative desert is somewhat problematic in a *definitional* role because its range does not extend beyond the limits set on punishment by the principles of justice, its proper role is a *justifying* one for the very same reason. But, as with all other accounts of retributivism, skepticism surrounds this idea. According to Cottingham, for example,

> viewed as an exercise in justification, this account shares the curiously jejune quality of theory (1) [the repayment theory]; and its detractors have made the complaint—not without force—that it reduces to the bald assertion that it is simply just that the offender should be punished.[20]

Mackie also dismisses the idea in barely more than one line in a footnote by saying that

> Desert Theory seems to be the bald, unexplained assertion that crime simply does deserve punishment.[21]

> This need not be the case, however. According to Honderich, for example, there are at least nine different ways of interpreting desert claims.[22] Also, Nozick has provided a detailed framework for retribution in an explicit attempt to answer the question: 'In what sense is punishment deserved?' Nozick formulates the moral retributivist thesis as the view that "people deserve punishment for their wrongful acts in accordance with r x H [the person's degree of responsibility weighted by the magnitude of the wrongness of the act], independently of the deterrent effect of such punishment."[23] Far from denying the need for a justification or rationale, Nozick then goes on to give an interesting and fairly complex rationale for the view by reference to the idea of connecting the wrongdoer with correct values:

> The wrongdoer has become disconnected from correct values, and the purpose of punishment is to (re)connect him. It is not that this connection is a desired further effect of punishment: the act of retributive punishment itself effects this connection. . . . When he undergoes punishment these correct values are not totally without effect in his life (even though he does not follow them), because we hit him over the head with them. Through punishment, we give the correct values, qua correct values, some significant effect in his life, willy-nilly linking him up to them.[24]

Whether this is a plausible way of explicating desert claims is a question that need not be decided here and it is not my intention to defend Nozick's rationale against criticisms.[25] I mention it to make the point that desert claims do not always come as bald, unexplained assertions in the way alleged by Cottingham and Mackie. What I propose now is to give a *moral explanation* of retribution, a kind of transcendental argument, along lines suggested by Oldenquist. This explanation appeals to notions of individual flourishing, life within a moral community and personal accountability, and the link that exists between them. I propose this explanation to be an explication of such shorthand, retributive justificatory claims as *'Retributive punishment is properly due as repayment for wrongs,' 'Retributive punishment is justified because it is deserved,'* and *'It is only fair, just and right that an offender should be punished.'* Such claims are often intended to justify a retributive approach to punishment. As they stand, however, they seem too lean to be satisfactory. They require further clarification and explanation. The following is an explication of such claims.[26]

1. Humans are innately social beings who can flourish and achieve their full humanity and potential in terms of moral and spiritual maturity, only in society.

2. A human society is a moral community.

3. A moral community is such that its members are mature, morally responsible individuals who hold one another accountable for wrongs to fellow members and to the common good.

4. To hold persons responsible and accountable for wrongs to fellow members and to the common good is to consider them liable for blame and punishment for such wrongs, independently of functionalist and instrumental considerations, such as expressing disapproval or deterrence—though obviously such considerations are not irrelevant to impositions of punishment.

5. To consider persons liable for blame and punishment for wrongs independently of functionalist and instrumental considerations is morally to accept retribution.

Using this explanation as part of an argument, there are two conclusions which follow:

6. Human individuals can flourish and achieve their full humanity, including moral maturity, only if they morally accept retribution and retributive liability for their wrongful actions.

7. Since individual flourishing and the achievement of one's full humanity, including moral maturity, are good things worthy of being pursued, retributive punishment within the limits set by the principles of justice is also a morally good thing which may be pursued and, unless contra-indicated by countervailing instrumental and functionalist considerations, or by the appropriateness of mercy and forgiveness, ought to be pursued.

This account does not fall into the trap of consequentialism. The central claim here is not a consequentialist one, that a good consequence of retributive punishment is individual human flourishing. Rather, it is the claim that life within a moral community with its attendant responsibilities and a liability for retribution within limits set by the principles of justice are ineliminable aspects of human flourishing and the achievement of full humanity, a very important part of which is moral maturity. The account is not jejune either. It is not a kind of "unexplained assertion" of which Mackie and Cottingham complained above. Nevertheless, the crucial analysis of personal accountability in premise four would benefit from the following explanation.[27] I start by quoting Kleinig and Bradley.

> The principle that the wrongdoer deserves to suffer seems to accord with our deepest intuitions concerning justice. While this may seem to conflict with another of our moral intuitions, viz. that it is bad to cause others to suffer, it does so only if an extreme form of the latter is adopted—the principle that it is always bad to cause another to suffer. The latter, however, is also implausible.[28]

> What is really true for the moral consciousness; what it clings to, and will not let go; what marks unmistakably, by its absence, a 'philosophical' or a 'debauched' morality, is the necessary connexion between responsibility and liability to punishment, between punishment and desert, or the finding of guiltiness before the law of the moral tribunal. For practical purposes we need make no distinction between responsibility, or accountability, and liability to punishment. Where you have the one, there (in the mind of the vulgar [ordinary people]) you have the other; and where you have not the one, there you can not have the other. And, we may add, the theory which will explain the one, in its ordinary sense, will also explain the other; and the theory which fails in the one, fails also in the other; and the doctrine which conflicts with popular belief as to one, does so also with regard to the other.[29]

Kleinig and Bradley are right, although the relationship between moral responsibility and liability to punishment is more complex than these quotations suggest. In the case of morally mature people (as distinct from, say, children and those who are mentally impaired), personal accountability is one aspect of the moral responsibility they bear for their actions. It is the retrospective part of it. For, when someone is considered morally responsible for something, there are two aspects to that responsibility. One is a prospective, forward-looking aspect which places that person under some kind of moral obligation or duty to act or not act in certain ways. But tied to such duties and obligations is a retrospective accountability which renders the person liable for moral censure in the form of condemnation, blame, and possibly punishment, if as a result of the person's fault the duty or obligation is not fulfilled.

For example, owning and using such items as guns and motor cars place people under moral, as well as legal, obligations to take all reasonable precautions to avoid injuring other people. Maintaining one's car in a roadworthy condition and not driving under the influence of alcohol are specific instances of such obligations. But such duties and obligations constitute only half of the story of what it is to be morally responsible as a car driver. The other half of the story is told, and it has to be told, in the event one fails to fulfill one's duties and someone gets hurt as a consequence. For instance, if George knowingly keeps driving his car with faulty brakes, or if he decides to drive under the influence of alcohol, and kills somebody as a consequence, it will not suffice as a response simply to shrug our shoulders and say something glib like *It is just too bad for that person that George did not take seriously his (forward-looking) responsibilities as a driver.* There is no getting away from the fact that George ought to have known better, and that his moral responsibility as a car driver exposes him to legitimate, *retrospective* moral censure, condemnation, blame and possibly punishment for his moral failure in forward-looking terms.[30] The appropriateness of such retrospective censure need not depend at all on potential benefits it may, or may not, have for George and others. Such moral censure is fully warranted by the fact that George bears responsibility for his actions. There is no further explanation required whatsoever.

Similarly, if George decides in a moment of frustration to shoot at passing motorists in his street, it will not suffice as a response to say something even more glib than before, like *Too bad for the motorists that they happened to be driving past just when George lost his temper.* George's moral responsibility as a member of the community exposes him to legitimate, *retrospective* moral censure, condemnation, blame, and punishment for his wrongful behaviour—and to an even greater degree if it resulted in injury or death to others.[31] What gives legitimacy to these responses is the responsibility George, as a whole-minded, mature individual, bears morally (and legally) for his actions, and quite independently of instrumental and functionalist considerations.[32] The possibility that, in addition, these responses might also have some instrumental value is neither here nor there. The expected benefits of some proposed punishment should, by all means, be taken into account. But, as the above examples illustrate, it would be mistaken to think that instrumental considerations were the only ones to have relevance. Moral censure, blame, and punishment can be mandated by the person's retrospective accountability for things done wrong and for which, as a mature member of a moral community, he or she bears a degree of responsibility.[33] As de Grazia argued the point against excessive forms of rehabilitationism,

> The social aspects of punishment have, for the most part, been ignored by their critics; their medical orientation serves to preoccupy them with the criminal *qua*

patient. They forget that he is first a social unit and that although he may ultimately be handed over to the doctor, demands of society ought first to be met. He does not have cancer or flu or dyspepsia; he has committed a crime, has injured someone, has damaged society according to its own definition. Because of this and irrespective of any moral taint, the criminal is obligated and must answer to society.[34]

This line of argument is not new. Many philosophers of distinction have argued that retributive accountability must be taken as the basis of punishment, if the dignity and inherent value in a human being is to be honored and treated with due respect. Thus, Kant argues against consequentialist justifications of punishment because such punishment treats the offender as a mere means to an end.

> Juridical Punishment can [should] never be administered merely as a means for promoting another Good either with regard to the Criminal himself or to Civil Society, but must in all cases be imposed only because the individual on whom it is inflicted *has committed a Crime.* For one man ought never to be dealt with merely as a means subservient to the purpose of another, nor be mixed up with the subjects of Real Right. Against such treatment his Inborn Personality has a Right to protect him, even although he may be condemned to lose his Civil Personality. He must first be found guilty and *punishable,* before there can be any thought of drawing from his Punishment any benefit for himself or his fellow-citizens.[35]

Similarly, Hegel argues that

> right and justice must hold their seats in freedom and volition, and not in unfreedom which is addressed by threat. In this [latter] way punishment is established as if we raised a stick at a dog, and man will not be treated according to his honor and freedom but like a dog.[36]

Also, although C.S. Lewis is critical of revenge—perhaps because he fails to see that revenge is a form of retribution—he argues strongly in defense of a retributive liability for punishment and against the deterrent and rehabilitative reasons proffered by theories of instrumental punishment for which, somewhat unfortunately, he uses the 'humanitarian' label.[37] Like Hegel, Lewis argues that punishing someone for the sake of good consequences, rather than for retributive reasons based on retrospective responsibility for their wrongful action, denies the inherently moral character of those actions. It denies the offender's status as a dignified, fully responsible human being.

> Their very kindness stings with intolerable insult. To be 'cured' against one's will and cured of states which we may not regard as disease is to be put on a

level with those who have not yet reached the age of reason or those who never will; to be classed with infants, imbeciles, and domestic animals. But to be punished, however severely, because we have deserved it, because we 'ought to have known better,' is to be treated as a human person made in God's image.[38]

Though they argue in their own respective ways, Kant, Hegel, and Lewis clearly converge on the central claim of the earlier outlined argument for retribution. This is the claim that retributive responsibility for one's actions is an ineliminable part of one's full humanity. A refusal to hold someone retributively responsible for his or her wrongful actions is tantamount to refusing to grant him or her the status of being a mature, fully developed human individual. From this perspective it is understandable why Lewis finds the instrumentalist's "humanitarian" kindness in matters of punishment so repulsive. Their kindness "stings with intolerable insult" because it is a kindness based on a paternalistic disrespect for the offender. By regarding the offender as someone in need of rehabilitation, or as someone who can be used as an instrument for purposes of deterrence, or both of these, the instrumentalist fails to respect and fails to take the offender seriously as a fully developed, mature, morally responsible person. While there may be cases where such an attitude may be warranted, it is indeed intolerably disrespectful to whole-minded, fully responsible adult individuals.

On that note, mention must also be made of Nietzsche's characteristically provocative position on resentment. The Nietzschean ideal and formula for overcoming resentment in the face of injustice is to become "*too pure* for the filth of the words: vengeance, punishment, recompense, retribution."[39] Without wishing to argue the point in detail here, it seems to me that the state of 'purity' recommended by Nietzsche is but a contemptuous, aristocratic arrogance which escapes resentfulness only to indulge in a worse emotion and attitude, an attitude which refuses to take other people seriously, viewing them instead like vermin that are unworthy of one's attention and resentment.

Mercy and the Liability for Punishment

None of the foregoing arguments for moral retributivism is incompatible with the importance of forgiveness and mercy. A recognition that offenders bear a retributive liability for their wrongful acts does not in any way entail that, therefore, come what may, they *must* be punished. Retribution is only one among a range of legitimate responses to wrongdoing and the retributive liability borne by offenders does not undermine the moral right, the power, or the prerogative, of victims to forgive and show mercy to them. This seems right, but some philosophers have tried to argue for a stronger position. Lewis, for example, holds the view that, far from being incompatible with mercy, a retributive liability for punishment is a *precondition* for it.

> The essential act of Mercy was to pardon; and pardon in its very essence involves the recognition of guilt and ill-desert in the recipient. If crime is only a disease which needs cure, not sin which deserves punishment, it cannot be pardoned. How can you pardon a man for having a gum-boil or a club foot?[40]

Similarly, Armstrong argues that

> The retributive theory is not . . . incompatible with mercy. Quite the reverse is the case—it is only the retributive idea that makes mercy possible, because to be merciful is to let someone off all or part of a penalty which he is recognized as having deserved.[41]

However, the view taken by Lewis and Armstrong may be too strong. They seem to assume that all just punishment must be retributive in nature. As I argued earlier, retributivism is not the only viable theory of just punishment. When punishment is imposed with defensible instrumental reasons, such as deterrence, rehabilitation, and correction of the offender, for instance, that punishment is still just if it does not violate the principles of justice, such as proportionality and punishing the right person. If so, there is no good reason to suppose that such non-desert based, non-retributive liability for punishment cannot replace retributive liability as a precondition of mercy. Therefore, it seems more reasonable and defensible to hold the weaker position that, while a wrongdoer's retributive liability for punishment is not a precondition of mercy, it is perfectly compatible with mercy. As Garcia put it,

> since desert renders punishment *prima facie* permissible but not *prima facie* obligatory, it poses no real danger to the normal acceptability (indeed, the praiseworthiness) of mercifully foregoing punishment.[42]

Nevertheless, it might be tempting to think that, since mercy and forgiveness are praiseworthy and, arguably, in some sense superior values to retribution, the best moral choice is always to place forgiveness and mercy ahead of punishment and retribution. This, however, does not follow. For, even though it is plausible to suppose that reaching a state of forgiveness (in terms of how one feels about the wrongdoer) is in many respects more desirable than being in a state of anger, indignation, or resentment, it does not follow that, therefore, the morally best course of action is always to let wrongdoers off all penalties and sanctions by exercising mercy. Mercy, it seems, can be rendered appropriate by considerations such as remorse, and inappropriate by a lack of it, as well as by misguided defiance, for instance.

The intrinsic and instrumental virtues of mercy have to be weighed against other considerations which have equally legitimate and important bearing on how a particular case should be resolved. Thus, it is reasonable to suppose that the value of retributive justice and the need for deterrence will outweigh the value of mercy in many cases. At a practical level, the moral and practical appropriateness of mercy does seem to depend very much on the circumstances of each individual case. It would be most inappropriate, it seems to me, if not repugnant, to go about unconditionally forgiving anything and everything, everywhere, at all times. Instrumental considerations alone seem to require that there must be some form of appropriate punishment for such crimes as, say, robbery, assault, child abuse, rape, and murder. To do otherwise is to breed moral monsters devoid of empathy and respect for the rights and needs of others, people who are unmoved by the suffering they cause around them—moral monsters who simply do not and, perhaps, cannot care. Confucius answered well, I believe, when he was asked:

'What do you say concerning the principle that injury should be recompensed with kindness?' The Master said, 'With what then will you recompense kindness? Recompense injury with justice, and recompense kindness with kindness.'[43]

Lewis echoes a similar sentiment concerning how we should think on a general level of the tension between the competing values of justice and mercy, and the way in which this tends to be handled in an anti-retributivist climate of punishment justification.

I think it essential to oppose the Humanitarian theory of Punishment, root and branch, wherever we encounter it. It carries on its front a semblance of Mercy which is wholly false. . . . [It] wants simply to abolish Justice and substitute Mercy for it. This means that you start being 'kind' to people before you have considered their rights, and then force upon them supposed kindnesses which they in fact had a right to refuse, and finally kindnesses which no one but you will recognize as kindnesses and which the recipient will feel as abominable cruelties. You have overshot the mark. Mercy, detached from Justice, grows unmerciful. That is the important paradox. As there are plants which will flourish only in mountain soil, so it appears that Mercy will flower only when it grows in the crannies of the rock of Justice: transplanted to the marshlands of mere Humanitarianism, it becomes a man-eating weed, all the more dangerous because it is still called by the same name as the mountain variety. But we ought long ago to have learned our lesson. We should be too old now to be deceived by those humane pretensions which have served to usher in every cruelty of the revolutionary period in which we live. These are the "precious balms" which will "break our heads."[44]

Some communities, of course, can be more forgiving than others. The reality is that there can be marked variations between the moral conventions

of various people, conventions which are embodied in their respective ide-
ologies and ways of life. It may even be the case that the degree of mercy
shown to wrongdoers is indicative of a community's moral evolution
towards humaneness and spiritual enlightenment. The question, however, is
whether our current human condition can realistically allow us as a community to embrace, for example, a philosophy of unconditional and universal
non-violence, or a Christ-like pacifism that enjoins us to love our enemies
and turn the other cheek? I wish it did, but I doubt it. While turning the
other cheek is, and must remain, an individual moral choice, it would be
often foolish and dangerous, and a moral community can rightly reserve the
right to overrule any such individual choice by victims of wrongdoing when
such forgiving personal decisions would undermine the public interest. I
will return to this theme again in the remaining chapters in the context of
considering the appropriate limits of victim empowerment.

I argued in the preceding chapter that revenge is personal retribution,
and that, to the degree that institutionalized personal punishment is done
with retributive reasons, it qualifies, and can properly be referred to, as
institutionalized revenge. In the present chapter I went on to clarify and
defend the notion of moral retributivism. Retribution within limits set by
the principles of justice is a legitimate, morally justifiable reason for punishment. A liability for retribution within limits set by the principles of justice
as a direct result of one's wrongdoing is part of what it means for an individual to be a fully responsible member of a moral community. In turn,
without being a fully responsible member of a moral community, individual
flourishing and the achievement of one's full potential as a human being are
impossible. It follows that such retributive liability for one's wrongful
behaviour is a necessary ingredient both for realizing one's individual
potential as a mature human being and for taking one's rightful and obligatory place in society as a fully responsible member of the moral community—a conclusion that accords well with the views of many philosophers of
distinction on the topic. Such retributive liability for wrongful behaviour is
also compatible with ideas of forgiveness and mercy. But, while forgiveness
and mercy are admirable and important moral ideals and values, a blanket
substitution of mercy for punishment, irrespective of the circumstances,
would be foolish and unacceptable.

If all this is correct, if wrongdoers do indeed bear a retributive liability
for punishment in proportion to the moral seriousness of their wrongdoing,
then what remains to be shown for a justification of institutionalized
revenge is that there are good reasons for putting the personal element back
into punishment.

9

Victim Justice and Institutionalized Empowerment

Justice is too important to be left to the judiciary.

Sir Ludovic Kennedy[1]

Revenge being personal retribution, in addition to justifying retributive motives and desert-based rationales for imposing punishment on an offender, a defense of institutionalized revenge requires good reasons for putting the personal element back into punishment by granting victims the legal right to have a substantial say in the handling and resolution of their cases. Of critical concern are matters of bail, prosecution, plea bargaining, sentencing, and parole. I show in this chapter that such empowerment is required for healing the effects of crime, and that without it justice to victims is incomplete. I discuss two main approaches for substantial victim involvement and empowerment. One is based on the concept of alternative dispute resolution (ADR), the other involves making substantial changes to the existing judicial system so that the decision making powers of judges and magistrates is shared with victims. These views and proposals are supported by social psychological research concerning the nature and dynamics of interpersonal relationships.

The Status of Victims in the Criminal Justice System

Abel and Marsh rightly point out the lack of status currently accorded to victims.

> Our present criminal justice system has, in effect, no law relevant to victims; it
> leaves them as they are, ignoring their plight in its zeal to punish, deter, and
> rehabilitate.[2]

Apart from the minor technicality that over the past decade many states
and countries have introduced low level victim-specific laws, that claim by
Abel and Marsh remains a fair description of the lack of status accorded to victims by contemporary criminal justice systems. To appreciate this point, it is
worth considering a 1995 newspaper report on the intended law reforms in
New South Wales (Australia) to establish a statutory charter of victims' rights.
According to the report, the new legislation was expected to give victims of
crime "the legal right to influence a court's sentencing of people convicted of
crime" and also "a say in parole and temporary leave for serious offenders."[3]
While such news reports sound impressive, actual legislation affords little
more to victims than a right to be *informed* about the various decisions made
by *others* (usually legal professionals and other bureaucrats). The so-called
"legal right to influence a court's sentencing" and the right to have "a say in
parole and temporary leave for serious offenders" simply means that a victim
may make written submissions expressing their views—submissions which
may, and may not, be taken seriously by the relevant decision makers in their
deliberations. Typically they are not required to justify their decisions by reference to the contents of such submissions.[4]

Such gestures towards victims of crime fall very much short of what is
required—a claim taken up in more detail below in connection with Victim
Impact Statements. The point emphasized here is that, notwithstanding
such low-level victim specific legislation, victims of crime continue to be
disempowered and marginalized in just the way described by Abel and
Marsh. In their turn, these authors argue for making restitution to victims
the primary focus of criminal law. But, while their proposal is a positive step
forward from a victim justice point of view, it still does not go far enough.
This is because being heard, respected, and recognized as an important par-
ticipant in the justice system matters to victims just as much as does the
receiving of adequate compensation.[5] This, in turn, can only be achieved by
making legal institutionalized punishment more personal by way of greater
victim participation in the process.

Such victim participation and empowerment, in turn, open up the possibility of revenge. This is true at least from the point of view of a victim
whose involvement in the process is motivated by a desire to get even with
the offender by giving them their just deserts. As I have argued in earlier
chapters, there is nothing intrinsically wrong with this, and the practical
challenges this may present will be discussed in the next chapter. Victim
participation, of course, need not be retributive, for victim reasoning in
terms of getting even, pay-back and desert may not be present in many

cases. But that is an entirely individual, and largely personal, matter for the victim. It is their prerogative to make sense of the situation and of their experience in terms of whatever ideas, concepts and attitudes make good sense to them. Telling aggrieved victims that they are wrong in wanting the retributive just punishment of their wrongdoers is deeply offensive. It literally adds insult to their injury. It is equally unhelpful, of course, when forgiving victims are told, often by close family and friends, that they are wrong in showing forgiveness towards their wrongdoers. Such matters are, or should be, the prerogative of the victim to decide. This point will be argued for and emphasized throughout this chapter. What needs to be recognized here is that greater victim involvement in the process is supported regardless of whether retributive considerations, or indeed forgiveness and mercy, happen to be present in a particular victim's reasoning or not. This, in a nutshell, is the main point of this section.

Certain basic human rights are specific to punishment contexts. Especially in criminal justice contexts, some such rights are specific to people accused of wrongdoing, examples being their right to a fair trial and, in the event of being found guilty, the right not to be punished out of proportion to the moral gravity of the offense. But victims also have comparable rights. It is at least arguable that victims have a fundamental, inalienable right to participate actively, and have a say, in the resolution of offenses committed against them. After all, the incident is *their* business first and foremost, and it is the rest of society's only after that. In a great number of cases of criminal wrongdoing the real or primary injury is to the victim and society is harmed, if at all, only secondarily and derivatively.[6] As some victims put it,

> Why didn't anyone consult me? I was the one who was kidnapped, not the state of Virginia.[7]
>
> [T]o hell with people saying society is the victim: it was *me*, not society, that got hurt.[8]

It would be misguided and futile to take issue with such claims. Their point is simple, yet compelling. Offenses are offenses against specific people, the victims, unless no identifiable person(s) got hurt. This idea is not new. As David Friedman has observed,

> The idea that law is primarily private, that most offenses are offenses against specific individuals or families, and that punishment of the crime is primarily the business of the injured party seems to be common to many early systems of law . . .[9]

Greater victim participation is further supported by instrumental considerations of victims' rights to restitution, compensation, and restoration in material, social and psychological terms. Broadly construed, their right is to be restored as much as possible to their original, pre-victim position economically, physically, psychologically, and socially. Such victim rights are clearly spelled out in the *United Nations Resolution on Victims of Crime and Abuse of Power*.[10] Victims have the moral right to get all the help and opportunities they need to rebuild their shattered lives as quickly as possible. To deny them this right is to deny them justice—justice which can be regarded as the other side of the coin of criminal justice: *criminal victim justice*. This is a concept which needs to be explored in detail.

Criminal injuries compensation schemes are an important step towards restitution and compensation to victims for harms and losses they sustained. However, while such schemes are necessary and welcome, they are not normally part of the judicial process which deals with the offense in question. Thankfully, there are exceptions to this, such as the one in Hanover where the Association for Conflict Mediation and Redress

> manages a fund for victims, from which offenders without means may receive an interest-free loan in order to pay compensation to the injured party. The offenders then either pay the money back through instalments or perform community service at a fixed hourly rate.[11]

There is a lot to be said for such schemes. Unfortunately, in many countries compensation is normally considered and granted by the state in complete isolation from, and well after, judicial proceedings have been finalised and the case is closed. These schemes, therefore, do not affect in any way the lack of status accorded to victims of crime in the judicial process. But, as pointed out earlier, research findings consistently show that victims' needs to be heard, respected, appreciated, and recognized as important and necessary participants in the judicial system are not less important to them than is the punishment of their offenders or the receiving of adequate compensation for losses and traumas endured. Consequently, victim dissatisfaction with judicial processes that do not accord them a role commensurate to their status as the persons who in fact have been wronged and whose lives have been the most affected by the crime, is understandable and invites consideration.

It is not difficult to see why, and how, victim dissatisfaction with the judicial processing and substantive resolution of their cases can be an obstacle to recovering their damaged sense of security, self-esteem, and peace of mind—all of which are necessary for them to be able to return to the quiet enjoyment of their lives. Satisfaction in the above terms is essential to engendering in victims a feeling that they can now put behind them whatever happened and get on with their lives, looking once again to the future, rather than being continuously preoccupied with the hurtful past because of a feeling that, in all fairness, justice still hasn't been done. In the absence of a feeling that their cases have been dealt with in a satisfactory manner, their recovery is likely to be protracted, if not impossible to achieve. Yet a crucial element of victim justice is victim restoration in the form of emotional and psychological recovery following an offense. In turn, victim restoration must start with resolving the conflict with as much satisfaction to the victim as possible.

In this regard it is crucial that the legitimacy of the victims' feelings of resentment and, where appropriate, their need for retributive justice receive proper acknowledgment and due consideration, rather than dismissal and trivialization. This is especially important, I suggest, in serious crime, such as assault, rape, and murder.[12] Otherwise victims are likely to feel victimized twice over: first by the original offender, and then by the legal system. It is the common experience of raped women, for example, that they are the ones on trial in the courtroom. As Holmstrom and Burgess concluded in their study, *Rape: The Victim Goes on Trial,*

> The rape victim is treated in the courtroom as if she had committed a crime. Technically, only the defendant is on trial. But socially and psychologically the victim is on the firing line too. It is her reputation against his. The defense lawyer's strategy is to blame the victim. . . . This strategy is devastatingly effective, as the attrition rate in the present sample shows. Sixty-one rape victims were admitted to the hospital. Twenty cases went through lower court, and seven through superior court. There was one conviction for rape: The man pleaded guilty.[13]

But even more generally, and this includes cases where convictions are in fact obtained, victim accounts of their experiences with the judicial system clearly indicate that unsatisfactory processes and resolutions generate severe feelings of injustice and, instead of soothing, tend to aggravate their feelings of disillusionment, anger, bitterness, and resentment.

> Where is the justice in the law that allows none of us to speak of the unimaginable horror of a father finding his dead daughter . . . ? At times it felt as though we were being punished twice, once by having our daughter murdered, and then having to go through the ordeal again in court. . . . I feel very angry and bitter about this and I would wish that the legal processes could be changed so that the families who are hurting so much could feel as though justice was indeed being done. To us, the victims, it appears as though the law does everything to protect the criminal and forgets about his victims.[14]

Contrast this with the satisfaction of a murdered young man's mother who was at least allowed to confront the offender with the consequences of his actions in court.

> For the first time in Queensland legal history, a sobbing mother was yesterday allowed to confront her son's murderer in court and tell of the tragedy caused

by the killing. . . . Mrs. Ward spoke for about 10 minutes from a typed statement, which had been approved by Justice Paul de Jersey who said he thought
the courtroom was "not inappropriate for those convicted of murder and the
public to be reminded of the consequences of these terrible crimes". . . .
Outside the court, Mrs. Ward said she wanted to congratulate Justice de Jersey
on taking Queensland a great step forward by allowing her to address her son's
killer.[15]

Such accounts indicate that giving victims the opportunity to take a
greater role in the resolution of their cases has strong potential to help them
feel that justice has been done, thus aiding their recovery and restoration.
In addition, giving them a substantial say in the handling and resolution of
their cases would be a further act of empowering them, as it would place
them in a position of strength where they once again could feel in control
of their lives and their situation, which has been wrongfully and grievously
disrupted by the wrongdoer. A very important aspect of this empowerment
would be that they would be able to establish a relationship of equality *vis-
à-vis* their wrongdoers, which would spare them from the role of being
helpless victims. As I argue further below, these measures would help them
regain their shaken confidence and, possibly, their damaged sense of self-
worth. As Braithwaite put it in the context of a need to empower similarly
disempowered offenders, "coherent strategies of empowerment can succeed
even with the most powerless."[16] If this is right, then denying victims the
opportunity to take an active and substantial role in the resolution of their
cases is inimical to according them justice.

A brief look at the nature and psychology of interpersonal relationships
and exchanges in general should help us to appreciate the importance of
substantial victim involvement and empowerment in the interests of victim
restoration. Although communal relationships, such as, for example, relationships between partners and between parents and their children, do not
depend so heavily on reciprocity,[17] the idea that equality, reciprocity, and
fairness ought to characterize human interactions is deeply ingrained in the
human psyche. Research in social psychology shows that equality and reciprocity are among the healthiest and most desirable features which can, and
ought to, characterize relationships and interpersonal exchanges. It is a
widely held belief among exchange theorists that relationships are in general
more satisfying and stable when reciprocity is perceived, and when the
rewards for each partner are perceived to be more or less equal.[18] For example, in relationships between colleagues at work "concerns of reciprocity are
of paramount importance."[19] In many different kinds of relationships, being
over-benefited, as well as being under-benefited have been found to create
negative feelings, distress, loneliness and a reduced sense of well-being. This
is as much true of able-bodied individuals as it is of people with disabilities
who have also been found trying to maintain reciprocal supportive relation-

ships.[20] The evidence suggests that, generally, giving more support than one receives leads to feelings of unfairness and resentment, whereas receiving more support than one gives results in feelings of guilt and shame,[21] as well as to feelings of obligation and owing, uncertainty, and fear of not being able to repay the debt.[22]

These findings allow an understanding of the social psychological realities created by crime. Offenses occur in social contexts and, therefore, in cases where victim and offender are clearly identifiable, the offense is a kind of interpersonal exchange, a social (or rather anti-social) exchange which creates a state of severe imbalance between offender and victim whereby the victim suffers undue and unjustifiable harms and losses in material and psychological well-being, a loss of trust and damaged sense of security. Unjust and unrectified interpersonal exchanges can also lead to a reduced sense of self-worth. Two notions are relevant here. One is respect from others, the other is self-worth, or self-esteem. To be treated with respect by others entails at the very least that one is treated justly by them. In turn, respectful, just treatment can consist in nothing less than equitable, reciprocal and fair treatment. Behavior which contravenes one or more of these values is disrespectful and can easily arouse feelings of indignation, resentment, anger and, not uncommonly, an urge to retaliate in order to even the scores with the wrongdoer. As Kim and Smith observe,

> Most people believe that they deserve respectful treatment from others. Cultural norms dictate that, fundamentally, everyone should be of equal worth as a human being. Thus, if the unjust act of a harmdoer serves to violate these beliefs, the threat and assault to the self can be severe. A large part of the message carried by the unjust act is that the victim is inferior and undeserving of respect. . . . Particularly when the wrongdoer's harm diminishes our self-worth, we are all the more angered and all the more compelled to avenge injustice, even at high personal cost.[23]

Still, it might be asked: Why should our sense of self-worth be sensitive to the opinions and attitudes of those around us, and given that it is, why don't we react to injustice and disrespectful treatment with acquiescence or unconditional and instant forgiveness, instead of anger, indignation, and resentment? Once again, social-psychological research suggests certain answers to these questions. Disrespectful, unjust treatment upsets the ideal state of equality and fairness between individuals (and groups) and the balance is tipped in favor of the offending party. A recognisable function of the retributive emotions, such as indignation, anger, and resentment, is to promote a rapid re-establishment of that balance which is especially important, as well as urgent, from the victimized persons' point of view. For, unless that balance is re-established soon, there is an increased probability that the victim of the original offense will be further victimized by the offender.

Laboratory experiments indicate that if the harm-doer doesn't compensate his victim, either because proper channels are not open or because he chooses to withhold compensation, he will then distort his perceptions in such a way as to justify his actions. Usually one justifies the harm he has done by derogating his victim, but one may also justify his behavior in other ways. He may minimize the harm he has done or he may deny responsibility for the harm. It appears that the harm-doer will attempt to eliminate, at least in his own mind, the inequity that he has created, either by compensating his victim or by justifying his act.

Removal of inequity through justification rather than compensation is potentially dangerous. Not only does the harm-doer end up with a distorted and unreal assessment of his actions, but he may commit further acts based on these distortions. When the harm-doer's response to his act is justification, the victim is likely to be left in sad straits. Not only has he been hurt, but as a result of justification of the harmful act the probability that the harm-doer will hurt him again has increased. Obviously, from the victim's point of view, it is desirable to have equity restored before the perpetrator is forced to justify what he has done.[24]

These findings explain why in the face of injustice we react with anger, indignation, and resentment. We are more likely to do something about restoring equity following unfair treatment as a result of having retributive feelings than we would be if we had no such feelings. Additional findings also explain why it is so tempting for victims to retaliate, sometimes at high risk and costs to themselves. If offenders are unable or unwilling to put right their wrongs, reciprocating through retaliation appears to be the next best option which may be open to victims, if equity is to be restored to the now inequitable relationship. The benefits of retaliation are not merely that the victim's sense of self-worth is restored, however. Retaliation also has the highly desirable effect of engendering respect for the victim in the offender. This is illustrated and supported by both anecdotal and experimental evidence from social psychology.[25] Research findings clearly show that in cases where other ways of redressing the offense are impossible, "a harm-doer will derogate a victim who is powerless to retaliate but will not derogate a victim from whom he anticipates retaliation."[26] Such findings confirm that retaliation can be an effective way to restore equity following an offense. To be derogated by one's wrongdoer following an offense is, literally, to be insulted on top of the injury, and is inimical in every way to victim interests and the principles of victim justice. Therefore, victims' desire for retaliation even in the face of further personal cost is entirely understandable and rational. Also, the victim-focused perspective afforded by the above findings provides an interesting context for interpreting and making sense of Solomon's following remarks on vengeance, retribution and punishment:

Vengeance is the emotion of 'getting even', putting the world back in balance, and this simple phrase already embodies a whole philosophy of justice, even if (as yet) unarticulated and unjustified. . . . 'Getting even' is and has always been one of the most basic metaphors of our moral vocabulary, and the frightening emotion of righteous, wrathful anger is an essential part of the emotional basis for our sense of justice . . . Our resentment of injustice is a necessary precondition of our passion for justice, and the urge to retribution its essential consequence. . . . The impulse to punish is primarily an impulse to even the score. [27]

Especially where serious crime is concerned, victims usually have a deep moral-psychological need to know that justice is done, in the sense that criminals are made to pay for what they have done, that they don't get away with it, but get their just deserts. If such deep-seated needs are not satisfied in victims, punishments imposed on their wrongdoers, no matter how harsh, are unlikely to be good enough for them, and their dissatisfaction with the criminal justice system will remain high. Unfortunately, as with the fear of crime, such feelings of dissatisfaction are often played on by politicians at election times who get considerable mileage out of promising tougher and tougher punishments for criminals. But, apart from perpetuating the frightful, if utterly unhelpful, image of the criminal as a monster, such policies are proven failures in terms of crime control, and it is doubtful that they will succeed in the long run in engendering more respect for the law and the criminal justice process.[28] A far more promising and honest approach is indicated by victim accounts, according to which a great deal of their dissatisfaction is due to their marginalization and disempowerment in the legal processing and resolution of their cases. My suggestion is that many sentences which currently leave victims dissatisfied would in fact more than satisfy them if they were made to feel genuinely valued by giving them an active role in the process of punishment with substantial decision making powers in matters such as bail, prosecution, plea bargaining, sentencing, and parole. As Braithwaite observes,

The surprising thing is that victims, who so often call for more blood in traditional Western justice systems, in New Zealand frequently plead with the police to waive punishment and 'give the kid another chance'.[29]

What this indicates is that it is very important from the point of view of victim satisfaction and social-psychological restoration that victims are appropriately empowered and involved. Victim involvement and empowerment must include the prerogative and the legal power to prosecute, settle with, or forgive their aggressors. As I pointed out earlier, in a great number of cases of criminal wrongdoing the real or primary injury is to the victims, and 'society' is harmed, if at all, only secondarily and derivatively. Therefore, victim decisions with regard to prosecution, punishment, and mercy should not be vetoed by police, judges, magistrates, or community representatives, unless those decisions are clearly reckless and unreasonable in that they harm the wider public's interests. Such extensive victim empowerment would not be without precedent. There are many historical examples of such legal systems, including classical Greece, Roman law, and medieval Iceland.

> . . . only under very special circumstances was homicide dealt with by the public authorities in classical Greece. The execution of the offender was essentially looked upon as a private affair, and no officially coded law was ever written which required the state to punish a murderer without there being an accuser. Roman law was also based on this premise, although it gradually gave way toward the end of the empire when the dictators took over.[30]

> The function of the courts [in medieval Iceland] was to deliver verdicts on cases brought to them. That done, the court was finished. If the verdict went against the defendant, it was up to him to pay the assigned punishment—almost always a fine [paid to the victim]. If he did not, the plaintiff could go to court again and have the defendant declared an outlaw. The killer of an outlaw could not himself be prosecuted for the act; in addition, anyone who gave shelter to an outlaw could be prosecuted for doing so. Prosecution was up to the victim (or h   i   s survivors). If they and the offender agreed on a settlement, the matter was set-tled. . . . If the case went to a court, the judgment, in case of conviction, would be a fine to be paid by the defendant to the plaintiff.[31]

Apart from acting as a boost to confidence and empowerment, giving victims the power of decision with regard to matters of prosecution, settle-ment, and mercy has the potential to aid in generating respect in offenders for victims. From the point of view of prevention alone it would make sense to make the prospect of personal victim retaliation a reality to offenders who at the moment don't even have to face the disastrous impact their actions have on others, let alone having to face directly their victims' anger, indignation, and resentment. Through substantial victim involvement and empowerment a legal justice system can send an unambiguous message to potential offenders that, by law, and in virtue of the power of the state, their victims (and potential victims) possess substantial powers of punishment and mercy and will respond effectively to wrongs committed against them. In light of research findings such as those quoted above, it is hard to think of a better way to teach offenders and impress upon them the value and respect which must be accorded to others whom they (might) victimize, intentionally or otherwise, through unlawful behaviour. And, as indicated, in addition to promoting a more realistic and healthier outlook towards others in potential and actual offenders, such victim empowerment would help in restoring victim confidence and dignity, and would promote in vic-tims a new, empowering self-image away from helpless victimhood. Thus, substantial victim empowerment offers many benefits to offenders and vic-tims alike.

Models of Victim Empowerment

1. Privatizing the Criminal Justice System

Greater victim involvement and empowerment could be achieved, for example, in the context of a privatized legal justice system. This could be modelled, for instance, on the medieval Icelandic system of law enforcement, along lines suggested by David Friedman.

> The first step in applying the Icelandic system of private enforcement to a modern society would be to convert all criminal offenses into civil offenses, making the offender liable to pay an appropriate fine to the victim. In some cases, it might not be obvious who the victim was, but that could be specified by legislation. . . . For some minor offenses anyone could sue; presumably, whoever submitted his case first would be entitled to the fine. It must be remembered that specifying the victim has the practical function of giving someone an incentive to pursue the case. The second step would be to make the victim's claim marketable, so that he could sell it to someone willing to catch and convict the offender. The amount of the claim would correspond approximately to the damage caused by the crime divided by the probability of catching the criminal. In many cases it would be substantial. Once these steps were taken, a body of professional 'thief-takers' (as they were once called in England) would presumably develop and gradually replace our present governmental police forces.[32]

Current debate on, and interest in, such models is focused on questions of comparative efficiency and cost-effectiveness, while the desirability of such privatization receives little or no attention from a victim justice point of view.[33] However, provided that the proposed victim involvement was there, it would be reasonable to expect that victim justice and empowerment would be prominent under such private law enforcement conditions. To be sure, without the appropriate shift in focus to enhance the victim's role, privatization would make little difference in terms of enhancing victim justice. Privatization, however, represents not only a radical departure from the dominant criminological theories of modern times but also from the experience of contemporary, urbanized societies in handling crime. This explains, perhaps, why the debate on privatization is slow to gather pace. Nevertheless, it is not unreasonable to expect that, in the long run, a complete privatization of the justice system may become reality. The price paid by the public for crime and law enforcement through our current institutions is inordinately high. Considering that the very same money supports chronic corruption, organized crime, and abuse of power in some of those institutions of enforcement, privatization which effects a shifting of the financial burden away from the taxpayer to the criminal is bound to look increasingly attractive not only to the average citizen and voter, and hence the political parties sensitive to their votes, but also to governments struggling to balance their budgets. But, whether, or how, such a system of justice would work today need not be decided here. There are at least two other approaches for facilitating adequate victim involvement and empowerment which do not require privatization of the criminal justice institutions involved. I consider them in turn.

2. Alternative Dispute Resolution Models

There are three main models based on the concept of alternative dispute resolution (ADR), which have been tried out and are being introduced at an increasing rate as permanent features of criminal justice systems in various states and countries. These are: Victim-Offender Mediation (VOM), Sentencing Circles, and Restorative Justice Conferencing (RJC).[34] VOMs are typically attended only by the offender and the victim, and their meeting is facilitated by trained mediators. If a support person is present on either side, they do not normally get involved in the discussion. In some contrast, Sentencing Circles and RJCs encourage the active participation of the respective communities of the principal parties, such as their respective families, close friends, trusted neighbours, teachers, employers, and so forth. However, the central idea behind all three models is that victim and offender meet each other face to face to discuss what has happened, who has been affected, and in what way, and to find an all-round satisfactory outcome to their conflict in a controlled and supportive environment, without interference from third parties, such as criminal justice professionals, who have no personal or special ties to either of them. Participation is voluntary and the above models may be used in three main ways.

1. As an outright alternative to court processing (diversion), provided that the parties reach agreement. If there is no agreement, the matter is referred back to court. Understandably, this option has been mainly used so far in the less serious offence categories, and even there predominantly with juvenile offenders.

2. As part of the court process, usually following a plea of 'guilty' but before sentencing, so that the agreement or recommendations of the meeting may be considered, and made use of, by the sentencing judge.

3. At any time after the court case is finalised in the interests of aiding people's recovery and healing from the effects of crime, but also to consider and decide important matters relating to release from prison and/or parole.

The *United Nations Resolution on Victims of Crime and Abuse of Power* strongly recommends the use of such alternative, and less formal, processes of conflict resolution in the interests of victims,[35] and various versions of the above models have already been successfully adopted in many countries, including the United States, Canada, England, Singapore, Austria, Belgium, Germany, New Zealand, and Australia. While there can be considerable variations between the various programs and their protocols with regard to the intake, preparation, facilitation and follow-up of cases, they all have the one core feature mentioned above, that they empower the principal parties to sort matters out between themselves in face to face discussions. In RJCs, for example, victim and offender, accompanied by their respective communities of supporters, meet each other face to face to discuss and find a solution to their conflict in a way that is acceptable to all parties involved. Conferences are prepared and facilitated by trained and skilled Facilitators. Conferencing allows an in-depth discussion and consideration of the offense, its causes, and its consequences. The aim is to empower participants so that they can present their respective points of view and work out an outcome that is acceptable to both sides. While such discussions and agreements typically address both the causes and the consequences of the wrongful behaviour in question, healing of the emotional harm from the wrongdoing is strongly dependent on the direct and active participation by the parties concerned. Through the experience of developing a shared, community-based understanding and appreciation of the moral, material, psychological and social dimensions of the offense through direct engagement and dialogue, negative emotions and attitudes, such as animosity, anger, resentment, humiliation, shame, defiance, indifference, and insecurity, are gradually replaced by more positive ones, such as respect, acceptance, remorse, forgiveness, self-forgiveness, and caring. Especially in cases where the offense in question has created a lot of emotional trauma and harm, traversing this emotional landscape in the context of a conference is a powerful and moving experience. High rates of satisfaction have been reported by all participants, including offenders, victims, and their respective supporters.[36]

Indeed, the greater the harm, the more important it is that there be such an experience of empowerment and healing for the parties concerned, especially for victims. Therefore, while it is understandable that early experimentation with conferencing must take place in the lower end of the spectrum of seriousness, the tremendous emotional harm which typically results from serious offenses creates an even greater need for conferencing at the upper end of that spectrum. If this is right, then conferencing for adult and serious crime cannot be introduced soon enough. The potential benefits are there for all parties concerned: the victim, the offender, and the broader community. Braithwaite's pioneering theory of *reintegrative shaming,* for example, explains why, in comparison to court, such alternative approaches are more likely to be successful in addressing criminal behaviour.

Crime is best controlled when members of the community are the primary con-
trollers through active participation in shaming offenders, and, having shamed
them, through concerted participation in ways of reintegrating the offender
back into the community of law abiding citizens. Low crime societies are societies where . . . communities prefer to handle their own crime problems rather
than hand them over to professionals.[37]

Shaming is a powerful mechanism of social control and, when combined
with appropriate efforts to reintegrate the offender into the community of
law-respecting citizens, it can be used as an effective method of crime control.[38] As Pincoffs put the matter,

The practice of leaving the punishment to the community has in its favour the
point that for any individual the most meaningful punishment is that which is
inflicted by those closest to him. It is the opinion of his peers that he values far
more than the opinion of some vast and faceless 'general public' represented by
the sentencing judge. It is a point in its favour, also, that it makes for no discon-
tinuity between the legal and moral community in the way that legal punishment does, in setting off some offences as subject to the sway of jails and jailers
while other offences, morally as heinous, are not so subject.[39]

From a victim justice perspective, an important reason for empowering
victims and, whenever possible, giving them the opportunity to discuss and
resolve the offense personally with their wrongdoers is that irrational and
unrealistic fears, apprehensions, anxieties and misconceptions about the
aggressor's person and power are likely to be dissipated in the victim's mind
when they see their offenders remorse and experience of shame for what
they did. Furthermore, such discussions also give an opportunity for symbolic reparation, which is the giving and accepting of apology. In their
study of conferencing, for example, Retzinger and Scheff found that there
are two processes occurring side by side: material and symbolic reparation.[40]
The process of material reparation results in a final settlement between
offender and victim and typically consists of specific agreements about compensating the victim, community service, and so forth. The process of symbolic reparation is less visible. It is composed of gestures and expressions of
courtesy, respect, remorse, and forgiveness. According to Retzinger and
Scheff, the core sequence, consisting of the offender's apology and the victim's forgiveness, is the key to reconciliation, victim satisfaction, and
decreasing recidivism.

The core sequence generates repair and restoration of the bond between victim
and offender. . . . Without the core sequence, the path toward settlement is
strewn with impediments; whatever settlement is reached does not decrease the
tension level in the room, and leaves the participants with a feeling of arbitrari-

ness and dissatisfaction. Thus, it is crucially important to give symbolic reparation at least parity with material settlement. Unless this is done, conferences may turn out, in the long run, to be only marginally better than traditional court practices. Symbolic reparation is the vital element that differentiates conferences from all other forms of crime control.[41]

Research by Estrada-Hollenbeck confirms the importance symbolic reparation in criminal justice disputes.[42] Apology is very important for overcoming the negative social-psychological effects of criminal victimization, and there can be little doubt that it is the most desirable way to redress psychological trauma and soothe hard feelings in victims. The power of apology as a mechanism of aggression control has been demonstrated through laboratory experiments in social psychology.[43] A sincere apology soothes hard feelings in victims, such as resentment and anger, and is very effective in controlling and diffusing retaliatory aggression. Sincere apologies take the wind out of the sails of resentment and obviate the need for retaliation to re-establish equity into inequitable relationships. The key messages conveyed in apology explain its almost magical ability to soothe hard feelings following an act of aggression. For example, by publicly admitting fault and wrongdoing through apology, the aggressor reduces the victim's sense of responsibility for the negative consequences of the act and, therefore, helps to restore the victim's self-respect and social identity. It is a common tendency among sexual assault victims, for example, to blame themselves for what happened. Apology expresses respect for the victim from the offender and publicly acknowledges the victim's moral and social status.

Apology from an offender also indicates self-disapproval on account of their wrongful act, and conveys the message that the wrongdoer is not such a bad person, after all. Acceptance of fault and responsibility by the offender in public and expressions of remorse may also be taken by victims and third parties as self-punishment for the transgression. This may reduce, if not altogether obviate, the need for imposing further penalties on the offender. Especially where remorse and sincere apologies are accompanied by adequate restitution and compensation, the need for retaliation or further punishment may well be redundant, since adequate compensation also addresses the need for social justice and equity.[44] While each case must be decided on its merits, there is a good chance that in such circumstances retaliation or further penalties become inappropriate.[45]

The benefits of symbolic reparation, and the benefits of direct victim-offender discussions generally, do not stop with the victim, however. Research clearly shows that this is very important to offenders as well.[46] Resolving conflicts in these ways holds the promise of being significantly less costly to offenders than court processing (on its own) would be, and it is also likely to be less disruptive for everyone concerned, including the respective families of the principal parties. Meeting their victims is good for offenders also, as it allows them a constructive approach to the wrong they did in three ways:

(a) it helps them to appreciate the damaging consequences their actions have had on others, including their victims and their own loved ones;

(b) it provides them with an opportunity to apologize and make good their actions by doing whatever may be necessary and fair in order to restore the victim;

(c) it provides them with the opportunity to receive signs and expressions of forgiveness from their victims which, in turn, make it easier for them to start being positive about themselves, to forgive themselves perhaps, and, having wiped the slate clean, return to living a life unfettered by the moral-psychological burden of the past.[47]

All these factors are important for the social reintegration and moral-psychological restoration of offenders. For, with very rare exceptions, offenders are not bereft of moral sensibilities. They realize that they have done wrong and that they need to make amends through adequate reparation and apology in order to put things right. In familiar jargon, offenders need to be given genuine opportunities to wipe the slate clean for a fresh start. Impersonally imposed punishment by a judicial system, which not only disempowers offenders but also shields them from the serious consequences of their actions on others, is more likely to produce a feeling of detachment and alienation in offenders than it is to engender in them constructive feelings and attitudes with regard to the wrongs they committed and the need to put them right.

It is not difficult to see that denying offenders the opportunity to make amends in appropriate ways is bound to make it harder for them to feel remorse and to forgive themselves. Worse, imposing on them penalties which may be wholly inappropriate in terms of meeting their needs in the above indicated ways is as likely to hinder their reintegration and rehabilitation as it is likely to hinder victim restoration and healing. The need for engendering constructive attitudes in the offender and the need for appropriate sentences highlight the importance of involving close family and friends from both sides of the conflict, since it is the opinions of close ones, and especially the views of respected others in their lives, that matter most to them. In addition, it is these people who are likely to know best what will be constructive, rather than destructive, in a given case. As an example, the traditional Maori followed these principles in their customary responses to wrongdoing.

In a Maori setting, offenders were never alienated from the victim of their actions or the authority which decided their fate. Their actions were the shared responsibility of a whanau [extended family] or iwi [tribe], and the consequences and judgement of them was similarly shared. ... Whanau involvement would both reinforce the idea of group responsibility and ensure the remorse and shame an offender needs to feel before effective rehabilitation and redress is possible.[48]

The needs of offenders and victims complement each other in that their respective giving and acceptance of appropriate apologies and reparation comprise the single most important and constructive first step towards resolving their conflict to the point where they can both leave the matter behind and get on with their lives. It stands to reason, therefore, that the first mission of any justice system ought to be to promote the resolution of conflicts in ways which most appropriately meet the needs of both offenders and victims. If this is right, it hardly needs further argument that we should promote the empowerment of both victims and offenders to the point where they can enter into civilized, constructive dialogue with each other. This is precisely what ADR processes seek to do. Having said that, it is reasonable to expect that in some cases of serious crime victims and offenders would not want to meet face to face with each other, or be able to work out a mutually agreeable resolution. Therefore, ADR processes on their own are not going to be appropriate or sufficient in all circumstances. They must be complemented with a court system as an alternative and backup measure, which brings us to the point of considering greater victim involvement under a *Modified court model* where victims may be similarly empowered and given opportunities to take an active role in the prosecution and sentencing of their offenders.

3. A Modified Court Model

The most obvious way to promote victim involvement in the court process would be by allowing them to contribute to the sentencing of their offenders. An increasingly common attempt to make judicial systems more victim-oriented is by way of Victim Impact Statements (VIS's). A VIS is a statement by the victim about the physical, financial, psychological, and social impacts of the crime on their lives. In some countries it may also include an expression of victim's feelings about the crime and the criminal, as well as a statement of opinion by the victim as to what they would consider to be an appropriate sentence. Normally, VIS's are submitted to the judge for consideration in sentencing, thus providing victims with an opportunity to make a contribution towards the final resolution of the case. While VIS's are by no means the most empowering way to involve victims in the judicial process, when they are properly administered, and are given due consideration by the sentencing judge or magistrate, they represent a step in the right direction. This is confirmed by research, which shows increased victim satisfaction levels with judicial outcomes as a result of their participation in the process by way of a VIS.[49]

Their undoubted value notwithstanding, VIS's are not, from a victim justice point of view, the ultimate answer. They do not, for example, compensate for the current lack of provisions for substantial victim input in the relevant decision making processes, such as bail, plea bargaining, sentencing, and parole, let alone the lack of direct victim representation in court by qualified legal counsel. Arguably, lack of such legal representation is one of the most important contributing factors in the continued marginalization and disempowerment that victims experience in the criminal justice process, and it cannot be overcome through VIS's alone. The severity of victim disempowerment is acutely felt, for example, by victims of sexual assault, especially under the adversary system:

> Many sexual assault victims who have given evidence at a criminal trial feel that they were the ones being judged, rather than the assailant. . . . women find that they are disbelieved, their allegations are trivialized, and their honesty and credibility are severely questioned.[50]

Such disempowerment is not restricted to sexual assault victims, however. The phenomenon is virtually universal, and the problem is structural. The following passage is indicative of the general disempowerment victims of serious crime experience with the judicial system as it stands.

> How devastating it was for me and for my family to sit in the court, day after day, feeling almost as though Leanne was on trial. To hear various witnesses speak on behalf of her murderer, while we are not permitted to say one word on Leanne's behalf.[51]

It would be naive to suppose that VIS's will overcome the damaging effects of such experiences in the court room. In addition, the effectiveness of the VIS tends to be undermined by two factors. One of these is that it is mostly left to the discretion of the sentencing magistrate or judge to read and take into account the contents of the VIS. This represents a problem, because

> victim participation and input into sentencing decisions challenge traditions and established patterns within the criminal courts, [and as a result] legislative reforms often amount to lip service; they typically lack remedies for non-compliance.[52]

The remedy to this is easy to see. Sentencing judges and magistrates must be required to address each element of the VIS as part of the sentencing process. No element of a VIS should be left without mention or dismissed without adequate justification. Proposed sentences should then be examined by the victim, with support from an appropriately qualified victim advocate. Sentences which do not display adequate awareness and consideration of the statement's contents should be returned to the sentencing judge or magistrate in question for proper consideration. To be truly effective, these requirements must be given appropriate legislative backing.

The other factor which tends to undermine the effectiveness of the VIS is that, all too often, victims either aren't adequately informed about the VIS, or they do not receive the necessary encouragement and support in their preparation. Thus, VIS's can become "well-kept secrets that only few victims know about, or make use of, to their advantage."[53] As before, the remedy to this problem is fairly straightforward. Victims must be provided with an appropriately qualified advocate who, besides keeping them informed at all stages of the court process and representing their interests in court, would consult with the victim for purposes of preparing a proper VIS according to the guidelines set out for the purpose. Once again, legislative backing would be required for such provisions to be truly effective.

Evidently, a key role in ensuring the safeguarding of victims' rights should fall on the victim's representative, or advocate. On a par with there being a qualified advocate for the offender, it ought to be the victim advocate's role and responsibility to provide the victim with all the relevant information, support, and representation with respect to all aspects of the court process. Essentially, this would only require a change in the public prosecutor's role, whereby they would represent the victim, rather than the state or the Crown. Victim justice requires that victims be empowered through such representation to speak up and take an active role in court proceedings. This would be the best way to safeguard and promote their interests throughout the process, and fundamental law reform in these areas is likely to aid their restoration, the very first step to which must be that victims are satisfied with both the processing and the substantive resolution of their cases.

The need for replacing public prosecutors with victim advocates is highlighted by a recent case in the Court of Appeal of New Zealand where, against the victim's expressed wishes, the solicitor-general's office succeeded in overturning a negotiated settlement the victim had reached with the offender in the context of a restorative justice conference.[54] As a result of this appeal, the victim, the offender, their respective families, as well as the general community are all worse off than before, and the victim was reported to be particularly upset with the overruling of their wishes and interests in the case.[55] This particular victim's dissatisfaction also contrasts with research findings which show that victim involvement and empowerment in both the court system and in ADR processes result in improved victim satisfaction.

> Studies of victims who participated as subsidiary prosecutors or who acted as private prosecutors (as several continental justice systems allow) reveal that their

satisfaction with justice is higher than those who did not actively participate in the proceedings.[56]

[V]ictims who were referred to VORP [Victim Offender Reconciliation Program] and participated in a mediation session with their offender were far more likely (by 2 to 1 margin) to have experienced fairness (80%) with the manner in which the criminal justice system dealt with their case than those victims who were referred to VORP but chose not to enter mediation (38%).[57]

Such findings, in my view, complete the case for greater victim participation and empowerment in the criminal justice system. Objections to these proposals are considered in the remaining chapter.

Summing Up This Chapter

There are good reasons, both instrumental and non-instrumental, for putting the personal element back into institutionalized legal punishment by way of greater victim involvement and empowerment in the criminal justice process. As one of the principal parties in a criminal justice dispute, a victim has an inalienable right to have a substantial say in matters affecting their interests in terms of restitution, compensation, and social-psychological restoration, which in many cases requires that they satisfy themselves with the knowledge that justice has been done. Such victim satisfaction with justice signifies closure and a readiness to move on, unshackled by the hurt of the past, but this is extremely difficult and sometimes impossible without an experience of real empowerment by having a substantial say in the way one's case is resolved. Increased victim empowerment is further supported by social-psychological research on the nature, dynamics, and psychology of interpersonal exchange.

There are two main models for constructive victim participation and empowerment. Neither of these requires privatization of the criminal justice system, although they would work equally well in a privatized environment. ADR models should be given first priority whenever possible, and a modified court model should be resorted to as a backup measure in cases where victim, offender, and their immediate communities do not wish to meet, or cannot reach agreement. A modified court model would see the victim placed at the centre of the court system and would invest them with substantial decision-making powers at all stages of the criminal justice process, such as bail, plea-bargaining, sentencing, and parole. Most importantly, a modified court model would see public prosecutors acting primarily as victim advocates, representing and safeguarding the legitimate rights and interests victims have in the handling and resolution of their cases. Nothing short of such measures is likely to meet the requirements of victim justice.

In the next and final chapter, I argue that such victim empowerment, with all the opportunities it presents for institutionalized revenge, would not jeopardise the other advantages of a good institutionalized justice system.

10

Beyond Restorative Justice: The Primacy of Empowerment

Now my hypothesis is not so much that the court is the natural expression of popular justice, but rather that its historical function is to ensnare it, to control it and to strangle it, by re-inscribing it within institutions which are typical of a state apparatus.

Michel Foucault[1]

The arguments of the previous chapter ought to be sufficient to justify enhanced victim empowerment in the legal resolution of their cases, and the defense of moral retributivism I gave in Chapter 8 provides additional grounds for making such victim involvement morally admissible. In turn, a substantial legal empowerment of victims in the criminal justice system opens up the real possibility of victims taking revenge on their wrongdoers within limits allowed by law, as major actors in the relevant institutions involved. Given the appropriate legal rights to make substantial decisions with regard to matters such as bail, prosecution, plea bargaining, sentencing, and parole, victims are immediately placed in a position of strength to deal with their wrongdoers in whatever way they think fair and appropriate. In such situations, their responses could range from forgiveness to punitiveness as a way of teaching the offender a lesson, or as a way of getting even with the offender by giving them their just deserts within limits allowed by law.

Such new possibilities, uncertainties, and realities can be disconcerting, especially to people whose understanding of justice is contained within an anti-revenge and anti-retribution paradigm. To them, the prospect of legally sanctioning or condoning revenge in our criminal justice institutions may seem abhorrent, and they are likely to resist *the idea* in some form or another. I emphasize the word 'idea' because, as in this case, a new idea may be resisted from within an established paradigm in more than one way. The new idea may be overtly resisted for what it is, or it may be resisted by denying its reality through wishful reinterpretation, a kind of conceptual gerrymandering. The anti-revenge paradigm shows signs of strong resistance to the idea of revenge in both these ways, and the following two sections address these two kinds of resistance to the idea and prospect of institutionalized revenge. The final section argues for a shifting of the newly emerging criminological focus on restorative justice to the more fundamental question of empowerment. Individual and community empowerment, I suggest, is the truly important question from all interested parties' point of view, not least of all from the point of view of the legal profession whose monopoly on criminal justice is threatened by restorative justice initiatives.

Victim Empowerment and the Dangers of Revenge

Though widely and often passionately held, the view that revenge is wrong, inherently or otherwise, is not self-evidently correct. An anti-revenge position cannot simply be assumed. Rather, it must be argued for, and I suggest that the arguments presented in this book place some onus on defenders of the anti-revenge paradigm to respond convincingly.

Absent good arguments to the contrary, victim empowerment should not stop short of granting victims the legal right to institutionalized revenge and, indeed, the legal right to forgive and be merciful to their offenders, as they, in good conscience, deem fit. Without such legal rights, victims are unnecessarily denied their rightful interests in justice. The question, therefore, is whether there are good arguments against substantial victim empowerment of the kind that would effectively give them the legal right to institutionalized revenge. I do not believe that there are.

The kind of victim empowerment envisaged under the empowerment paradigm of justice would not jeopardize any of the advantages of a good institutionalized system of criminal justice. This point is worth considering in detail, as there have been concerns raised in connection with the possible dangers involved in revenge. For example, having unregulated, raw revenge in mind, rather than the kind of legal institutionalized forms of revenge I have been defending, Russell talks about revenge as "a very dangerous motive."[2] Hume similarly cautions against it with the words,

Who sees not that vengeance, from the force alone of passion, may be so eagerly pursued as to make us knowingly neglect every consideration of ease, interest, or safety?[3]

Again, according to Siebers,

[T]he fear of revenge may be the emotion that underlies moral philosophy in the West. A society can survive arbitrary acts of violence; it may even withstand warfare, since battle often strengthens the unanimity of a group. But no society can withstand the premeditated and organized violence of revenge because it initiates menacing cycles of conflict from within. Blood feuds, cycles of revenge, and other forms of organized violence endure for generations; as Greek tragedy dramatically illustrates, they place a curse on the house of mankind.[4]

More recently, Wallace has emphasized that in unregulated revenge

there is always the danger of vendettas developing and spirals of violence. . . . When personal relations have deteriorated so much that violent revenge is on the agenda proportionality is unlikely.[5]

Wallace does recognize, however, that when there is no system of law, or when the law is "discriminatory by failing to offer equal protection to all citizens," or when some class of harms are "legally ignored no matter who suffers them, . . . revenge, with all its drawbacks, is then the only form of retribution available."[6] But because of the dangers involved in unregulated revenge, Wallace argues that

injustice is the probable outcome. So even if it is sometimes possible to justify harmful revenge, a general right to be revenged cannot be sustained.[7]

I agree that any form of retaliation or punishment which is outside a formalized and fair institutionalized framework, such as unregulated, raw revenge and vigilante punishment, for example, has many dangers and ills and, therefore, generally, taking the law into our own hands would not be a good idea. Injustices, wrongs, and losses being very close to home, the need to 'even the score' in revenge is likely to be driven by powerful retributive emotions, such as resentment, indignation, and anger. In the heat of the moment, judgment and control can be easily affected and more can be inflicted in retaliation, for example, than what, in all fairness, would be due. Such factors are bound to increase the dangers of escalation also. Therefore, even though there is nothing *inherently* wrong with non-institutionalized acts of revenge which observe the requisite principles of justice, the need for structural controls by means of institutionalization and formalization of processes dealing with offenses requires no further argument.

That point conceded, none of these considerations give good grounds for marginalizing and disempowering victims from the processes of the justice system, and it is doubtful that there should ever emerge an *all-things-considered* justification for such victim marginalization and disempowerment. There are a number of reasons for this, and it will be worth listing them again briefly. First, the claims and requirements of victim rights and victim justice outlined in the previous chapter alone are sufficient to cast serious doubt on the defensibility of the current marginalization and disempowerment victims experience with the judicial processing of their cases. It is increasingly recognized that more attention must be paid to the rights of the wronged individuals in question and those closely related to them. The introduction of low-level victim rights legislation in many states and countries is evidence of this growing recognition. To reiterate an earlier point, given that it is the victims who in fact have been wronged and that they are the ones most affected by the crime in question, justice must be primarily *theirs*, not society's; and it must be at least as much theirs as it is their wrongdoers'.

Second, the fear of vengeful victims being unreasonable and unduly harsh on their offenders has no rational basis. Apart from the fact that the power of victims is still very limited under both models discussed and that, therefore, there is virtually no chance that they can abuse their enhanced status to bring about unfair outcomes for offenders, research into attitudes to sentencing consistently shows that "victims of crime are no more punitive than others."[8]

> The message from studies in several countries is that first-hand experience of crime as a victim does not, in general, fuel a desire for heavy sentences. Furthermore, victims have not been found to be more punitive than the general public.[9]

Third, there are no good reasons to think that victim involvement would jeopardize any of the principles of offender justice, if it all took place within a fair, properly structured institutionalized framework. For, notwithstanding victim involvement, the usual safeguards of a well-constructed system in guarding against violating principles of justice would continue to be present. In other words, there are no reasons to think that victim justice and justice to offenders are incompatible with each other under either of the two institutionally based models I have described in the previous chapter. Admittedly, this point has been vigorously contested from an adversarial stance. For example, in *Booth v. Maryland (1987) 482 US 496* it was successfully argued that the introduction of a VIS at the sentencing phase of a capital murder trial violated the defendant's rights under the Eighth Amendment of the U.S. Federal Constitution. While this decision and a similar decision reached in *South Carolina v. Gathers (1989) 490 US 805* were both overruled by *Payne v. Tennessee (1991) 501 US 808*, there is evidence of growing concern of "the potential damage caused by giving victims too much control over the criminal justice system" because of the accurate recognition that this would increasingly allow "seeking revenge on the defendant" and an alleged "unacceptable skewing of the criminal justice process in favor of victims."[10] While such concerns and arguments should not be dismissed out of hand, they clearly reflect a point of view heavily biased in favor of defendants—a recognizable and deeply ingrained feature of the traditional adversarial approach to criminal justice in our courts. I do not accept for a moment that greater victim involvement and empowerment in our courts would unacceptably skew the process in favor of victims, though no doubt it would effect a significant shift in the myopic preoccupation our courts tend to have with the legal rights of the accused in terms of due process, especially in sentencing and while their 'guilt' is established or tested.

Why is this myopic? There are a number of reasons. One is that it ignores the victims' interests and it does untold damage to them through marginalization and disempowerment in the course of such court proceedings. Another is that it fails to consider properly the interests of the broader communities involved on both sides of the criminal justice dispute, as well as the general public's interests, all of which would be much better served by processes and resolutions that left the principal protagonists satisfied that the matter has been resolved and that justice has been done. To these reasons we must add that, while protecting the offender's due process rights is important, such focus is too narrow even from the point of view of the offender's own, broader interests. As John MacDonald has argued, in connection with conferencing for young offenders,

> No one will argue against the right to silence, the right to legal representation, and competent counsel. But what we also suggest, and which lawyers can't offer, and don't want to offer, is the opportunity for the young offender to be educated from this experience. Young offenders have the right to learn the consequences of their crime. They have the right to understand how many other people it affects. They have the right to develop as full human beings through this process. Now if you let the opportunity slip by by handing it over to lawyers, you deny them all those developmental rights.[11]

In addition to these considerations, perhaps the most pertinent point is that the narrow preoccupation with the offender's due process rights flies in the face of community values and good moral sense because it largely ignores the offender's moral responsibilities for putting things right with the people they harmed. The starting point here surely must be that the criminal is in the wrong. They have unjustifiably harmed others, and this creates a moral obligation on their behalf: the responsibility to put things right with the people they have hurt. Therefore, morally speaking, requiring offenders to put things right in this way should be our first priority, and it certainly should not come second in importance to the protection of their rights. Having it any other way is like allowing the tail to wag the dog. What the critics of victim empowerment fail to recognize is that a shift in focus as just described is highly desirable in terms of giving the criminal justice process more balance, and there can be little doubt that a more balanced approach is long overdue. To the degree that the legal profession fails to recognize and correct this myopic imbalance, it shows itself to be out of touch with both community values and the broader interests of the offender in putting things right with the people they have harmed, let alone the damage done to victims by court processes heavily skewed against them. Tom Campbell made a telling remark, I believe, when he suggested that

> those who object to victim participation on the grounds that it distracts attention from doing justice to the accused, may simply be begging the crucial questions against victim justice.[12]

Lastly, the fourth major reason why it is unlikely that there should ever emerge an all-things-considered justification for the continued marginalization and disempowerment of victims is that under the two models I have covered, the danger of escalation would be contained. Because of the institutionalized nature of the system there would be an built-in finality which ends the process. Thus, the danger of conflict escalation which is ever-present in raw, unregulated revenge, for example, is no longer a problem and, therefore, cannot serve as an objection against institutionalized forms of revenge. As a practical matter, the enhanced scope for mild forms of institutionalized revenge within the justice system is now a foregone conclusion. Its entry onto the moral stage through the back door, as it were, was unintended, has gone largely unnoticed, and may even be denied, which brings me to consider the second way in which the established paradigm resists the idea of institutionalized revenge.

The Denial and Reality of Institutionalized Revenge

In an ironic turn, the ailing criminal justice systems of the Western world, which pride themselves on having eliminated all traces of revenge from the criminal justice process, are increasingly propped up by ADR models, the historical and philosophical roots of which are found in traditional practices by indigenous people. This is ironic because the traditional practices in question were strongly victim-focused, and it cannot be plausibly disputed that the fundamental premise of such practices was that, unless victims could be satisfied in other ways, they had the right to revenge.

In practice, the same reality is recreated by diversionary programs that employ ADR models as a way of dealing with crime. Such diversionary programs operate now in many countries (including the United States, Canada, New Zealand, Australia, and Britain), and in some cases as permanent features of the Youth Justice System. One of the benefits of such programs for offenders is that they are spared a criminal conviction, and sometimes detention or incarceration, provided that they put things right with the victim in the course of their facilitated meeting. Typically, when the meeting is an attempted diversionary measure, the victim's consent is required to resolve the matter out of court. In more serious cases where the meeting was requested by a judge for purposes of more informed and appropriate sentencing, the victim's plea on behalf of the offender can spare the latter from bearing the full brunt of the penalties that otherwise would be their due in court.

In the context of such programs, victims are already in a powerful position to exercise mercy or demand satisfaction in a fair and civilized manner as they, in good conscience, deem fit. Their satisfaction need not be limited to restitution and compensation alone, but may include fair penalties which are accepted as fair and just by all participants in the facilitated meeting, including the offender. If the victim thinks that the offender should be given some appropriate penalty for what they did (such as a substantial donation to charity, or community service), they are quite within their rights to say so, and then it is up to the offender and their family to agree or disagree with the fairness of the proposal in light of the offense they committed, the harm they caused, and the likely outcome of going to court instead. And, while it is true that penalties agreed upon in such meetings are constructive in instrumental ways, they can also be, and I suggest that they frequently are, seen by participants as the retributive price the offender rightfully pays for their wrongdoing, in accordance with their just deserts. In addition, if the victim finds no satisfaction at the conference, they can send the offender back to court, thus forcing on the offender a criminal conviction, or a more serious sentence by the judge than would be otherwise possible, or both. While such outcomes are far less satisfactory than a mutually satisfying agreement, it is nonetheless an empowering last resort for the victim to get even personally with the offender.

Such institutionally sanctioned opportunities for revenge, however, should not cause alarm. First, as we have seen earlier, victims generally are not more punitive than others. Second, whether they think about the whole matter in retributive terms or not makes no practical difference, as long as their proposals and requests are reasonable and are fair to offenders in light of prevailing community standards. Third, should an offender find the victim's position unacceptable, they have the option of going to court instead. This very rarely happens, however. Experience shows that offenders are more than willing to accommodate the victim's position, which is further confirmation that victims are not unreasonable in their own cases,[13] even though they effectively have the powers of revenge and mercy as explained.

Nevertheless, in a culture where the very concept of justice is colored by anti-revenge myths, and even by anti-revenge hysteria, this will be greeted as mixed news at best. Worse, in such an environment, the very reality of institutionalized revenge as I have described it may be denied. In fact, it would be naive not to expect such denials. Well-established paradigms are resilient, and the anti-revenge paradigm is no exception. Resisting the idea of institutionalized revenge by denial and conceptual gerrymandering need not involve a rejection of it in practice, but only a redescription of it (or whatever is happening in practice) in terms that identify the practice as something other than revenge. Perhaps it is not a coincidence that this tends to be a favoured approach by advocates of restorative justice, who all too readily resort to retribution-bashing as a way of making restorative justice more appealing.[14] Discussing one example in detail will help to illustrate the point.

As mentioned earlier, punishment practices in pre-colonial, indigenous cultures generally guaranteed the rights of victims to revenge, as prescribed and sanctioned by indigenous customary laws. Many of these practices have survived, especially in remote areas, and are gaining increased recognition by the courts as part of respecting indigenous peoples' rights to cultural autonomy. It can happen, for example, that a sentencing judge makes allowances for, and takes into account, any retaliatory punishment the victim will need to inflict on the offender to fulfil the requirements of their community's sacred, customary laws, such as the spearing of the wrongdoer's thigh by the victim's family as payback in indigenous Australian communities. Suppose that such traditional practices received full institutional recognition in the criminal justice systems of the relevant countries concerned. The reality of institutionalized revenge in such cases, it seems to me, ought to be beyond question, but, as I go on to explain further below, at least one prominent advocate of restorative justice holds a different view. In his book *Restorative Justice: Healing the Effects of Crime*, Jim Consedine argues that the criminal justice system is only concerned with retribution and vengeance and he blames these for being the main obstacles to restorative justice.[15] At the very core of Consedine's thinking and arguments is the assumption that retribution and restorative justice are incompatible, and that the former is the antithesis of the latter.

Consedine's analysis is open to question in a number of ways. First, many victims of crime would disagree with his claim about the orientation of contemporary justice systems. The earlier quoted comment that "the law does everything to protect the criminal and forgets about his victims" is not an atypical impression among victims of crime. Second, legal professionals would similarly disagree with Consedine's claim. To repeat an earlier remark by Pincoffs, "defenders of the institution of punishment may be defending it precisely on the ground that it rules out vengeance-taking as a practice."[16] Third, Consedine, confuses punitiveness with retribution. But the former may be present in a criminal justice system purely as a result of instrumental reasoning in terms of deterrence and rehabilitation, and may have nothing to do with retribution in the repayment or just deserts sense. This point can be illustrated by the Young Offenders Act 1993 in South Australia, which provides exclusively instrumental rationales and guidelines for imposing punitive sanctions on young offenders. The overall aim and rationale of the Act is "to secure for youths who offend against the criminal law the care, correction and guidance necessary for their development into responsible and useful members of the community and the proper realization of their potential."[17] The more specific and most important purposes specified by the Act are:

(a) to make the young person aware of the consequences of breaking the law;
(b) to impose sanctions which are severe enough for purposes of deterrence;
(c) to ensure that the community is protected against juvenile wrongdoing.

These aims or rationales have nothing to do with retributivism in the repayment sense, or even with the principle of giving offenders their just deserts. They express an entirely consequentialist frame of thinking and it therefore confuses the discussion to call such legislation 'retributive'. The Act is not retributive, not even in part, unless retribution is loosely equated with any punitiveness, as is done to some extent by Consedine, but also by other writers,[18] including Wundersitz and Hetzel who specifically characterize the above Act as partly retributive in character.[19]

Put differently, insofar as Consedine and other critics of the so-called 'retributive' system really mean to say that the current criminal justice system is retributive in the sense that it is mostly interested in giving offenders their just deserts, they are mistaken. If anything, state-based justice systems generally have been strongly consequentialist in their orientation. This is an important point and has been convincingly argued by Newman. He points out that

the principle of retribution is incorrectly believed to be something awful that the state demands of the individuals in society. . . . [O]n the contrary, the role of the state in punishment has, by and large, required utilitarian rather than retributive justifications of punishment . . . and there is little doubt that it has always been the most dominant guiding principle of punishment in Western civilization. Much confusion over this point has arisen because very often the politicians, administrators, and students of criminal law have used the principle of retribution for utilitarian ends, so people (including academics) have come to think of retribution as 'evil' or 'oppressive' and utilitarianism as 'progressive' and 'humanitarian'.[20]

Newman, I believe, is right, and the instrumentalist trend in punishment justification is set to persist into the foreseeable future. In addition to the South Australian example just discussed, it is not unusual to hear arguments by lawyers that 'the sentence should reflect a *general deterrent.*'[21] The claim that contemporary criminal justice systems are retributive is similarly at odds with Doolan's plausible observation about discriminatory and harmful practices in pursuit of *rehabilitation*, rather than retribution and revenge.

> In New Zealand, Maori and Pacific Island youth are more fundamentally at risk of the more coercive, intrusive welfare dispositions . . . *in pursuit of rehabilitation,* than are their Caucasian counterparts.[22] (My emphasis.)

But perhaps the most telling example of instrumental reasoning being dominant in our courts is the earlier-mentioned case, *The Queen v. Clotworthy,* where the New Zealand Court of Appeal sent an offender to gaol against the wishes of the primary victim. After discussing the matter with the offender in a conference, the victim considered imprisonment useless and inappropriate. In return, the offender undertook to pay the victim's medical bills by remaining employed. The District Court approved the agreement and the matter was settled to everyone's satisfaction, except the Crown, who subsequently had the agreement overturned in the Court of Appeal. The following excerpt captures the Justices' reasons for their decision.

> We record that Mr Cowan [the victim] was present at the hearing. We gave him the opportunity to address us. He reiterated his previous stance, emphasizing his wish to obtain funds for the necessary cosmetic surgery and his view that imprisonment would achieve nothing either for Mr Clotworthy or for himself. We can understand Mr Cowan's stance. He is to be commended for having forgiven Mr Clotworthy and for the sympathetic way he has approached the matter. It must be said, however, that a wider dimension must come into the sentencing exercise than simply the position as between victim and offender. The public interest in consistency, integrity of the criminal justice system, and deterrence of others are factors of major importance.[23]

The instrumental nature of the reasoning behind this judgement is clear. There is no mention of the offender having to 'pay' for his wrongful action through a harsher punishment, or of the offender's 'just deserts' anywhere in the summary of arguments, or in the justification of the decision to impose a three-year custodial sentence. On the contrary, there is much weight given to consequentialist considerations in terms of the need to maintain sentencing consistency in the interests of the public and of the criminal justice system, and the deterrence of others from committing similar crimes. Interestingly, arguments that Mr Clotworthy was not in danger of re-offending and that he presented no risk to the public by staying out of gaol were accepted by the prosecution and by the Court. Notwithstanding, the Court concurred with the prosecution that "This was more than moderately serious offending, and the need to deter others for public safety reasons is too important."[24] In view of such exclusively consequentialist reasoning by sentencing judges, it is simply not credible to blame retribution for the ills of the court system. To be sure, there are many things wrong with the wisdom of the Justices in the above decision and I shall return to them shortly. Retribution, however, is not one of them.

Lastly, the fourth, and perhaps most serious point on which Consedine's analysis is flawed is the mistaken assumption that retribution and restoration are incompatible. As before, this is an assumption that most writers on restorative justice share with Consedine. But they are wrong. The need for retribution and for restoration, as well as for deterrence and rehabilitation, often coincide, and all these values, goals and ideals will be simultaneously served by any enlightened response to crime. While punitiveness need not always be resorted to, that victims have a right to retributive justice is fundamental. A clear acknowledgment of this right is the cornerstone of their social-psychological restoration, and of the restoration of social peace, especially where serious crime is concerned. Judge McElrea's position on this point provides a refreshing and welcome contrast to the views I am contesting here. In connection with conferencing rape cases, he makes the telling point that conference outcomes might still include imprisonment as part of a sentencing package. Punishment can still play a part in restorative justice without it being the dominating influence it is today.[25]

This point should be well taken, especially by advocates of restorative justice. It is vitally important because resolution of serious offences through ADR processes will never be an accepted practice, unless punitive outcomes are allowed to be part of agreements. It is mistaken to think that punitive elements of an agreement automatically undermine or weaken its restorative potential. Quite the contrary. Some appropriate level of punitiveness will often have to form part of agreements to be acceptable to the relevant parties in the first place. That wrongdoing deserves punishment is a fundamental aspect of our reality, even if that reality is in part socially constructed. Our liability to punishment is an ineliminable part of what defines us as mature and responsible members of the moral community. As a result, in many cases of serious victimisation, no amount of therapy, or indeed conference discussion, may replace a victim's and the community's need to know that wrongdoing is punished, that justice, including justice in the retributive sense, is done. This unambiguously comes through in Umbreit's surveys of crime victims.

> Without question, nearly all citizens at large and crime victims specifically want criminals to be held accountable through some form of punishment. . . . Oftentimes, the need for punishment was expressed in terms of 'accountability'. 'Justice to me requires some punishment.' 'It doesn't have to be severe but has to be something that causes them to know they did something wrong and they have to pay for that.'[26]

What needs to happen, therefore, is that any punitive response to wrongdoing be complemented by genuine caring, acceptance, and reintegration of the person, as opposed to rejecting or crushing them. In this way, far from defeating restoration, a well-pitched punitive measure will form part of, and will enhance restoration for everybody involved. By failing to recognize and appreciate this point, advocates of restorative justice often hinder their own cause. But they are also creating confusion. Especially because of the mistaken belief that retribution and restoration are incompatible, Consedine and other authors, for example, tend to give severely distorted interpretations of traditional revenge practices of indigenous people. These misinterpretations are what I have earlier referred to as paradigm resistance by denial and conceptual gerrymandering—something that can take place, as in this case, in the face of overwhelming evidence to the contrary. Such gerrymandering is evident, for instance, in Wundersitz and Hetzel who describe and identify as "appropriate reparation by the 'offender'" the Australian Aboriginal practice of "pay-back" which, as they admit, "could include some physical 'reprisal' such as ritual spearing."[27] Consedine goes even further when he explicitly denies the retributive nature of payback in Aboriginal Australia.

> In all cases we have outlined, while there is so much verbal emphasis on revenge, it is plausible to infer that underlying this is a general aim of achieving order and balance. An injury is done, the status quo is upset, retaliation provides a means by which this may be restored. . . . [This] is essentially a restorative process, not a retributive one.[28]

These are confused and misleading interpretations of what, clearly, are retributive practices. The process of payback, is indeed highly ritualized and is closely monitored and controlled by the community. It is important, however, that the word 'ritual' does not mislead the reader. Such 'ritual spearing' signifies real spearing, and sometimes multiple spearing of the wrongdoer, often resulting in very serious injuries and sometimes death.

More to the point, while such payback is restorative in the sense that it restores social peace between the conflicting parties and between the wrongdoer and the rest of their community, it is neither credible, nor helpful to describe it as "reparation by the 'offender'," or worse, to assert that it is not retributive. The Aboriginal Australians themselves call it 'pay-back' and their justification for it is deontological, rather than instrumental in the way Consedine's reinterpretation suggests. Their customary laws, which they refer to as 'The Law', require that wrongs *must* be punished through payback. This is a sacred duty and it is accepted and insisted on by all members of the community, wrongdoers and victims included, as being right on account of The Law. And, while it is true that the restoration of social order and social peace are unthinkable without fulfilling the requirements of The Law in terms of payback, the inevitable restorative function of payback is no ground for a redescription of its basic character as if it was a consequentialist practice.

The basic character of an act of punishment, as I have argued in Chapter 7, is best determined by the reasons and motives behind it. The fact that an essentially retributive act can also serve a multitude of other functions, such as restoration, correction, and deterrence, only shows that its basic retributive character is compatible with other important instrumental and functionalist reasons, goals, and values, which, at least in principle, all forms of punishment are capable of serving simultaneously. If this is right, then what Consedine is describing is restoration through proportional and controlled personal retribution, restoration through what all involved accept as fair and just revenge. It is payback by means of which the wronged party gets even with the perpetrator.

The same distorting effects come through where Consedine considers pre-English law in Ireland. While he acknowledges that in cases where the prescribed compensation for murder "could not be paid or there were special circumstances, the family of the victim could kill an offender," he proceeds to assert that "Retaliation and retribution based on vengeance were not part of that philosophy."[29] This cannot be right. In the absence of commensurate compensation, retaliation by way of revenge was the old Irish way to restore balance. It was the only way of getting even, the only way to even the score with the wrongdoer. While killing the offender in retaliation may not have been obligatory, it is surely not credible to assert that the right of the victim to kill the offender was not a right to retribution and revenge.

Again, by interpreting the New Zealand Maori practice of *utu* as "compensation and satisfaction," Consedine seriously underdescribes and misrepresents the true retributive nature of *utu* as negative repayment for insults and other wrongs.[30] '*Utu*' can mean positive reciprocity, as when gifts and favors are returned in kind, but it is most commonly used in the negative repayment sense and is most frequently translated as 'revenge.' Even if we grant that some wrongs might have been settled through compensation rather than retaliation, translating 'utu' as compensation and satisfaction is most misleading. This point was underscored to me in a colorful way by a recent incident in New Zealand. I was looking for a car, and a well-travelled and very articulate Maori gentlemen in his seventies kindly brought around his daughter's car to show me. I did not buy the car, but we talked and talked for the next two hours. When he found out that I was writing a book in defense of *utu* as a moral practice, his eyes lit up with recognition, and with a wide, mischievous grin on his face he lifted a clenched fist in front of him, shook it gently and chuckled with obvious relish in his voice as he repeated the words: "Pay-back time! Pay-back time!" There was no mistaking the kind of compensation and satisfaction he had in mind in thinking about *utu*.

Consedine does say, however, that "muru, a formalized concept of *retributive* compensation, was a feature central to Maori . . . law."[31] Even so, and leaving aside what might be meant by 'retributive compensation', it is puzzling why Consedine should say that such a retributive feature was "alien to English law,"[32] especially since he condemns all justice systems based on English law precisely because, in his view, they are "retributive" in character.

To sum up this section, analyses and arguments such as those put forward by Wundersitz, Hetzel, Consedine, and other authors criticizing the criminal justice system for being 'retributive' are conceptually confused and lacking in rigour. It would be unduly tedious to try to straighten out every conceptual knot created by describing as 'retribution' and 'retributive' any legislation, practice, or punitive court decision, without considering or recognizing the essentially instrumental nature of the policies which underpin them, and without considering the reasons given by sentencing judges for their decisions. Such sloppy critiques of the justice system are little more than populist retribution-bashing—the appeal of which is rooted more in the cultural and religious myths and dogmas of Western civilization than reason. While the dissatisfaction shown with the criminal justice system by Consedine and other advocates of reform is fully understandable, they miss the mark in blaming retribution for every unenlightened or punitive court decision, completely disregarding the reasons behind those decisions, and the legislation underpinning them, which, on closer examination, are replete with instrumental justifications

Changing Paradigms in Criminal Justice: The Primacy of Empowerment

As the reasoning by the Judges in the Clotworthy case illustrates, the difficulty with the traditional criminal court system is not retribution. Focusing on, and blaming retribution is a distraction which obscures the real source of the problems that Consedine and other advocates of reform want to see addressed through restorative justice initiatives. I suggest that their quarrel should not be with retribution at all, but with the disempowerment inherent in the judicial status quo, a status quo which disempowers the very people who have the most to lose and gain by any decisions made, the very people who stand the best chance of making a positive difference in terms of addressing both the causes and the consequences of criminal wrongdoing. It is on this point, it seems to me, that the Judges' reasoning in the Clotworthy case is flawed. They *presumed* to know better than the offender and the victim as to how their dispute would be best resolved. Because of this presumption, and because they approached the matter with their own set of priorities—priorities which were priorities only to them and to the Solicitor-General, it seems to me—they discounted and overruled the primary stakeholders' agreement, which, in the circumstances, would have been maximally restorative to all involved. The problem with this judgment is not retribution, but the disempowerment of the principal stakeholders by the Court, which chose to judge the case with its own set of priorities based on its own established tradition—a tradition which is evidently out of touch with what is important for the people at the receiving end of their decisions.

Especially since there was no trace of retributive reasoning in the Judges' justification, the Clotworthy case illustrates just how mistaken it is to blame retribution for the ills of a state-controlled judicial system which has been obsessively consequentialist in its aims and ideals. The aims, values, and ideals of state-based criminal justice systems of the Western world, I suggest, have been predominantly in terms of crime control, the protection of people's rights, lives, and property, the rehabilitation and correction of offenders, and general deterrence, rather than in terms of giving wrongdoers their just deserts, or paying them back what they have merited. This is as much true today as it was half a century ago when no scholarly journal in England would publish C.S. Lewis's essay in defense of retributivism as the only morally acceptable theory of punishment justification.[33] On this point, I concur with Braithwaite, Pettit, and Newman:

> Until the 1970s retributivism—the idea that criminals should be punished because they deserve it—was something of a dead letter in criminology; there were a few scholars in jurisprudence and philosophy who continued to dabble with retributive theories but they did so in ways that had little impact on public policy. During and since the Victorian era retributivism had become increasingly disreputable, probably unfairly, as an unscientific indulgence of emotions of revenge.[34]

> Historically, the state turned out to have very definite utilitarian purposes in mind as far as punishment was concerned, so the pure reciprocity of criminal punishment has never really been given a chance.[35]

What must be targeted, therefore, is the systematic, institutionalized disempowerment of the principal parties by a legal profession that has positioned itself at the centre of the criminal justice process to the exclusion of the principal protagonists in the dispute, who have the most to gain or lose from any decisions made. Framing the issues and problems as if our critical choices were to be made between restoration and retribution is implausible, it lacks conceptual clarity and rigor, and it distracts us from the real issues. These are best understood and addressed when the critical choices are seen in terms of empowerment versus disempowerment of the principal stakeholders in a criminal justice dispute.[36] This is another way of saying that, in order to get a proper understanding of the newly emerging phenomenon of restorative justice in relation to the traditional criminal justice systems, a paradigm shift is needed in the way we understand and frame the problem. That shift must be from an anti-revenge and anti-retribution paradigm to an empowerment paradigm of justice with a legitimate place for revenge.

Such a shift is evident in the thinking of Judge McElrea who not only recognizes that punishment has a place in restorative justice but places the emphasis where it needs to be placed as a matter of priority.

> Thus we come at once to the heart of restorative justice, which I define as involving three radical changes to the mainstream western model of justice:
>
>   1) The transfer of power (principally the courts' power) from the State to the community;
>
>   2) The use of FGC [Family Group Conferences] or some other mechanism to produce a *negotiated* community response; and
>
>   3) The involvement of victims as key participants, thereby enabling a healing process to occur.[37]

The primary focus has to be on questions of empowerment and disempowerment. Without such a shift in conceptualizing and framing the new phenomenon of restorative justice, the potential of the concept will not be fully realized in practice, and there is every danger of its being hijacked and subverted by interests that fear the loss of authority and control over the criminal justice process, and indeed the criminal justice industry, if key decision making powers are given, as Judge McElrea suggests, to victims, offenders, and their respective communities of support and care. Blaming the ills of the criminal justice system on retribution and revenge creates ambiguity and confusion. It also misses the mark in a major way, especially when it is not clear just what may be meant by retribution in such contexts.

Blaming retribution, and even punitiveness, is a red herring, a distraction, and it runs the risk of losing us the single most important target of reform, the transfer of power, essentially the state's power which is currently invested in the courts and the legal profession, to the primary protagonists in any criminal justice dispute, namely the offender, the victim, and their respective families and immediate communities of support and care. Without such transfer of power, the potential benefits of restorative justice for individuals and communities affected by crime cannot be realized. In terms of actual reform, the difference in the end can be like the difference between the rebuilding of an ailing ship and the rearrangement of its deck chairs.

A clear, philosophically sound definition of our target is vitally important. If we don't know where we are going, we may more easily lose our way. Such target definition is impossible from within an anti-revenge and anti-retribution paradigm, as this is riddled with myths and misconceptions, and it shows increasingly serious signs of conceptual deterioration. This is evidenced by the false dichotomy it creates between retribution and restoration, and by other fantastic assertions, the most striking of which is that the traditional revenge practices of indigenous people had little to do with revenge and retribution, while at the same time blaming Western justice systems for being interested mostly in retribution and revenge, when in fact these have done just about everything in their power to eliminate revenge-taking as a form of justice.

By contrast, an empowerment paradigm of justice has every potential to keep the focus of reform sharply on what ultimately is important in any response to criminal wrongdoing. This is the achievement of closure and satisfaction for the principal protagonists in the knowledge that justice has been done. The best way to do this is to empower them and their respective communities of support to settle their dispute to their satisfaction. This is as much true of empowerment in the context of a modified court system as it is in ADR approaches. There are good reasons to believe that such empowerment will also prove to be effective in terms of preventing crime, something in which the wider community has a legitimate, but by no means overriding, interest. That personal retribution may form part of such processes and settlements is acceptable as long as such retribution or instrumental punitive measures are within limits allowed by the moral community's values and the law. And, since this condition can be met perfectly well by appropriate institutionalisation, there is no excuse for disempowering and marginalising the key stakeholders in the resolution of their dispute.

Key Points of Chapters 8–10

I will now review and summarize the main ideas of the last three chapters. The moral permissibility of institutionalized revenge is justified by reference to two basic factors. One is the retributive liability borne by wrongdoers for their wrongful actions. The other is the importance of victim justice and

victim restoration, which require the involvement and substantial empowerment of victims in the processes of the criminal justice system. These two
factors were argued in Chapters 8 and 9, respectively. Chapter 10 considered the question of paradigm change in criminal justice. There are two
ways in which the established anti-revenge paradigm resists the idea of institutionalized revenge. These are overt resistance, including resistance at the
level of practice, and resistance by denial and distorted reinterpretation.

Overt resistance sees a rejection of substantial victim involvement and
empowerment on the practical level as a way of blocking the very possibility
of institutionally sanctioning, or even condoning, revenge. But, as maintained in Chapter 9, in view of weighty arguments for greater victim
involvement and empowerment, the continued marginalization and disempowerment of victims is indefensible. For while substantial victim empowerment in the processes of the justice system do indeed open up the real possibility of institutionalized revenge, the supposed evils and dangers of
revenge are more fictional than real. In addition to the debunking of the
many myths and misconceptions of revenge in the Western world, even the
briefest consideration of the practicalities involved reveals that the dangers
involved in raw, unregulated revenge are no longer present in its institutionalized variant. For one thing, the image of unreasonable, vengeful victims
who would want to see injustices being perpetrated on their wrongdoers is a
myth, and it has been consistently exposed as such by research. Preoccupation with revenge and retribution is also a distraction, a red herring. For,
regardless of whether in a victim's mind retributive considerations play a
role or not, victim empowerment under the two models described in Chapter 9 would not jeopardize any of the advantages of a good institutionalized
system. One of the primary functions of institutionalisation would be to
provide appropriate safeguards, so that important principles and goals, such
as ensuring justice to offenders and the need to prevent conflict escalation,
are not endangered as a result of such empowering victim participation.

By comparison to overt resistance, the resistance displayed through
denial and conceptual gerrymandering may seem at first harmless. However, because such resistance involves false categorizations and arbitrary shifting of the boundaries of our key punishment concepts, a great deal of additional confusion is generated in an already difficult area where clarity of
thinking is sorely needed. This confusion is most evident where the traditional revenge practices of indigenous people are redescribed in ways that
hide and obfuscate their retributive character, as well as outright assertions
that those revenge practices in fact were not revenge practices after all. Such
claims border on the absurd. Coupled with the equally misguided blaming
of retribution for the ills of an unsatisfactory criminal justice system, which,
on closer analysis, turns out to have been driven mostly by instrumental reasoning and considerations and by a desire to eliminate revenge taking altogether, makes the position of some advocates of restorative justice on these

matters doubly distorted. Under the opposing pressures of wanting to renounce everything that has to do with retribution and revenge while at the same time also wishing to embrace restorative justice philosophy which has its origins in revenge-based traditional approaches to settling disputes and restoring social peace, restorative justice advocates working within an anti-revenge paradigm of justice are tying themselves into a conceptual Gordian knot.

There are dangers in confusion, the most serious one in this instance being that the restorative justice initiatives that have mushroomed in the past decade throughout the Western world will not reach their full potential in criminal justice. Confusion is the ideal state for the subversion and hijacking of the restorative justice vision by powerful interest groups that would prefer to see control and decision making powers being retained in the hands of professionals, instead of handing them over to the primary stakeholders in criminal disputes who have the most to lose and gain from the relevant criminal justice processes and the outcomes generated by criminal justice proceedings.

To start seeing our way clear of the confusion and also to keep the opponents of positive reform honest, we require a paradigm shift in the way that we think about criminal justice in general, and the emergence of restorative justice initiatives in particular. The shift must be from an anti-revenge and anti-retribution paradigm, to an empowerment paradigm of justice. At the highest level of generality, this must start with a recognition of two basic truths. One is that, far from being incompatible, the claims of just retribution and the need for restoration often coincide. They especially coincide where personal retribution is concerned, as recognition of a victim's right to retributive justice is part of their substantial empowerment, which, in turn is a fundamental precondition of their social-psychological restoration. How far they exercise their right to such justice within limits allowed by law is entirely up to them, as that is their prerogative as an essential constituent of their empowerment. The second basic truth is that not all punitiveness is retribution and, therefore, the ills of the current justice system may not lie with retribution at all. Especially in light of the emerging conflict between restorative justice initiatives and the traditional approach prevalent in our courts, as can be seen in the Clotworthy case, it is clear that the most serious problems of court-based criminal justice systems are due to the inherent disempowerment by professionals of the primary stakeholders in the conflict, rather than a supposed preoccupation with retribution for which there is little evidence. Therefore, the terms of the debate for meaningful reform must be set around the question of appropriate forms and degrees of legal empowerment by the justice system of the principal protagonists and their respective communities.

To empower or not to empower the principal protagonists in a criminal justice dispute—that is the question. The rest is distraction. As to answering that all-important question, in light of the reasons discussed in this book it would be hard not to concur with Sir Ludovic Kennedy that justice is too important to be left to the legal profession alone. It properly belongs to the people who have the highest stakes in it: the victim, the offender, and their respective communities of influence and care.

Afterword

Implications for Policy and Practice

The primary focus of reform and criminal justice policy in the new millennium ought to be the empowerment of the principal stakeholders in a criminal justice dispute. These are the victim, the offender, and their respective communities of concern and care. It is these people who are most affected by criminal wrongdoing and the subsequent handling and resolution of their case. These are the people who have the most to lose and gain by the relevant criminal justice processes and their outcomes, and this fact makes them the principal stakeholders in the dispute. Their interest, in terms of knowing that justice is done, is high and therefore their views, wishes, and priorities in terms of how their dispute should be resolved must take precedence over the views and priorities of third parties, such as legal professionals and other agents of the state.

Promotion of a feeling of satisfaction with justice in the principal stakeholders is best achieved through such empowerment so that they can deal with the causes and consequences of the criminal wrongdoing in question to their satisfaction, in a way that is right for them. While the state should ensure that there are both formal and informal processes of dispute resolution available for the resolution of criminal justice disputes in culturally appropriate ways, professionals and agents of the state ought not to take over the parties' dispute. Their stake in justice is secondary and therefore their proper role is a supportive one and must be confined to the smooth running of the dispute resolution processes in question, ensuring that all parties to the dispute act within the law, that everybody's rights and responsibilities are properly observed, and that agreements between the parties are not obviously harmful to the public good.

The use of ADR (alternative dispute resolution) processes in the resolution of criminal justice disputes by the principal stakeholders should be encouraged regardless of the degree of seriousness of the crime or the age of the offender. However, face to face discussions among the principal protagonists must be conducted by highly skilled and appropriately trained facilitators. Control and administration of such ADR programs should be placed in the hands of community groups, rather than centralized state bureaucracies, as this will maximise a program's flexibility to the socio-cultural and other environmental characteristics of the local community. The participation of the principal protagonists' respective communities (family members and trusted friends, colleagues, teachers, coaches, and so forth) is important, especially in the more serious offence categories. It is the community of such supporters that is the best insurance that the voice of reason prevails in all matters and that stable and workable resolutions are reached. The content and outcome of such facilitated meetings must not be determined by secondary stakeholders, such as the facilitator, social workers, legal advocates, and the police, as that would disempower the principal parties in dispute and their satisfaction with justice would be significantly less likely to be served.

Criticisms of retribution and punitiveness in general alleging that these are inappropriate responses to criminal wrongdoing are conceptually confused and are largely beside the point. Punitive responses to wrongdoing are often essential and cannot be eliminated or ruled out. Therefore, the full range of sanctions allowable by law must be made available to the community of participants in ADR forums. Without this, their empowerment is incomplete and their ability to resolve the matter to everybody's satisfaction is limited.

Criminal justice disputes that are unresolvable by ADR processes can be dealt with through a modified court process. Criminal offences are, principally, wrongs done to specific people, the victim of the crime, not the letter of the law, the Queen, or even the people and the state. Therefore, the focus of the court process must be the victim and the wrong that was done to them. This should be reflected in a real transfer of the state's power to the victim, which implies two major changes to the current system. First, the victim must be given qualified legal representation by changing the role of the public prosecutor from being a representative of the state to being the victim's advocate. Second, the sentencing powers of judges must be shared with, and possibly transferred to, the victim; and offenders must be given the opportunity even in the sentencing stage to negotiate. As in ADR processes, the proper function of the professionals in a modified court process is to assure the smooth running of the dispute resolution process, ensuring that all parties act within the law, that everybody's rights and responsibilities are observed, that sentences are within limits set by law, and that they do not obviously undermine the public good.

While such substantial empowerment of victims does open the possibility for personal retribution under both types of processes of dispute resolution, the fear of vengeful victims is a myth, as is the belief that revenge is somehow evil and barbaric, something that must be rejected by civilized society. Let each and every victim of a crime decide those fundamental philosophical and spiritual questions for themselves. Our half-baked and half-believed cultural myths and dogmas are poor reasons for allowing the continued marginalization and disempowerment of victims of crime. If, and since, civil society has failed to protect them from being wronged and hurt, it is civil society's foremost obligation to ensure that they get every opportunity to satisfy themselves that things are put right and that justice is done. Most importantly, appropriate institutionalized frameworks, whereby victims' compliance with community values and the law are aided and monitored by communities of participants and legal experts, are sufficient to ensure that such victim empowerment does not result in an overstepping of the acceptable boundaries set by morality and law, resulting in an injustice to the offender. But once the requisite safeguards are in place, the rest is the prerogative of the victim, in negotiation with the offender. As with judges under the traditional court system, unless they demonstrably display unreasonable degrees of leniency or harshness, a victim's decision must be final.

Notes

1. Freud's quotation of Heine in Freud 1961, p. 57.
2. Elizabeth Bowen, "Making Arrangements" (In *Early Stories*, 1951).
3. Alexandre Dumas, *The Count of Monte Cristo*. Translated by Robin Buss. (Penguin, 1996 [1844–45]), p. 1024.

Introduction: Empowering the Victim

1. Kant 1965, p. 100.
2. Judicial System a Joke: Detective. *The Canberra Times* (5 July 1995), p. 5.
3. Braithwaite 1993, pp. 33, 34.
4. The inquiry system is commonly referred to as the 'inquisitorial' system. This latter expression has unfortunate connotations. The expression I use is accurate and more appropriate.
5. Kennedy 1989, p. 322.
6. Whitton 1994.
7. Braithwaite 1993, p. 37.
8. Severin 1995.
9. R. Duce, Man Who Shot Son's Killer Is Cleared: Crowd Cheers Cleared Father on Way to Start a New Life. *The Times* (23 May 1992), pp. 1, 2. See also R. Duce, Father Says He Was Almost Insane as He Shot Killer. *The Times* (21 May 1992), p. 3. For a critical and in my view unconvincing evaluation of the jury's decision, see J. Daley, Blinded by Emotion. *The Times* (26 May 1992), p. 12.

1: Paradigms of Justice

1. On hearing of Riccio's death, 9 March 1566.
2. Bacon 1985, p. 72.
3. Spencer 1966, p. 363.
4. Boehm 1984, p. 89.
5. See, for example, Spencer 1966, p. 362.
6. The laws regulating revenge in traditional China provide us with a very interesting alternative to the outright and complete suppression of it by contemporary criminal justice systems in the West. Traditional Chinese laws recognized the moral and legal legitimacy of just revenge under clearly defined conditions and the protection of the law was extended to those who killed in revenge within the guidelines allowed by law (Dalby 1981).
7. Nozick 1981, p. 366.
8. Glover 1970, p. 145.
9. Lewis 1957, p. 109.
10. Lewis 1957, p. 82.

11. Nietzsche 1993, p. 122 (*Thus Spake Zarathustra*, Chapter 29: 'The Tarantulas'). Nietzsche mostly uses the word 'revenge' to indicate a psychological state of resentfulness which is born of envy and jealousy but which takes on the cloak of goodness through self-deception, rather than to mean acts of revenge as we commonly do. He talks with disdain only about people who self-deceptively regard themselves to be good on account of not retaliating when maltreated by others, but who, at the same time, deceive themselves about the impotent resentment they feel and are too cowardly to express openly. They decide instead to hide it even from themselves by attributing their lack of action to some imagined virtue, such as humility or long-suffering. By contrast, in some places he talks disparagingly of the doglike people who allow themselves to be maltreated and who are too afraid to revenge themselves. His examples include the person "who does not outrage, who harms nobody, who does not attack, who does not requite, who leaves revenge to God" (Nietzsche 1989, p. 46). In such passages, where he talks of individual acts of revenge, rather than the destructive and contorted psychological state of *ressentiment* and the actions which spring from it, his attitude to revenge seems to be more accepting, if not approving.

12. Wallace 1995, p. 369.
13. *The Merchant of Venice*, Act 4, Scene 1, Line 180.
14. Solomon 1990, p. 294.
15. Severin 1995, p. 17.
16. Severin 1995, p. 17.
17. Severin 1995, pp. 16–17.
18. See an extensive discussion of this point in Chapter 10 below.
19. Throughout this book I occasionally employ the plural form to indicate the singular of either gender: 'they' for 'he or she', 'their' for 'his or her', and so on. Though most English speakers adopt this construction from time to time in ordinary speech, its use in written work is still controversial. But no doubt there are other aspects of this book which will prove even more controversial.

2: Pious Myths about Revenge

1. Solomon 1990, p. 293.
2. Nozick 1981, p. 367.
3. Glover 1970, p. 145.
4. Lewis 1957, p. 109.
5. Lewis 1957, p. 82.
6. Lewis 1957, p. 82.
7. The quotation is from *Leviathan*, Pt. I, Chapter 6.
8. Lewis 1957, p. 82.
9. Lewis 1949, p. 10.
10. Lewis 1949, p. 10.
11. Lewis 1957, pp. 81–82.
12. Man Stabbed Over Rape, Court Told. *The Canberra Times* (29 May 1991), p. 4.
13. Carlyle, quoted in Rashdall 1924, p. 304.

14. Lewis 1957, p. 81.
15. Lewis 1957, pp. 81–82.
16. Lewis 1957, p. 82.
17. Lewis 1949.
18. Hedenius 1973, p. 13. The concept of honorification will be discussed in more detail with regard to punishment further below.
19. Wallace 1995, pp. 369–370.
20. Glover 1970, p. 145.
21. Wallace distinguishes between vindictive and non-vindictive revenge. The latter, according to him, consists merely in finding satisfaction in evening the scores with someone, such as when one wins a squash game after losing one. While I find it implausible to regard such competitively, as opposed to morally, grounded acts of payback to be revenge, except in a metaphorical or derived sense, I merely wish to point out that Wallace uses 'vindictive' and 'malicious' to mean about the same thing as 'hurtful' or 'harmful,' and that he accepts that such cases of revenge may, on occasions, be justifiable (Wallace 1995, pp. 372–73).
22. Nozick 1981, p. 367.
23. As John Braithwaite pointed out to me, the suggestion in question should also "cause us to be puzzled about how as a species we have survived this long."
24. Milgram 1974.
25. Milgram 1974, p. 167.
26. Milgram 1974, p. 167.
27. Milgram 1974, p. 107.
28. Milgram 1974, p. 72.
29. Milgram 1974, p. 92.
30. Milgram 1974, p. 97.
31. Milgram 1974, pp. 97–98.
32. Milgram 1974, p. 104.
33. Kahn 1984, p. 186 (Figure 7.3).
34. Kahn 1984, p. 170 (Table A).
35. Nozick 1981, p. 367.
36. This was pointed out to me by Bob Goodin.

3: Punishment and Revenge

1. Solomon 1990, p. 292.
2. Newman 1978, p. 291.
3. Hobbes 1962, Part 2; Rawls 1955.
4. Mill 1962, p. 307; Kleinig 1973, p. 39.
5. Hobbes 1962, pp. 277–79.
6. Hobbes 1962, p. 278.
7. Kleinig 1973, pp. 19–20.
8. The following argument by Morris also confirms these criticisms: "Criminal punishment will normally be authorized and carried out by the state, though this need not be the case; to make it part of the proper characterization of the notion would be to beg the question against anarchists" (Morris 1991, p. 55).

9. Hedenius 1973, p. 13.

10. This dubious technique of conceptual misappropriation is recognisably similar to the appropriation and reservation of such expressions as 'justice' and 'doing justice' by judicial systems which try to honorify all their decisions and activities with such positive labels—including decisions and activities which are blatantly wrong and unjust in a more neutral, ordinary sense of the word.

11. Quinton 1954, p. 140.

12. Hart 1968, p. 6.

13. Kleinig 1973, p. 13. For expressions of similar views, see Hart 1968; Armstrong 1969.

14. Hedenius 1973, pp. 28–29.

15. Kleinig 1973, p. 39.

16. Mill 1962, p. 307.

17. Kleinig 1973, p. 39.

18. Butler 1896, *Upon Resentment* (Sermon VIII), p. 96.

19. Rashdall 1924, p. 304.

20. Richards 1971, p. 253; Gaus 1990, pp. 284–86.

21. Note that this view can accommodate even Nietzsche's claim that slave morality, such as Christian morality, originated with the *ressentiment* of the herd—the frustrated and impotent feelings of envy, jealousy, resentment, and rancour generated in the ugly, the weak, the untalented, and the poor towards the beautiful, the strong, the talented and the well off. For, in so far as they are part of *ressentiment*, feelings of resentment can be attributed to the social injustices and the discrimination to which common people felt exposed at the hands of the master class or the aristocracy. (See 'On the Genealogy of Morals' in Nietzsche 1989.)

22. Murphy and Hampton 1988, p. 16.

23. Murphy and Hampton 1988, p. 18.

24. Adam Smith, as quoted in Solomon 1990, p 293.

25. Butler 1896, *Upon Resentment* (Sermon VIII), p. 96.

26. For an interesting and detailed account of such a cognitivist account of the retributive emotions, see Mackïe 1985.

27. Murphy and Hampton 1988, p. 16.

28. Hampton in Murphy and Hampton 1988, p. 55.

29. Murphy and Hampton 1988, p. 16.

30. Carlyle quoted in Rashdall 1924, p. 304.

31. Bacon 1985, p. 72.

32. Russell 1961, p. 561.

33. Marongiu and Newman 1987, p. 9.

34. Solomon 1990, pp. 292–93.

35. Jacoby 1983, pp. 12–13.

36. Oldenquist 1986, p. 76.

37. Solomon 1990, pp. 292–93.

4: Rationality and Revenge

1. Newman 1978, p. 290.

2. Accordingly, the basic sense embodied in this reportive definition should be

taken into account in assessing the proper scope and merit of any theory of rational choice attempting to give a more detailed account of what this attribute called 'rationality' is. Such a theory can be criticised for being too narrow, if it fails to explain actions which are rational in this pre-theoretical, but plausible and intuitively correct, sense. It can be similarly criticised for being too wide, if it deems rational those actions which are not rational in this pre-theoretical and intuitively correct sense. But a wider theory of rational *behavior* may have less stringent conditions of rationality than would a theory of direct rational choice. The details and significance of the differences between direct rationality in rational choice actions and indirect rationality in rational behaviour have been discussed elsewhere (Barton 1996).

3. Singer 1993, p. 316.

4. Black 1982, p. 162.

5. Sen 1977, p. 332.

6. Johansen 1987, p. 664.

7. Elster 1990, p. 863.

8. Elster's claims and arguments will be considered in detail in Chapter 5.

9. Hare 1981.

10. Elster 1990, p. 862.

11. Elster 1990, p. 863.

12. For detailed refutations of Elster's arguments, see Barton 1996; Hamlin 1991.

13. For the technically minded, this example shows the possibility of rational revege in terms of material interests alone in a one-shot game of a prisoner's dilemma situation. The rationality of revenge in prisoner's dilemma situations is fully discussed in Barton 1996.

14. Spencer 1966, p. 362.

15. Rashdall 1924, p. 304.

16. Boehm 1984, pp. 88, 183.

17. A defence of honour as a moral value is undertaken further below, while an explanation and defence of moral retributivism is provided in Chapter 8.

18. These will be discussed in more detail in Chapter 9.

19. See, for example, Dickie 1989; Kennedy 1989; Whitton 1994.

20. Elster 1990, pp. 883–84.

21. Berger 1984, pp. 153, 154.

22. Ayers 1984, p. 20.

5: Retribution and Justice

1. Newman 1978, p. 287.

2. Cottingham 1979, p. 238.

3. Wolgast 1987, pp. 147ff; Cottingham 1979, pp. 238–39.

4. The fact that the imagery of the repayment metaphor runs in the other direction as well, in that the wrongdoer is also said to pay with suffering for the wrong committed, does not undermine this way of understanding what retributive punishment is.

5. Cottingham 1979, p. 245.

6. For example, Nozick 1981, p. 36; Braithwaite and Pettit 1990, p. 2.

7. A more provocative example is the notion of eternal suffering in hell as punishment for a brief, sinful life.

8. The views of these authors will be discussed in detail further below.

9. Braithwaite and Pettit 1990.

10. Mackie 1985, p. 207.

11. Hart 1968, p. 12.

12. Walker 1980, p. 26.

13. Golding 1975, p. 85.

14. Quinton 1954, p. 136.

15. Braithwaite and Pettit 1990, p. 35.

16. Mackie 1985, p. 207.

17. Walker 1980, p. 26.

18. Newman 1978, p. 309 n.21.

19. Walker 1980, p. 26.

20. Braithwaite and Pettit 1990, p. 33.

21. While Armstrong refers to Lewis's article only in other contexts, in my opinion it was C.S. Lewis who first made the crucial point at the heart of the quoted passage. Lewis writes: "The Humanitarian theory removes from Punishment the concept of Desert. But the concept of Desert is the only connecting link between punishment and justice. It is only as deserved or undeserved that a sentence can be just or unjust. . . . There is no sense in talking about a 'just deterrent' or a 'just cure'" (Lewis 1949, p. 6).

22. Armstrong 1969, p. 155.

23. It may be of interest to scholars to examine the possibility of grounding these principles in some kind of notion of desert. For, if there is an initial ring of plausibility to the claim in question, I suggest that this is largely due to the idea that the principles of justice are somehow desert-based. Lewis and Armstrong make a strong appeal to this idea when they claim that *only as a punishment/sentence is deserved or undeserved can it be just or unjust.*

While non-desert-based groundings of the principles of justice render the Lewis-Armstrong claim ultimately untenable, their argument nevertheless retains an appearance of plausibility for two reasons. One is that appealing to a notion of desert is a familiar and simple way of grounding the principles in question. The second reason is that this appeal to desert is easily confused with the concept of *negative* desert which is frequently used to justify the thesis of moral retributivism. The distinction between the two kinds of desert is subtle, but significant. Insofar as the notion of desert is appealed to by an account of moral retributivism as a justificatory reason for imposing punishment, the appeal is to a *negative* notion of desert. But, while this notion may be used to justify imposing punishment on the guilty, it is hard to see how it could be taken to forbid the punishment of the innocent. *The claim that the guilty should be punished because they deserve it does not entail that, therefore, the innocent should not be punished because they do not deserve it.* For there may be good reasons for imposing punishment on people other than their negative deserts. Denying this would be implausible. Indeed, consequentialists in general would consider people's negative deserts to be the least of the reasons justifying punishment.

If this is right, then desert claims embodied in the principles of justice, such as the claim that the innocent should not be punished because they do not deserve to be punished, must be grounded in a somewhat different notion of desert from that of the justificatory negative desert claim of moral retributivism. This notion, I suggest, is a *positive* notion of desert, for the reasoning here is no longer about what the guilty deserve in a negative way, but rather about what the innocent and the guilty may be said to deserve in a more positive way in matters of punishment: If someone has been law-abiding in the sense that they have not broken the law, they deserve not to be framed or punished. If someone is guilty, then they ought not to be over-punished, either as a way to serve the interests of utility (deterrence), or as a way to impose on them the negative deserts of others.

But, even though the grounding of the principles of justice in a notion of positive desert is possible, it is only in a very old fashioned sense of *bestowing* that this sense of 'desert' may still be called 'retributive'—a sense akin to the one used in the phrase "never did a charitable act go away without the retribution of a blessing" (a seventeenth-century example quoted from the OED by Cottingham in his 1979, p. 239). There may be other ways, of course, to link the principles of justice to the notion of desert. It may be possible, for example, to construe retribution in such a way that both its justification and the limiting principles of justice issue from a common, more basic principle, such as the principle that *Happiness and unhappiness should be proportioned to virtue and vice (or right and wrong, or good and bad conduct), respectively.* While such appeals to a cosmic sense of fairness and justice may be workable, and even plausible, the pertinent point remains: non-desert-based groundings of the principles of justice render ultimately untenable the second interpretation of the Lewis-Armstrong claim that only as a punishment/sentence is deserved or undeserved can it be just or unjust.

24. Mackie 1985, p. 208.

25. Cottingham 1979, p. 241.

26. Braithwaite and Pettit 1990, p. 207.

27. Walker 1991, pp. 92–95. Walker develops this idea only in relation to the principle that the innocent should not be punished.

28. Arguably, the ultimate viability of the Rawlsian approach may be suspect. Michael Tooley suggested to me that it might be reasonable to expect that B-type societies would have a lower crime rate than would A-type societies, which could make rational choice in this instance much harder than it would at first appear.

29. Walker 1991, p. 93. Walker makes out a good case for distinguishing between two versions of the principle that the innocent should not be punished. One is what he calls 'the wrong-person rule', the other one 'the blameless-doer rule' (pp. 88–95). But then, for some unexplained reason, he unnecessarily weakens the force of his Rawlsian account of these rules by construing type B societies to be ones in which law-abiding citizens do not run the risk of being framed for things they did not do. Only if a person "was incarnated as a law-breaker [would he] be at risk of being penalized not only for his own offences but also for those which the authorities found it difficult to pin on anyone else" (p. 93). It is clear, however, that a world in which all citizens run the risk of being penalised for things they did not do is even less preferable than a world in which this is true only of law-breakers.

30. At the same time, in the interests of restoration, it is highly desirable that there be provisions for flexibility and plurality in sentencing in order to take advantage of diverse cultural and community values. Such flexibility is necessary, for

instance, for models of justice based on reintegrative shaming. As Braithwaite puts it in the context of youth justice, "because the whole idea of the process is to empower local communities to come up with their own approach to dealing with the life problems of a particular young person and their victims, plurality and unpredictability is inherent in the strategy" (Braithwaite 1993, p. 40). Also, in response to criticisms that community- and family-based diversionary conferences (to be described in more detail in Chapter 9) may impose harsher or lighter penalties on offenders than a court would, McElrea made the telling point that "sentencing is not an exact science and there can be considerable disparity between the sentences imposed by different judges in similar cases" (McElrea 1993, p. 4).

31. However, many believers from both faiths have rejected this view.

32. A secular interpretation of the notion of Divine Retribution is the normative, if sometimes wishful, notion of Cosmic Justice, that the good (ought to) prosper while the wicked (ought to) suffer in some way in proportion to their respective deserts. This is what Lewis refers to when talking about "the universal human feeling that bad men ought to suffer" (Lewis 1957, p. 81).

33. Jacoby 1983, p. 115.

34. A point also acknowledged by Golding in a footnote: Golding 1975, p. 85.

35. A similar point is made in Cottingham 1979, p. 241.

6: *Retribution and Revenge*

1. Newman 1978, p. 287.

2. Nozick 1981, p. 367. See also Kleinig 1973; Van den Haag 1975; Wallace 1995.

3. Jacoby 1983, pp. 4, 6.

4. Solomon 1990, p. 302.

5. Solomon 1990, p. 300.

6. Solomon 1990, p. 301.

7. Solomon 1990, p. 300.

8. Pincoffs 1966, p. 48.

9. Oldenquist 1986, p. 76.

10. Dimsdale 1866.

11. Oldenquist 1986, pp. 76–77. See also his 1988, on some formally set out conditions of this sanitising process (p. 474).

12. On the various construals of retribution see Cottingham 1979.

13. Oldenquist 1986, p. 77.

14. However, closeness need not always be along biological or family lines. One may feel much closer to a good friend, for instance, than to some members of one's family. I consider in more detail the nature of the relevant personal or special tie further below.

15. We have three familiar forms of retribution, namely, institutionalized, vigilante, and personal retributive punishment. Recognizably, this last one is what normally goes by the name 'revenge'. A less familiar form of retribution, however, is a combination of the first and last of these: institutionalized personal retribution or *institutionalized revenge*. These points will be discussed in more detail in the next chapter.

16. Mill 1962, p. 307.

17. Nozick 1981, p. 36. We must always clearly distinguish between retribution as an act, or practice, of punishment, which might be defensible on various different grounds, and retributivism, a philosophical thesis which explains and possibly justifies the practice. A defence of moral retributivism is provided in Chapter 8.

18. Nozick 1981, pp. 366–68.

19. Ten 1987, pp. 42–43.

20. Ten 1987, p. 43.

21. Nozick 1981, p. 366.

22. M. Cockerill, Soccer Scandal: Judge Urges Police Investigation/ Involvement. *The Sydney Morning Herald* (11 January 1995), p. 1.

23. M. Brown, Informers Face Retribution. *The Sydney Morning Herald* (14 December 1994), p. 9.

24. Nozick 1981, p. 367

25. Boehm 1984, p. 70. See also the rest of Boehm's Chapter 5.

26. Nozick 1981, p. 367.

27. Nozick 1981, p. 367.

28. Nozick 1981, p. 368.

29. I examine the link between wrongdoing and liability for punishment in Chapter 8.

30. I cover vigilante punishment in more detail in Chapter 7.

31. Hasluck 1954, pp. 231–32.

32. The institutionalisation of punishment will be covered in more detail in Chapter 7.

33. Ten 1987, p. 43.

34. The notion of epistemic identity was discussed in Chapter 4 in connection with the importance of honor in such cultures.

35. Patterson 1992a, p. 130.

36. John Braithwaite drew this to my attention.

37. Benedict 1977.

38. Patterson 1992a, p. 140.

39. Patterson 1992b, p. 15.

40. For a defence of collective responsibility in Maori tribal contexts, see Perrett 1992. Perrett shows that the Maori concept of collective responsibility is not unlike the collective responsibility borne by corporations-an account of which has been articulated and defended, for example, by French (French 1984). It is also important to note that "The Maori view recognises both the tribe and its individual members as moral subjects. Thus, in the collective's external relations (as in intertribal matters) utu is exacted at the collective level, rather than simply directed at the individual offender. However, in the collective's internal relations the individual offender is not treated as if he had no individual responsibility: hence the practice of muru" (Perrett 1992, p. 37). Obviously, the Maori used *muru* (plunder) to punish groups, as well as individuals.

Note also that one of the central criticisms made by Moana Jackson of the criminal justice system of New Zealand is its refusal to accept the concept of collective responsibility. It's hard to disagree with Jackson that the resultant alienation of offenders from their families and victims has disastrous results in terms of rehabilitation and reintegration (Jackson 1988).

41. For instance, by Philip Pettit.

7: Revenge: Its Nature and Definition

1. Newman 1978, p. 192.

2. P. Cockburn, Mutilation for Iraqi Thieves, Deserters. *The Sydney Morning Herald* (14 January 1995), p. 15.

3. I will discuss Mackie's position with regard to the justification of retribution in Chapter 8.

4. Lewis 1949, p. 12.

5. I have already discussed the moral status of resentment, arguing that it is a kind of moral indignation over perceived injustice or unfairness done to oneself or those close to oneself.

6. Dimsdale 1866.

7. Kenney 1987.

8. Friedman 1979; Foote 1970; Miller 1990; Benedict 1977; Patterson 1992a; Patterson 1992b.

9. These were covered in Chapter 3.

10. Foote 1970; Gragas 1980; Benedict 1977.

11. Boehm 1984, p. 84.

12. Zeid 1965, p. 259.

8: A Defense of Moral Retributivism

1. As quoted in Kleinig 1973, p. 125.

2. Oldenquist 1986, p. 76.

3. For instance, deterrence, or rehabilitation of the wrongdoer. An undesirable consequence of imprisonment as a form of punishment seems to be that, far from being rehabilitated, the wrongdoer learns how to be more efficient at criminal activity. This suggests, among other things, that there is more to take into account in the justification of the modality of punishment in any given case than whether or not the mode of punishment is a humane one or not.

4. For example, expression of disapproval, or symbolic and ritualised affirmation of correct values. Arguably, an undesirable function of (at least some) forms of punishment might be the implicit message that violence is an acceptable response to conflict situations.

5. Wolgast 1987, pp. 160–62.

6. For a detailed, philosophical discussion of this point, see Kleinig 1973, esp. pp. 72–77.

7. Cottingham 1979, p. 242.

8. Braithwaite and Pettit 1990, p. 48.

9. Honderich 1984, p. 34.

10. Honderich 1984, pp. 233–34.

11. Atkinson 1974, p. 81.

12. Hampton 1991, pp. 405, 414.

13. Hume 1975, *Enquiry Concerning the Principles of Morals,* Section III, 'Of Justice,' Part I, § 10; Morris 1991.

14. Mackie 1985, p. 208.
15. Mackie 1985, p. 207.
16. Mackie 1985, pp. 209–212.
17. For the details of these explanations see Mackie, 1985, pp. 215–18.
18. Mill 1962, p. 296.
19. Mackie 1985, pp. 209–212.
20. Cottingham 1979, p. 239.
21. Mackie 1985, p. 209.
22. Honderich 1984, pp. 26–33.
23. Nozick 1981, p. 366.
24. Nozick 1981, pp. 374–75.
25. See, for example, Ten 1987, p. 45; Oldenquist 1988, pp. 470–71. In addition to these criticisms we could ask Nozick, tongue in cheek, whether there is a point or further rationale to connecting someone up with correct values by *hitting him over the head with them*. There is an interesting parallel here between Nozick's rationale and Kafka's story 'In the Penal Settlement', in which punishment consists in literally inscribing messages about values into the living flesh of the condemned person—such as, for example, HONOUR THY SUPERIORS and BE JUST (Kafka 1961). But, while the understanding or 'enlightenment' which is generated in the person by the slow and painful carving of the message deep into his body seems to be the central point of the punishment in Kafka, Nozick's rationale for retribution does not incorporate an analogous point about effecting in the wrongdoer through punishment similar realisations about correct values. Thus, Nozick's rationale seems wanting of a further rationale, because its very point seems so pointless.
26. For the following, I am indebted to Oldenquist's first argument in his 1988, pp. 464–65. However, there are at least two important difference between us: 1. While Oldenquist uses the notion of 'harm' in his argument, I appeal to the stronger notion of a moral wrong. 2. Oldenquist refers to desert as part of his explanation of retribution, while I take desert to be the object of the explanation. This means that my account is not vulnerable to criticisms by Cottingham and Mackie that desert claims are "jejune" or mere "bald assertion[s]."
27. There are also other important aspects to moral responsibility, such as free will and choice, which are not immediately relevant to this discussion and which fall outside the scope of this book.
28. Kleinig 1973, p. 67. See also Davis 1972.
29. Bradley 1927, pp. 4–5.
30. Husak (1994) has argued that drunk driving is not as serious an offence as people generally believe it to be. He does not dispute, however, that when disastrous consequences result because of drunk driving, the responsibility of the driver renders him liable to blame and punishment in the way suggested above.
31. This last claim may raise the question of moral luck—an interesting issue which falls beyond the scope of this book.
32. Cupit has argued (1996) that moral responsibility is not presupposed or necessitated by moral desert. I tend to agree and, transposed into Cupit's framework, my claim is almost the mirror image of his. Whereas Cupit's position is that someone doesn't have to be responsible to be deserving, may argument is that, if someone is responsible for a morally unjustifiable act, then they are liable to (deserv-

ing of) moral censure and possibly punishment simply in virtue of the responsibility they bear for their wrongful behavior as a whole-minded member of the moral community. Thus, in a sense, these two positions are complementary.

33. Retrospective moral accountability is rarely strict, however. We do recognise certain excuses for failure to fulfil an obligation. Rather, the line is drawn at, or with, the notion of 'fault'—analysis of which is beyond the scope of this book.

34. de Grazia, as quoted in Pincoffs 1966, p. 104.

35. Kant 1974, p. 195.

36. Hegel, as quoted in Heller 1987, p. 160.

37. Lewis 1949.

38. Lewis 1949, p. 10.

39. Nietzsche 1993, p. 116 (*Thus Spake Zarathustra*, Chapter 27: 'The Virtuous').

40. Lewis 1949, p. 11.

41. Armstrong 1969, p. 155.

42. Garcia 1989, p. 264. See also Garcia 1986; Brien 1998.

43. As quoted in Spencer 1966, p. 366.

44. Lewis 1949, pp. 11–12.

9: Victim Justice and Institutionalized Empowerment

1. Kennedy 1989, p. 321.

2. Abel and Marsh 1984, p. 160. See also Harding 1982.

3. Victims of Crime Get Rights in Sentencing. *The Canberra Times* (5 October 1995), p. 5.

4. *Victims Rights Act 1996*. New South Wales, Australia.

5. Erez 1991, p. 2.

6. Braithwaite and Pettit 1990, p. 91.

7. As quoted in Erez 1991, p. 2.

8. As quoted in Consedine 1995, p. 82.

9. Friedman 1979, p. 401.

10. General Assembly 1985.

11. Severin 1995, p. 21.

12. In line with established usage, a victim is any person who suffers harm as a result of an offense. In cases such as murder, "any person who was financially or psychologically dependent on the primary victim immediately before his or her death", is also a victim (*Victims of Crime Act 1994 [ACT]*, No. 83. §3, 1). Accordingly, considerations of victim involvement and empowerment are as applicable to them as they are applicable to (living) primary victims. It would be implausible, and wrong, to say that in a case of murder, for example, there are no living victims to consider. This is acknowledged not only in legislation such as the above, but also by the *United Nations Resolution on Victims of Crime and Abuse of Power* (General Assembly 1985).

13. Holmstrom and Burgess 1975, p. 46.

14. R. Harvey, How Murder Hits the Victim's Kin. *VOCAL Newsletter* (ACT) (1994–95), Vol. 5. No. 3–4, pp. 14–15.

15. Court Allows Mum to Confront Son's Killer. *The Courier Mail* (11 November 1995, p. 3.

16. Braithwaite 1995, p. 68.

17. Clark and Mills 1979.

18. Buunk, Doosje, Jans, and Hopstaken 1993, p. 801. See also, LaGaipa 1977.

19. Buunk at al. 1993, p. 802.

20. Antonucci and Jackson 1990.

21. Rook 1987.

22. Greenberg and Westcott 1983; Hatfield and Sprecher 1983; as reported in Buunk at al. 1993, p. 801.

23. Sung Hee Kim and Smith 1993, pp. 39, 41.

24. Berscheid, Boye, and Walster 1968, p. 370.

25. For anecdotal evidence see Sung Hee Kim and Smith 1993, p. 40.

26. Berscheid et. al. 1968, p. 370.

27. Solomon 1990, pp. 293, 292.

28. However, Block and Lind argue that "for any punishment harsh enough so that no individual would commit these crimes if he were certain to be punished there also exists a probability of punishment less than unity that will deter all such criminal acts" (Block and Lind 1975, p. 247). If this is right, then increasing the chances of apprehension above a certain level would bring about more positive results in terms of deterrence than does the increasing of the severity of punishment. Most criminal justice systems seem to be headed in the other direction.

29. Braithwaite 1993, p. 39. Braithwaite seems to attribute this phenomenon to people being "enmeshed in institutions that invite them to care about each other instead of hate each other" (p. 39). However, it would be more appropriate to say that the two systems *allow* and *engender* the development of different attitudes. Under restorative justice processes victims and offenders do not have to be (and most of the time are not) explicitly invited to care about each other. They naturally start to care as a result of new perspectives afforded to them by their direct involvement and empowerment.

30. Newman 1978, p. 104.

31. Friedman 1979, pp. 405–06.

32. Friedman 1979, pp. 414–15 (Appendix B). For more details, and arguments in favour, of a completely private system, see Friedman 1973; Becker and Stigler 1974. For a discussion of an historical example of a private system from the nineteenth-century American West, see Anderson and Hill 1979.

33. See, for example, Becker and Stigler 1974; Landes and Posner 1975; Block and Lind 1975; Schwartz and Tullock 1975; Polinsky 1980; Friedman 1984.

34. Judge F.W.M. McElrea, in a draft paper "Restorative Justice: A Peace Making Process," has highlighted the many parallels between restorative justice initiatives in criminal justice contexts and alternative dispute resolution processes in other jurisdictions. As a researcher and practitioner of these processes both within and outside the criminal justice contexts, I fully agree with Judge McElrea's assessment, and believe that there is every reason to identify these processes outright as alternative dispute resolution processes, regardless of whether they are being employed in criminal justice contexts or not. After all, they are alternatives to the disempowering processes where key decision making powers lie with professionals, as typified by our courts.

35. General Assembly 1985.
36. Sherman and Strang 1997a; Sherman and Barnes 1997; Strang and Sherman 1997.
37. Braithwaite 1989, p. 8.
38. Sherman and Strang 1997b; Sherman and Barnes 1997.
39. Pincoffs 1966, pp. 125–26.
40. Retzinger and Scheff 1996.
41. Retzinger and Scheff 1996, pp. 316, 317.
42. Estrada-Hollenbeck 1996.
43. See, for example, Sung Hee Kim and Smith 1993; Ohbuchi, Kameda, and Agarie 1989.
44. Ohbuchi, et. el. 1989, pp 219–220.
45. Possible concerns that greater victim involvement will lead to vindictiveness and to the endangerment of offender rights and offender justice will be covered in the remaining chapter.
46. Estrada-Hollenbeck 1996.
47. Sherman and Strang 1997a, p. 4.
48. Jackson 1988, pp. 234, 242.
49. Erez 1991, p. 5.
50. McCarthy 1994, p. 180.
51. R. Harvey, How Murder Hits the Victim's Kin. *VOCAL Newsletter (ACT)* (1994-95), Vol. 5. No. 3, 4, p. 14.
52. Erez 1991, p. 6.
53. Erez 1991, p. 6. See also Kelly 1990.
54. The Queen v. Clotworthy (1998) 114/98. Wellington, New Zealand.
55. Jonathan Milne. 'Appeal Court Quashes "Justice Deal," Jails Man.' *The Dominion*. Wellington, New Zealand (1 July 1998), p. 1.
56. Erez 1991, p. 5.
57. Umbreit 1989, p. 56.

10: Beyond Restorative Justice: The Primacy of Empowerment

1. Foucault 1980, p. 1.
2. Russell 1961, p. 561.
3. Hume 1975, Appendix II, p. 302.
4. Siebers 1988, p. 124.
5. Wallace 1995, p. 374.
6. Wallace 1995, p. 374.
7. Wallace 1995, p. 375. Similar views are expressed in Primoratz 1989, p. 84.
8. Hough and Moxon 1988, p. 147.
9. Erez 1991, p. 4. See also Gardner 1990; Walker and Hough 1988; Kelly 1990; Shapland, Willmore, and Duff 1985, esp. pp. 72–74; Umbreit 1989.
10. Long 1995, pp. 225–26, 229, 189.
11. John MacDonald in 'An Introduction to Family Group Conferencing'. Video by REAL JUSTICE.
12. Campbell 1984, p. 359.
13. Sherman and Strang 1997b.

14. It appears as though advocates of restorative justice are not merely looking for a contrast, something that restorative justice may be compared to, but also for a target of attack, the enemy that stands in the way of positive change and reform. Retribution, much maligned already, appears to be an obvious and easy target. But this misses the mark, as I go on to argue below.

15. Consedine 1995.

16. Pincoffs 1966, p. 48.

17. Young Offenders Act 1993 (South Australia), s 3.

18. See Zehr 1990; Umbreit 1989; Van Ness 1990; 1996; 1997; Wright 1996; Munn 1993; Galaway and Hudson 1996, p. 10; Dignan and Cavadino 1996; Jones 1996; and generally most authors on restorative justice. See also the articles by Bowen, Consedine, Lapsley, Boyack, Hayden and Henderson, and Hickey in Consedine and Bowen 1999.

19. Wundersitz and Hetzel 1996, pp. 113–17.

20. Newman 1978, pp. 193, 202.

21. N. Leedham, Jail 'Unduly Harsh' for Guilty Officer. *The Canberra Times* (22 June 1995), p. 4 (my emphasis).

22. Doolan 1993, p. 18.

23. The Queen v. Clotworthy (1998) 114/98 (Wellington, New Zealand), p. 12.

24. The Queen v. Clotworthy (1998) 114/98 (Wellington, New Zealand), p. 14.

25. McElrea 1996, p. 7.

26. Umbreit 1989, pp. 52, 54.

27. Wundersitz and Hetzel 1996, p. 136.

28. Consedine 1995, p. 113.

29. Consedine 1995, p. 145.

30. Consedine 1995, p. 89.

31. Consedine 1995, p. 89.

32. Consedine 1995, p. 89.

33. Lewis 1949. Lewis was a man of deep Christian convictions and was fully aware of the value of forgiveness and mercy. But he was also a fierce defender of moral retributivism, which was already unpopular at the time. He concludes his article by saying: "You may ask why I send this to an Australian periodical. The reason is simple and perhaps worth recording; I can get no hearing for it in England" (p. 12).

34. Braithwaite and Pettit 1990, p. 2.

35. Newman 1978, p. 192. Note that the former quotation focuses on retributivism as a criminological theory of punishment justification, while the latter makes a historical claim about the application of that theory, or rather the lack of it, in practice.

36. The potential subtleties that may be contained in this point are highlighted by Cunneen in connection with indigenous people. He rightly points out that restorative justice initiatives which are centrally imposed on indigenous communities without prior consultation with them, especially initiatives that employ ADR processes that are culturally inappropriate or alien, may be little more than just another aspect of their ongoing disempowerment (Cunneen 1997).

37. McElrea 1996, p. 1. The same points are made in McElrea 1999, p. 57.

Bibliography

Abel, C.F. and F.H. Marsh. 1984. *Punishment and Restitution: A Restitutionary Approach to Crime and the Criminal.* Westport: Greenwood.

Acton, H.B. (ed.) 1969. *The Philosophy of Punishment.* London: Macmillan.

Adams, R.M. 1985. Involuntary Sins. *Philosophical Review 94:* 3–31.

Agassi, J. 1987. Theories of Rationality. In Agassi and Jarvie 1987.

Agassi, J. and I.C. Jarvie (eds.) 1987. *Rationality: The Critical View.* Dordrecht: Nijhoff.

Allen, C.K. 1958. *Aspects of Justice.* London: Stevens and Sons.

Anderson, T.L., and P.J. Hill. 1979. An American Experiment in Anarcho-Capitalism: The *Not* So Wild, Wild West. *Journal of Libertarian Studies, 3:* 9–29.

Antonucci, T.C., and J.S. Jackson. 1990. The Role of Reciprocity in Social Support. In Sarason and Pierce (eds.) 1990.

Armstrong, K. G. 1968. The Retributivist Hits Back. In Acton 1969.

Arrow, K.J. 1977. Current Developments in the Theory of Social Choice. *Social Research 44:* 607–622. Reprinted in Barry and Hardin 1982.

Atkinson, M. 1974. Interpreting Retributive Claims. *Ethics 85:* 80–86.

Axelrod, R. 1984. *The Evolution of Cooperation.* New York: Basic Books.

Ayers, E.L. 1984. *Vengeance and Justice: Crime and Punishment in the 19th-Century South.* Oxford: Oxford University Press.

Bacon, F. 1985. *The Essays.* Edited by J. Pitcher. Harmondsworth, England: Penguin.

Bar-Elli, G., and D. Heyd. 1986. Can Revenge be Just or Otherwise Justified? *Theoria, 52:* 68–86.

Barry, B., and R. Hardin (eds.) 1982. *Rational Man and Irrational Society?* Beverly Hills: Sage.

Barton, C. 1996. *Revenge and Victim Justice.* Ph.D. thesis. Canberra: The Australian National University.

Beccaria, C. 1995. *Crimes and Punishments and Other Writings.* Translated by R. Davies and V. Cox. Edited by R. Bellamy. Cambridge: Cambridge University Press.

Becker, S. and G.J. Stigler. 1974. Law Enforcement, Malfeasance, and Compensation of Enforcers. *Journal of Legal Studies 3:* 1–18.

Benedict, R. 1977. *The Chrysanthemum and the Sword.* London: Routledge.

Berger, P. 1984. On the Obsolescence of the Concept of Honour. In Sandel 1984.

Berkowitz, L. 1962. *Aggression: A Social Psychological Analysis.* New York: McGraw-Hill.

Berofsky, B. 1987. *Freedom from Necessity.* New York: Routledge.

Berscheid, E., D. Boye, and E. Walster. 1968. Retaliation as a Means of Restoring Equity. *Journal of Personality and Social Psychology 10:* 370–76.

Best, B. 1952. *The Maori as He Was.* Wellington: R.E. Owen, Government Printer.

Bird, O.A. 1967. *The Idea of Justice.* New York: Praeger.

Bishop, J. 1985. Review of Elster 1983. *Australasian Journal of Philosophy 63:* 245–48.

Bishop, J. 1986. Review of Schick 1984. *Australasian Journal of Philosophy, 64:* 238–39.

Black, M. 1982. Why Should I Be Rational? *Dialectica, 36:* 147–168.

Black-Michaud, J. 1975. *Cohesive Force: Feud in the Mediterranean and Middle East.* Oxford: Blackwell.

Block, M.K., and R.C. Lind. 1975. Crime and Punishment Reconsidered. *Journal of Legal Studies 4:* 241–47.

Boehm, C. 1984. *Blood Revenge.* Lawrence: University Press of Kansas.

Bourdieu, P. 1977. *Outline of a Theory of Practice.* Translated by R. Nice. Cambridge: Cambridge University Press.

Bradley, F.H. 1927. The Vulgar Notion of Responsibility. In *Ethical Studies.* Second edn. Oxford: Clarendon.

Braithwaite, J. 1979. *Inequality, Crime, and Public Policy.* London: Routledge.

———. 1989. *Crime, Shame, and Reintegration.* Cambridge: Cambridge University Press.

———. 1993. What Is to Be Done about Criminal Justice? In Brown and McElrea 1993.

———. 1995. Corporate Crime and Republican Criminological Praxis. In F. Pearce and L. Snider (eds.), *Corporate Crime: Ethics, Law, and State* (Toronto: University of Toronto Press).

Braithwaite, J., and P. Pettit. 1990. *Not Just Deserts.* Oxford: Clarendon.

Brien, A. 1998. Mercy within Legal Justice. *Social Theory and Practice 24:* 83–110.

Brown, B.J., and F.W.M. McElrea (eds.) 1993. *The Youth Court in New Zealand: A New Model of Justice.* Publication No. 34. Auckland: Legal Research Foundation.

Buss, A.H. 1961. *The Psychology of Aggression.* New York: Wiley.

Butler, J. 1896. Upon Resentment (Sermon VIII); Upon Forgiveness of Injuries (Sermon IX). In *The Works,* Vol. 2. Edited by W.E. Gladstone. Oxford: Clarendon.

Buunk, P.B., B.J. Doosje, L.G.J. Jans, and L.E.M. Hopstaken. 1993. Perceived Reciprocity, Social Support, and Stress at Work: The Role of Exchange and Communal Orientation. *Journal of Personality and Social Psychology, 65:* 801–811.

Calhoun, C. 1992. Changing One's Heart. *Ethics 103:* 76–96.

Campbell, T. 1984. Compensation as Punishment. *UNSW Law Journal 7:* 338–361.

———. 1988. *Justice.* London: Macmillan.

Carthwright, D. 1985. Revenge, Punishment, and Mercy: The Self-Overcoming of Justice. *International Studies in Philosophy 17:* 17–26.

Carthwright, D.E. 1984. Kant, Schopenhauer, and Nietzsche on the Morality of Pity. *Journal of the History of Ideas 45:* 83–98.

Clark, M.S. and J. Mills. 1979. Interpersonal Attraction in Exchange and Communal Relationships. *Journal of Personality and Social Psychology 37:* 12–24.

Consedine, J. 1995. *Restorative Justice: Healing the Effects of Crime*. Lyttleton, New Zealand: Ploughshares Publications.

Consedine, J., and H. Bowen (eds.) 1999. Restorative Justice: Contemporary Themes and Practice. Lyttleton, New Zealand: Ploughshares Publications.

Copeland, J. (ed.) 1996. *Logic and Reality: Essays in Honour of Arthur Prior*. Oxford: Oxford University Press.

Cottingham, J. 1979. Varieties of Retribution. *The Philosophical Quarterly 29:* 238–246.

Cunneen, C. 1997. Conferencing and the Fiction of Indigenous Control. *Australian and New Zealand Journal of Criminology 30:* 292–311.

Cupit, G. 1996. *Justice as Fittingness*. New York: Oxford University Press.

Dalby, M. 1981. Revenge and the Law in Traditional China. *American Journal of Legal History 25(4):* 267–307.

Davidson, D. 1980. *Essays on Actions and Events*. Oxford: Clarendon.

Davis, L.H. 1972. They Deserve to Suffer. *Analysis 32:* 136–140.

de Sousa, R. 1987. *The Rationality of Emotion*. Cambridge, Ma: MIT Press.

Del Mar, F. 1924. *A Year among the Maoris*. London: Ernest Benn.

Dennis, A., P. Foote, and R. Perkins (trans.) 1980. *Laws of Early Iceland: Gragas*. Winipeg: University of Manitoba Press.

Dickie, P. 1989. *The Road to Fitzgerald and Beyond*. Brisbane: University of Queensland Press.

Dignan, J., and M. Cavadino. 1996. Toward a Framework for Conceptualizing and Evaluating Models of Criminal Justice from a Victim's Perspective. *International Review of Victimology 4(3):* 153–182.

Dimsdale, T.J. 1866. *Vigilantes of Montana*. Virginia City: Montana Post Press.

Doolan, M.P. 1993. Youth Justice: Legislation and Practice. In Brown and McElrea 1993.

Drapkin, I. and E. Viano (eds.) 1975. *Victimology: A New Focus: Vol. 3: Crimes, Victims, and Justice*. Lexington, Ma: Lexington Books.

Ellis, A. 1995. Recent Work on Punishment. *Philosophical Quarterly 45:* 225–333.

Elster, J. (ed.) 1986. *Rational Choice*. Oxford: Basil Blackwell.

———. 1983. *Sour Grapes*. Cambridge: Cambridge University Press.

———. 1990. Norms of Revenge. *Ethics 100:* 862–885.

Erez, E. 1991. Victim Impact Statements (Issue paper No. 33). In P. Grabosky (ed.), *Trends and Issues in Crime and Criminal Justice* (Canberra: Australian Institute of Criminology).

Estrada-Hollenbeck, M. 1996. Forgiving in the Face of Injustice: Victims' and Perpetrators' Perspectives. In Galaway and Hudson 1996, pp. 303–313.

Evans, D.A. 1977. *Retributive Theories of Punishment Justification*. Thesis. Detroit: Wayne State University.

Ezzat, A. F. (ed.) 1986. *From Crime Policy to Victim Policy: Re-orienting the Justice System*. Basingstoke: Macmillan.

———. (ed.) 1989. *The Plight of Crime Victims in Modern Society*. New York: St. Martin's Press.

Fawcett, S.B., T. Seekins, P.L. Whang, C. Muiu, and Y.S. de Balcazar. 1984. Creating and Using Social Technologies for Community Empowerment. In Rappaport *et al.* 1984.

Feibleman, J.K. 1985. *Justice, Law, and Culture*. Dordrecht: Martinus Nijhoff.

Feinberg, J. 1970. *Doing and Deserving*. Princeton: Princeton University Press.

Foote, P. 1970. *The Viking Achievement*. London: Sidgwick and Jackson.

Foucault, M. 1977. *Discipline and Punish*. New York: Pantheon.

———. 1980. On Popular Justice: A Discussion with Maoists. In C. Gordon (ed.), *Power/Knowledge, Selected Interviews and Other Writings 1972-1977* (New York: Pantheon).

Frankfurt, H.G. 1969. Alternate Possibilities and Moral Responsibility. *Journal of Philosophy 66:* 829–839.

French, P.A. 1984. *Collective and Corporate Responsibility*. New York: Columbia University Press.

Freud, S. 1961. *Civilization and Its Discontents*. Translated by James Strachey. New York: Norton.

Frey, R.G., and C. Morris (eds.) 1991. *Liability and Responsibility: Essays in Law and Morals*. Cambridge: Cambridge University Press.

Friedman, D. 1973. *The Machinery of Freedom: Guide to a Radical Capitalism*. New York: Harper and Row.

———. 1979. Private Creation and Enforcement of Law: A Historical Case. *Journal of Legal Studies 8:* 399–415.

———. 1984. Efficient Institutions for the Private Enforcement of Law. *Journal of Legal Studies 13:* 379–397.

Galaway, B. and J. Hudson (eds.) 1996. *Restorative Justice: International Perspectives*. Monsey, NY: Criminal Justice Press.

Garcia, J.L.A. 1986. Two Concepts of Desert. *Law and Philosophy 5:* 219–235.

———. 1989. Deserved Punishment. *Law and Philosophy 8:* 263–277.

Gardner, J. 1990. *Victims and Criminal Justice*. Adelaide: South Australian Attorney-General's Department, Office of Crime Statistics.

Gaus, F.G. 1990. *Value and Justification*. Cambridge: Cambridge University Press.

General Assembly. 1985. *Resolution Adopted by the General Assembly, 40/34. Declaration of Basic Principles of Justice for Victims of Crime and Abuse of Power Annex. Declaration of Basic Principles of Justice for Victims of Crime and Abuse of Power.* Document No. A/RES/40/34 (11 December 1985). United Nations.

Gensler, H.J. 1986. Ethics is Based on Rationality. *Journal of Value Inquiry 20:* 251–264.

Glover, J. 1970. *Responsibility*. New York: Humanities Press/London: Routledge.

Golding, M.P. 1975. *Philosophy of Law*. Englewood Cliffs: Prentice-Hall.

Greenspan, P.S. 1988. *Emotions and Reasons*. New York: Routledge.

Griffin, J. 1986. *Well-Being: Its Meaning, Measurement, and Moral Importance*. Oxford: Clarendon.

Hamlin, A.P. 1991. Rational Revenge. *Ethics 101:* 374–381.

Hampton, J., and J.G. Murphy. 1988. *Forgiveness and Mercy*. Cambridge: Cambridge University Press.

Hardin, R. 1991. Trusting Persons, Trusting Institutions. In R. Zeckhauser (ed.), *Strategy and Choice* (Cambridge, Ma: MIT Press).

Harding, C. and R.W. Ireland. 1989. *Punishment: Rhetoric, Rule, and Practice*. London: Routledge.

Harding, J. 1982. *Victims and Offenders*. London: Bedford Square Press.

Hare, R.M. 1981. *Moral Thinking: Its Levels, Method, and Point*. Oxford: Clarendon.

Harsanyi, J.C. 1977. Morality and the Theory of Rational Behavior. *Social Research* 44: 623–656.

———. 1986. Advances in Understanding Rational Behavior. In Elster (ed.) 1986, 82–107.

Hart, H.L.A. 1968. *Punishment and Responsibility*. Oxford: Clarendon Press. Oxford.

Hasluck, M. 1954. *The Unwritten Law in Albania*. Cambridge: Cambridge University Press.

Hedenius, I. 1973. The Concept of Punishment. In *Modality, Morality, and Other Problems of Sense and Nonsense: Essays Dedicated to Soren Hallden*. Lund: Gleerup.

Hegel, G.W.F. 1942. *The Philosophy of Right*. Translated by T.M. Knox. Oxford: Oxford University Press.

Heider, F. 1958. *The Psychology of Interpersonal Relations*. London: Wiley.

Heil, J. 1992. Believing Reasonably. *Nous 26:* 47–61.

Heller, A. 1987. *Beyond Justice*. Oxford: Blackwell.

Hobbes, T. 1962. *Leviathan*. Edited by J. Plamenatz. London: Collins.

Holmstrom, L.L., and A.W. Burgess. 1975. Rape: The Victim Goes on Trial. In Drapkin and Viano 1975.

Honderich, T. 1984. *Punishment: The Supposed Justifications*. Harmondsworth: Penguin.

Hough, A.B., and C.D. Moxon. 1988. Dealing with Offenders: Popular Opinion and the Views of Victims in England and Wales. In Walker and Hough 1988.

Houston, J. 1965. *Maori Life in Old Taranaki*. Wellington: A.H. and A.W. Reed.

Hudson, J., A. Morris, M. Gabrielle, and B. Galaway (eds.) 1996. *Family Group Conferences: Perspectives on Policy and Practice*. Australia: The Federation Press.

Hume, D. 1975. *Enquiries Concerning Human Understanding and Concerning the Principles of Morals*. Third edn., edited by L.A. Selby-Bigge. London: Oxford University Press.

Husak, D.N. 1994. Is Drunk Driving a Serious Offence? *Philosophy and Public Affairs 23:* 52–73.

Jackson, F. 1987. Group Morality. In Pettit, Sylvan, and Norman 1987, pp. 91–110.

Jackson, M. 1988. *The Maori and the Criminal Justice System, a New Perspective: He Whaipaanga Hou*. Wellington: Department of Justice.

———. 1992. The Colonisation of Maori Philosophy. In Oddie and Perrett 1992, pp. 1–10.

Jacoby, S. 1983. *Wild Justice: The Evolution of Revenge*. New York: Harper and Row.

Johansen, L. 1987. The Theory of Public Goods: Misplaced Emphasis? In F.R. Forsund (ed.), *Collected Works of Leif Johansen*. Volume 2. Amsterdam: Elsevier Science.

Johnson, C.D. 1975. Moral and Legal Obligation. *Journal of Philosophy 72:* 315–333.

Jones, K. 1996. Restorative Justice: The Theoretical Dream of Idealism. LLB (Hons) Research Paper; Criminal Law and Procedure (LAWS 511) Law Faculty. Victoria University of Wellington, New Zealand.

Kafka, F. 1961. In the Penal Settlement. In *Metamorphosis and Other Stories*. Harmondsworth: Penguin.

Kahn, A.S. (ed.) 1984. *Social Psychology.* Dubuque, Iowa: W.C. Brown.

Kamler, H. 1985. Strong Feelings. *Journal of Value Inquiry 19:* 3–12.

Kant, I. 1965. *The Metaphysical Elements of Justice.* Translated by J. Ladd. Indianapolis: Bobbs-Merrill.

———. 1974. *The Philosophy of Law.* Clifton, NJ: Augustus M. Kelley.

Kaufmann, W.A. 1950. *Nietzsche: Philosopher, Psychologist, Antichrist.* Princeton: Princeton University Press.

———. 1959. *The Owl and the Nightingale.* London: Faber and Faber.

Kelly, D.P. 1990. Victim Participation in the Criminal Justice System. In A.J. Lurigio, W.A. Skogan, and R.C. Davis (eds.), *Victims of Crime: Problems, Policies, and Programs.* Newbury Park, Ca: Sage.

Kelly, J., J. Kitchin, and R. Cahill. 1993. *Report on Victims of Crime.* Report No. 6. Community Law Reform Committee. Australian Capital Territory.

Kelsen, H. 1957. *What is Justice?* Berkeley: University of California Press.

Kennedy, L.H.C. 1989. The Advantages of the Inquisitorial over the Adversary System of Criminal Justice. In Whitton 1994, Appendix I.

Kenney, D.J. 1987. *Crime, Fear, and the New York City Subways.* New York: Praeger.

Kleinig, J. 1973. *Punishment and Desert.* The Hague: Martinus Nijhoff.

Körner, S. (Ed.) 1974. *Practical Reason.* Oxford: Blackwell.

LaGaipa, J.J. 1977. Interpersonal Attraction and Social Exchange. In S. Duck (ed.), *Theory and Practice in Interpersonal Attraction.* San Diego: Academic Press.

Landes, W.M., and R.A. Posner. 1975. The Private Enforcement of Law. *Journal of Legal Studies 4:* 1–46.

Lave, L.B. 1962. An Empirical Approach to the Prisoners' [sic] Dilemma Game. *Quarterly Journal of Economics 76:* 424–436.

Lewis, C.S. 1949. The Humanitarian Theory of Punishment. *Twentieth Century: An Australian Quarterly 3:* 5–12.

———. 1957. *The Problem of Pain.* London: Fontana.

Long, K. 1995. Community Input at Sentencing: Victim's Right or Victim's Revenge. *Boston University Law Review 75(1):* 187–229.

Lovibond, S. 1990. True and False Pleasures. *Proceedings of the Aristotelian Society 15:* 213–230.

Lucas, J.R. 1980. *On Justice.* Oxford: Clarendon.

Luce, D., and H. Raiffa. 1957. *Games and Decisions.* New York: Wiley.

Lycan, W.G. 1986. Moral Facts and Moral Knowledge. *Southern Journal of Philosophy 24 (Supplement):* 79–94.

Lynd, H.M. 1958. *On Shame and the Search for Identity.* London: Routledge.

MacIntyre, A. 1981. *After Virtue.* Notre Dame, Indiana: University of Notre Dame Press.

Mackie, J.L. 1985. Morality and the Retributive Emotions. In J. and P. Mackie (eds.), *Persons and Values, Volume 2* (Oxford: Clarendon).

Magnus, B. 1978. *Nietzsche's Existential Imperative.* Bloomington: Indiana University Press.

Malony, J.N. 1980. *I Am Ned Kelly.* Sydney: Allen Lane.

Margolis, J. 1966. *Contemporary Ethical Theory.* New York: Random House.

Marongiu, P. and G. Newman. 1987. *Vengeance, The Fight Against Injustice.* Lanham: Rowman and Littlefield.

Mawby, R.I., and M.L. Gill. 1987. *Crime Victims: Needs, Services, and the Voluntary Sector.* London: Tavistock.

McCarthy, T. 1994. Victim Impact Statements: A Problematic Remedy. *Australian Feminist Law Journal 3:* 175–195.

McElrea, F.W.M. 1993. A New Model of Justice. In Brown and McElrea (eds.) 1993.

———. 1996. Rape: Ten Years' Progress? An address to the Interdisciplinary Conference. 29 March 1996. Wellington.

———. 1999. Taking Responsibility in Being Accountable. In Consedine and Bowen 1999.

Mellema, G. 1985. Shared Responsibility and Ethical Dilutionism. *Australasian Journal of Philosophy 63:* 177–187.

Milgram, S. 1974. *Obedience to Authority.* London: Tavistock.

Mill, J.S. 1962. *Utilitarianism.* Edited by M. Warnock. London: Collins.

Miller, W.I. 1990. *Bloodtaking and Peacemaking: Feud, Law, and Society in Saga Iceland.* Chicago: University of Chicago Press.

Ministry of Justice. 1995. *Restorative Justice: A Discussion Paper.* Wellington: Ministry of Justice.

Morris, C.W. 1991. Punishment and Loss of Moral Standing. *Canadian Journal of Philosophy 21:* 53–80.

Mundle, C.W.K. 1954. Punishment and Desert. In Acton 1969.

Munn, M. 1993. Restorative Justice: An Alternative to Vengeance. *American Journal of Criminal Law 20:* 99.

Munson, M.E. 1985. Power and Virtue: Institutional Ascent or Individual Decline? *International Studies in Philosophy 17:* 27–31.

Murphy, J.G. 1979. *Retribution, Justice, and Therapy.* Dordrecht: Reidel.

Murphy, J.G., and J. Hampton. 1988. *Forgiveness and Mercy.* Cambridge: Cambridge University Press.

Newman, G. 1978. *The Punishment Response.* New York: Lippincott.

Nietzsche, F. 1966. *Beyond Good and Evil.* Translated by W. Kaufmann. New York: Vintage.

———. 1967. *The Will to Power.* Translated by W. Kaufmann and R.J. Hollingdale. New York: Vintage.

———. 1968. *Twilight of the Idols* and *The Anti-Christ.* Translated by R.J. Hollingdale. Harmondsworth: Penguin.

———. 1989. *On the Genealogy of Morals* and *Ecce Homo.* Translated by W. Kaufmann and R.J. Hollingdale. New York: Vintage.

———. 1993. *Thus Spake Zarathustra.* Translated by T. Common. Buffalo: Prometheus.

Nozick, R. 1974. *Anarchy, State, and Utopia.* New York: Basic Books.

———. 1981. *Philosophical Explanations.* Oxford: Clarendon.

Nyberg, D. 1981. *Power Over Power.* Ithaca: Cornell University Press.

Oddie, G. 1996. The Consequences of Action. In Copeland 1996.

Oddie, G., and P. Menzies. 1992. An Objectivist's Guide to Subjective Value. *Ethics 102:* 512–533.

Oddie, G., and R.W. Perrett (eds.) 1992. *Justice, Ethics, and New Zealand Society.* Oxford: Oxford University Press.

Ohbuchi, K., M. Kameda, and N. Agarie. 1989. Apology as Aggression Control. *Journal of Personality and Social Psychology 56:* 219–227.

Olafson, F. 1961. *Society, Law, and Morality.* Englewood Cliffs: Prentice-Hall.

Oldenquist, A. 1986. The Case for Revenge. *The Public Interest 82:* 72–80.

———. 1988. An Explanation of Retribution. *Journal of Philosophy 85:* 464–478.

Parfit, D. 1986. Prudence, Morality, and the Prisoner's Dilemma. In Elster 1986: 34–59.

Patterson, J. 1989. Utu, Revenge, and Mana. *British Review of New Zealand Studies 2:* 51–61.

———. 1992a. *Exploring Maori Values.* Palmerston, New Zealand: The Dunmore Press.

———. 1992b. A Maori Concept of Collective Responsibility. In Oddie and Perrett 1992.

Pears, D. 1984. *Motivated Irrationality.* Oxford: Clarendon.

Peristiany, J.G. (ed.) 1965. *Honour and Shame: The Values of Mediterranean Society.* London: Weidenfeld and Nicolson.

Perrett, R.W. 1992. Individualism, Justice, and the Maori View of the Self. In Oddie and Perrett 1992.

Perrett, R.W., and J. Patterson. 1991. Virtue Ethics and Maori Ethics. *Philosophy East and West 41:* 185–202.

Pettit, P. 1986. Free Riding and Foul Dealing. *Journal of Philosophy 83:* 361–379.

Pettit, P., and J. Braithwaite. 1990. *Not Just Deserts.* Oxford: Clarendon.

Pettit, P., and R. Sugden. 1989. The Backward Induction Paradox. *Journal of Philosophy 86:* 169–182.

Pettit, P., R. Sylvan, and J. Norman. 1987. *Metaphysics and Morality.* Oxford: Blackwell.

Pincoffs, E.L. 1966. *The Rationale of Legal Punishment.* New York: Humanities Press.

Plott, C.R. 1976. Axiomatic Social Choice Theory: An Overview and Interpretation. *American Journal of Political Science 20:* 511–527.

Polinsky, A.M. 1980. Private versus Public Enforcement of Fines. *Journal of Legal Studies 9:* 105–127.

Poundstone, W. 1992. *Prisoner's Dilemma.* New York: Doubleday.

Primoratz, I. 1989. *Justifying Legal Punishment.* Atlantic Highlands, NJ: Humanities Press International.

Quinton, A. 1954. On Punishment. *Analysis, 14:* 133–142. Reprinted in Acton 1969.

Rachels, J. 1993. *The Elements of Moral Philosophy.* Second edn. New York: McGraw-Hill.

Railton, P. 1984. Alienation, Consequentialism, and the Demands of Morality. *Philosophy and Public Affairs 13:* 134–171.

Raphael, D.D. 1955. *Moral Judgement.* London: Allen and Unwin.

Rapoport, A., and A.M. Chammah. 1965. *Prisoner's Dilemma: A Study in Conflict and Cooperation.* Ann Arbor: University of Michigan Press.

Rappaport, J., C. Swift, and R. Hess. 1984. *Studies in Empowerment: Steps Toward Understanding and Action.* New York: Haworth Press.

Rashdall, H. 1924. *The Theory of Good and Evil.* Volume 1. London: Oxford University Press.

Rawls, J. 1955. Two Concepts of Rules. *Philosophical Review 64:* 3–32.

———. 1984. The Right and the Good Contrasted. In Sandel 1984.

Retzinger, S. M., and T.J. Scheff. 1996. Strategy for Community Conferences: Emotions and Social Bonds. In Galaway and Hudson 1996, pp. 315–336.

Richards, D.A.J. 1971. *A Theory of Reasons for Action.* London: Oxford University Press.

RISE Working Papers 1997. Papers #1–#4. *A Series of Reports on Research in Progress on the Reintergrative Shaming Experiment (RISE) for Restorative Community Policing.* Law Program, Research School of Social Sciences, Institute of Advanced Studies. Canberra: Australian National University.

Rizzo, M.J. 1979. The Cost of Crime to Victims: An Empirical Analysis. *Journal of Legal Studies 8:* 177–205.

Rook, K.S. 1987. Reciprocity of Social Exchange and Social Satisfaction Among Older Women. *Journal of Personality and Social Psychology 52:* 145–154.

Ross, W.D. 1930. *The Right and the Good.* Oxford: Clarendon.

Russell, B. 1961. *History of Western Philosophy.* Second edn. London: Allen and Unwin.

Samuelson, P.A. 1948. *Foundations of Economic Analysis.* Cambridge, Ma: Harvard University Press.

Sandel, M.J. (ed.) 1984. *Liberalism and its Critics.* New York: New York University Press.

Sandel, M.J. 1984. Justice and the Good. In Sandel 1984.

Sarason, B. R. and G.R. Pierce (eds.) 1990. *Social Support: An Interactional View.* New York: Wiley.

Satz, D. and J. Ferejohn. 1994. Rational Choice and Social Theory. *Journal of Philosophy 91:* 71–87.

Schaefer, D.L. 1979. *Justice or Tyranny?* New York: Kennikat Press.

Scheff, T.J. 1994. *Bloody Revenge: Emotions, Nationalism, and War.* Boulder: Westview.

Schick, F. 1984. *Having Reasons.* Princeton: Princeton University Press.

Schwartz, W.F., and G. Tullock. 1975. The Costs of a Legal System. *Journal of Legal Studies 4:* 75–82.

Sen, A.K. 1974. Choice, Orderings, and Morality. In Körner 1974.

———. 1977. Rational Fools: A Critique of the Behavioural Foundations of Economic Theory. *Philosophy and Public Affairs 6:* 317–344.

Seneca. 1958. On Clemency. In M. Hadas (ed.), *The Stoic Philosophy of Seneca* (New York: Doubleday).

Severin, P. 1995. *Report on the Visit to the United States of America and Germany.* Brisbane: Queensland Corrective Services Commission.

Shapland, J., J. Willmore, and P. Duff, 1985. *Victims in the Criminal Justice System.* Aldershot: Gower.

Sherman, L.W., and G.C. Barnes. 1997. Restorative Justice and Offenders' Respect for the Law (Paper #3). In RISE 1997.

Sherman, L.W., and H. Strang. 1997a. The Right Kind of Shame for Crime Prevention (Paper #1). In RISE 1997.

Sherman, L.W., and H. Strang. 1997b. Restorative Justice and Deterring Crime (Paper #4). In RISE 1997.

Siebers, T. 1988. The Ethics of Criticism. Ithaca: Cornell University Press.

Singer, P. 1993. *Practical Ethics*. Second edn. Cambridge: Cambridge University Press.

Smith, A. 1971. *The Theory of Moral Sentiments*. New York: Garland.

Smith, J.C. and B. Hogan. 1983. *Criminal Law*. London: Butterworth.

Solomon, R.C. 1989. *A Passion for Justice*. Redding, Ma: Addison-Wesley.

———. 1990. Justice and the Passion for Vengeance. In Solomon and Murphy 1990.

Solomon, R.C., and M.C. Murphy (eds.) 1990. *What Is Justice?* Oxford: Oxford University Press.

Spencer, H. 1966. *The Principles of Ethics*. Volume 1. Osnabruck: Otto Zeller.

Stambaugh, J. 1972. Thoughts on Pity and Revenge. *Nietzsche-Studien: Internationales Jahrbuch fur die Nietzsche-Forschung I:* 28–35.

Stocker, M. 1973. Rightness and Goodness: Is there a Difference? *American Philosophical Quarterly 10:* 87–98.

Strang, H., and L.W. Sherman. 1997. The Victim's Perspective (Paper #2). In RISE 1997.

Sung Hee Kim, and R.H. Smith. 1993. Revenge and Conflict Escalation. *Negotiation Journal 9:* 37–43.

Tahtinen, U. 1982. *Non-Violent Theories of Punishment, Indian and Western*. Delhi: Motilal Banarsidass.

Tan, A. 1981. *Revenge Among the Tausug*. Thesis. Australian National University Library.

Taylor, A., T. Rosegrant, A. Meyer, and B.T. Samples. 1977. *Communicating*. Englewood Cliffs: Prentice-Hall.

Taylor, G. 1985. *Pride, Shame, and Guilt: Emotions of Self-Assessment*. Oxford: Clarendon.

Ten, C.L. 1987. *Crime, Guilt, and Punishment*. Oxford: Clarendon.

Thornton, C. 1993. *Family Group Conferences: A Literature Review*. Wellington: Practitioners' Publishing.

Tversky, A. and D. Kahneman. 1986. The Framing of Decisions and the Psychology of Choice. In Elster 1986.

Umbreit, M.S. 1989. Crime Victims Seeking Fairness, Not Revenge: Towards Restorative Justice. *Federal Probation 53(3):* 52–57.

Vallentyne, P. 1987. The Teleological/Deontological Distinction. *Journal of Value Inquiry 21:* 21–32.

———. 1988. Teleology, Consequentialism, and the Past. *Journal of Value Inquiry 22:* 89–101.

Van Ness, D.W. 1986. *Crime and Its Victims*. Leicester: Inter-Varsity Press.

———. 1990. Restoring the Balance: Tipping the Scales of Justice. *Corrections Today 52:* 62–66.

———. 1993. New Wine and Old Wineskins: Four Challenges of Restorative Justice. *Criminal Law Forum 4*.

———. 1996. Restorative Justice and International Human Rights. In Galaway and Hudson 1996.

———. 1997. *Restoring Justice*. Cincinnati: Anderson.

Van den Haag, E. 1975. *Punishing Criminals*. New York: Basic Books.

Vivas, E. 1963. *The Moral Life and the Ethical Life*. Chicago: Henry Regnery.

Walker, N. 1980. *Punishment, Danger, and Stigma*. Oxford: Blackwell.

———. 1991. *Why Punish?* Oxford: Oxford University Press.

Walker, N., and M. Hough. 1988. *Public Attitudes to Sentencing: Surveys from Five Countries*. Aldershot: Gower.

Wallace, G. 1995. Wild Justice. *Philosophy 70:* 363–375.

Whitton, E. 1994. *Trial by Voodoo*. Sydney: Random House.

Williams, G. 1983. *Textbook of Criminal Law*. Second edn. London: Stevens and Sons.

Wilson, B.R. (ed.) 1974. *Rationality*. Oxford: Blackwell.

Wilson, R.W. 1988. *Labyrinth: An Essay on the Political Psychology of Change*. New York: M.E. Sharpe.

Wiseman, R. 1995. The Megalab Truth Test. *Nature 373:* 391.

Wright, M. 1996. *Justice for Victims and Offenders: A Restorative Response to Crime*. Second edn. Winchester: Waterside Press.

Wolgast, E.H. 1987. *The Grammar of Justice*. Ithaca: Cornell University Press.

Wundersitz, J., and S. Hetzel. 1996. Family Conferences for Young Offenders: The South Australian Experience. In Hudson et. al. 1996, Chapter 7.

Zehr, H. 1990. *Changing Lenses*. Scottdale: Harold Press.

Zeid, A.A.M. 1965. Honour and Shame Among the Bedouins of Egypt. In Peristiany 1965.

Index